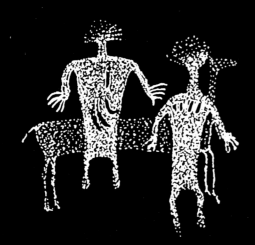

TAPAMVENI

Unlike Figure 2.16, which features a quadruped overlaying a Basketmaker anthropomorph, the human figures in this Basketmaker panel at the "Steps" site are clearly superimposed on the animals. Superimposition of one image upon another typically occurs in deep trance and may be evidence for the visual synesthesia that the shaman-artist experienced in this stage of his hallucinatory vision quest. Height of anthropomorph in top corner 44 cm.

TAPAMVENI

THE ROCK ART GALLERIES
OF PETRIFIED FOREST
AND BEYOND

TEXT AND DRAWINGS BY
PATRICIA MCCREERY

PHOTOGRAPHY AND CAPTIONS BY
EKKEHART MALOTKI

FOREWORD BY
STEWART UDALL

135. Colletto. Crete. Silk on silk woven with a cotton stripe, satin, four-sided, double running and Italian two-sided cross stitches. Red, blue, green, yellow, pink, salmon pink and black. Insertions and border of Cretan bobbin lace, over-embroidered in coloured silks. Two loops with tying cords are attached to the inside of the back above the lace border. Length at outer edge 161 cm. Centre back 23 cm. Sandwith Collection. 2028-1876

136. Colletto. Crete. Silk with insertions and border of Cretan bobbin lace, over-embroidered in red and green silk. Two loops with tying cords are attached to the inside of the back above the flounce. Length at outer edge 182 cm. Centre back 38 cm. Sandwith Collection. 2016-1876

Publisher: Petrified Forest Museum Association
Petrified Forest, Arizona

Some material from Chapter Nine was published previously in a different form
by the American Rock Art Research Association

Satellite photograph on page x courtesy of U.S. Geological Survey, EROS Data
Center, Sioux Falls, South Dakota

Credits:
Design and concept: Dena Dierker and Ekkehart Malotki
Typography: Dierker Design
Printed in Hong Kong through Asiaprint/Everbest
Project manager: Al Richmond
Copy editor: Rose Houk

ISBN: 0-945695-05-5
Library of Congress Number: 94-17796 CIP
1. Pueblo art — Themes, motives.
2. Pueblo Indians — Antiquities.
3. Petroglyphs — Arizona — Petrified Forest National Park.
4. Rock drawings — Arizona — Petrified Forest National Park.
5. Petrified Forest National Park (Ariz.) — Antiquities.
I. Malotki, Ekkehart.
II. Petrified Forest Museum Association.
III. Title.
E99.P9M23 1994
709'.01'130979137—dc20

CONTENTS

FOREWORD   vii

ACKNOWLEDGMENTS   viii

1   THE FACE OF THE LAND   1

2   ARCHAIC AND BASKETMAKER STYLES   13

3   PUEBLO II-PUEBLO III STYLES   33

4   PUEBLO IV STYLE   51

5   HUNTERS AND ANIMALS   67

6   MALE AND FEMALE   105

7   GEOMETRIC DESIGNS   119

8   ARCHAEOASTRONOMY   133

9   CEREMONIAL IMAGES   139

10   THE FUNCTION AND AESTHETICS OF ROCK ART   175

AFTERWORD—PROTECTING ROCK ART   182

NOTES TO CHAPTERS   184

BIBLIOGRAPHY   187

INDEX   191

This row of gigantic Linear Style Basketmaker figures projects an impressive aura of spiritual potency. Among the tiny animals associated with the anthropomorphs are several birds and dragonflies, possible graphic metaphors for the shaman's soul as it departs from his body and embarks on an extra-corporeal journey to the spirit realm. Betraying their shamanistic origin, all the elements of this panel at the "Jabberwocky" site represent Palavayu trance imagery at its best. Height of second anthropomorph from right 117 cm.

My native ground encompasses the unique region of the Colorado Plateau described in this timely book. I spent the first eighteen years of my life in St. Johns, a village on the Little Colorado River about forty miles east of the Petrified Forest in Arizona.

Nature is stingy in this sparse land, but it contains one of our nation's richest treasure troves of aboriginal art. The rock art depicted in this book is the work of Indian artisans whose displays might properly be characterized as one of the oldest art galleries on the North American continent. One of the mysterious, exciting experiences of my youth involved rambles into remote canyons where I and my friends found arrowheads, petroglyphs, potsherds, and the remains of Indian dwellings.

This book informs us that, despite the despoilment which has occurred in some areas, there are still national parks and monuments—and hidden recesses on the Plateau—where vintage art of those who came before us can be photographed and studied. The Petrified Forest was my introduction to the natural wonders of my home region, and one of the most satisfying moments of my tenure as Secretary of the Interior came when I was able to get it elevated to the status of a national park in recognition of its serene beauty and rich fossil and cultural resources.

A big challenge faced by future conservationists is the task of protecting our legacy of archaeological sites and the artwork of the first settlers of our land. This must be an unending effort, and it must encompass both the sites that lie within national or state parklands and areas such as those shown in this book that lie outside lands managed by public stewards. Vandalism is always a threat, and future generations and private property owners will inevitably confront a delicate, unavoidable dilemma between the desire to share these wonders and the need to keep some sites hidden or inaccessible. This explains why the authors wisely opted not to identify the locations of many of the objects of art which are the subject of this splendid book.

As a consequence, we can all rejoice that through his exceptional photographs Ekkehart Malotki has enabled us to vicariously enjoy art treasures we may never see with our own eyes. It is my hope that this publication will bring new appreciation for the work of these ancient artisans and underscore the need to preserve and protect this priceless legacy.

— Stewart Udall
Santa Fe
April 1994

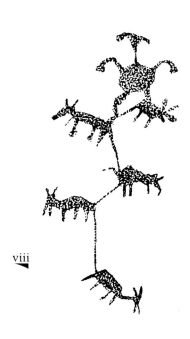

viii

I have many people to thank for their aid in the writing of this book. I am especially grateful to the archaeologists at the Western Archeological and Conservation Center in Tucson who supervised our volunteer group for ten years of survey, excavation, and rock art recording at Petrified Forest National Park. In describing the cultural background of the Palavayu region, I have relied greatly on their project reports and on the field experience each has afforded me. In particular, I thank Trinkle Jones, who initiated the surveys, supervising or directing most of the projects. Trinkle, Jeffery Burton, Marty Tagg, Susan Wells, and Don Christensen, made archaeology a continuing adventure while giving our group a painless education in the prehistory of Petrified Forest.

Former Park Superintendent Ed Gastellum and many other park personnel participated in these projects and assisted in locating rock art sites within the park. Many thanks to them and to the group of volunteers; we have enjoyed many exciting off-and-on duty rock art explorations together, and I have profited from their individual perceptions.

We were often helped by local residents who shared their rock art discoveries with us. These same generous people helped Ekkehart Malotki when he and I joined forces in planning this book; their names are included in his acknowledgments. I am grateful to Ekkehart, whose more than twenty years of research into the Hopi language and culture provided invaluable insights; as co-author he has contributed immensely to our view of Palavayu rock art, expressed in the captions he has composed for his photographs.

Bob Preston offered helpful suggestions on the archaeoastronomy of Petrified Forest. Don Christensen, Ken Hedges, Jerry Brody, and Peter Pilles read and commented upon portions of my text. I am especially indebted to Don Weaver, who meticulously critiqued each draft and whose meaningful advice is reflected throughout the book. My thanks to all who advised me on science and archaeology and who are blameless for any errors or shortcomings on my part.

Special thanks to Al Richmond for much-needed editorial advice, and to Rose Houk, who made it all come together.

Finally, I thank my husband Jack, who provided understanding, support and unfailing good humor through it all.

— Pat McCreery

The idea for this book arose during my photographic quest for the rock art motif of the flute player in northeastern Arizona in 1990. Enchanted by the petroglyphic imagery of Petrified Forest National Park and excited by the discovery of new rock art galleries on adjacent land, I invited Pat McCreery to team up with me in the realization of the book. Pat, an artist in her own right, has a longstanding enthusiasm for Southwestern rock art which allowed her to be easily persuaded. Not only did she agree to take on the formidable task of writing the text, she also volunteered to execute the many drawings for the book. Collaboration with Pat was a delight, her sensitivity to the subject matter and her diligence in carrying out the research an inspiration. Now that the task is completed, my foremost gratitude must go to her.

In the course of the project, during which I spent some 225 days in the field, clocked nearly 30,000 miles on paved and dirt roads, and walked two pairs of hiking boots to shreds, many other people became involved. All of them, in their own way, shared in its successful completion. To each one of them I am greatly indebted.

To owners in the vast territory of the Palavayu beyond the park, who graciously allowed entry to their land: Brantley Baird, Michael Breeze, Raymond Fitzgerald, Jim Gray, Bud Hunt, Bill Jeffers, Mick Maguire, Molly McLean, John McCauley, Michael O'Haco, Doy Reidhead, and Daniel Vizcaya. Concerned about the protection of their precious sites, they all received assurances that the exact locations of rock art would not be publicized.

For specific leads that often became departure points for further discoveries: John Parsons who, with great determination, is exploring the length of Silver Creek; Darlene Brinkerhoff, Steve Faust, Doug Johnson, Ferral Knight, Dot Reidelbach, and Lee Young for steering me to worthwhile destinations.

To friends who not only provided vital companionship while we trekked canyons and scoured every mesa and rock outcropping in the research area, but who also assisted in various ways: Peter Blystone, Helmbrecht Breinig, Kim Brown, Ken Gary, Jack Gondek, Chad May, and Claudette Piper for learning how to manipulate a light reflector; Bob Dawson, who introduced me to the art of rappeling, enabling me to overcome a fear of heights and record a number of otherwise inaccessible and often striking rock art panels; Glenn Cottle, who came to the rescue when the only way to panels was by canoe; Ted Bolich, Sharon Warneca, Mike Horton, and Mike Minnerath who held a ladder at several dangerous spots; and my son Patrick, who not only drove when I was tired, but who also ventured onto ledges where I dared not go, to photograph or measure many an enticing design.

For arranging lodging at the park on a number of occasions: Carl Bowman and Vincent Santucci; and Bill and Lois Jeffers of Holbrook, who generously offered their guest room.

To Al Richmond, Research Projects Manager at NAU, for being a valuable pointman and facilitator. With Merilee Sellers, he also provided the electron microscope photo of desert varnish. Jana Ruhlman and Linda Dellisime at the U.S. Geological Survey in Flagstaff assisted in selecting the color infrared satellite photograph.

To Henry Hooper, Vice President for Academic Affairs at NAU, who wholeheartedly endorsed the book and provided much-needed encouragement and moral support. To Robyn O' Reilly for producing the map; and to Dena Dierker, who translated many of my own design and layout ideas into reality, and who was in charge of all technical aspects of the book—a special thanks.

To Stewart Udall, whose willingness to write the foreword to the book both Pat and I consider a personal honor and reward.

To Ronda Millward, Production Manager at Asiaprint. Her competent counsel in the course of the book's production was a constant source of reassurance.

And finally, to all the board members of the Petrified Forest Museum Association, who, under the directorship of Marian Elson, demonstrated faith in the book idea and had the courage to underwrite it financially.

— Ekkehart Malotki

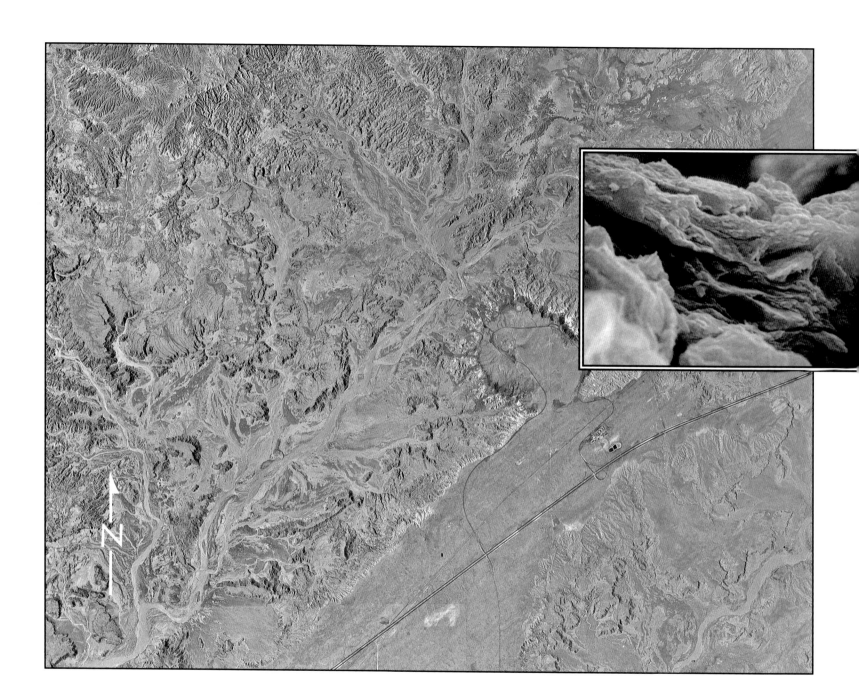

One inch in the adjacent color infrared photograph equals 0.9 mile on the ground. Taken from an altitude of 40,000 feet as part of the National High Altitude Photography Program, the territory shown includes most of the northern wilderness area of Petrified Forest National Park. Clearly visible are the park headquarters along Interstate 40 and the Painted Desert Rim Drive. Prominent among the clay hills, mesas, and buttes of the western part of the park is the multifingered drainage system of Lithodendron Wash. A section of Dead Wash is in the lower right-hand corner.

Inset in this geologic macrocosm, is the microscopic world of desert varnish. Adorning many rock formations in the park, this coating provides the necessary "canvasses" for rock art. Seen here through an electron microscope (at a 9,500 X magnification), this cross-section varnish looks very similar to stromatolites, fossilized algal growths. It gives credence to the theory that desert varnish is of a bacterial-assisted origin. Current thought is that airborne bacteria oxidize and concentrate manganese and iron, and then use clay minerals to cement them to rock surfaces, while adding other waterborne and airborne particles to the mix. The process is extremely slow; the result is a hard, weather-resistant, black or brown veneer, that provided a perfect medium for the petroglyphic artist.

Figure 1.1. Like this panel at "Slab Crest," most rock art sites within Palavayu are oriented toward the sun. This heliotropic orientation, comprising compass directions from northeast to northwest, may have a simple geologic explanation: rocks facing north usually lack a dark varnish, are often covered with lichen, or both.
This particular orientation, however, may have been triggered by reasons still anchored in Puebloan ideology. According to Hopi mythology, for example, Taawa, the sun god, is believed to "pick up" the people's wishes and desires in the form of prayer sticks or prayer feathers as he begins his diurnal journey across the sky. Because prayer items are vulnerable to the elements, animals, and other forces, it may have been considered more effective to engrave one's prayer on a rock surface exposed to the celestial divinity. Traveling across the land, the sun sweeps over the petroglyphic prayer on a daily basis, and is thereby compelled to receive the supplicant's message each day anew. Height of archer 41 cm.

The world over, early peoples left engravings and paintings on the stone faces of caves, cliffs, and boulders. This legacy is testimony of their need to communicate basic concerns; to invoke their gods; to depict their vision quests; to induce, by magical means, fertility, health, and success; to perpetuate myths and legends; to identify and claim territory; to record deeds, or simply to say "I was here."

The American Southwest is especially rich in the rock art of ancient people. A region well known for the abundance and diversity of its rock art is the land situated along the southern edge of the Colorado Plateau, a region termed here "Palavayu."[1] Certain petroglyph images are found only here and not in surrounding areas. Palavayu has a long history of human presence, from the big-game hunters of the Clovis era to the Pueblo farmers of the closing chapter of Southwestern prehistory. The region, centered around Petrified Forest National Park in northeast Arizona, includes lands adjacent to the park, as well as the Little Colorado River tributaries in the area south of the towns of Holbrook and Winslow.

Travelers on Interstate 40 through east-central Arizona are often completely unaware of the dramatic terrain of Palavayu. Between the red cliffs of the New Mexico border and the soaring heights of northern Arizona's San Francisco Peaks, the land subsides into a rolling grassy plain, broken by shallow washes and low rock-capped mesas. Pinyon and juniper trees, which abound at either end of this 160-mile stretch of highway, dwindle to a scattered few. Rocks, grass, and soil blend into a muted monotone. Heading west the route lies close to the Puerco River, a usually dry and sandy arroyo that joins the Little Colorado River near Holbrook. Cottonwoods and salt cedar mark the rivercourses. At Winslow, the Little Colorado swings north, and a long, low bridge spans the wide river bed. Here the traveler gains a first and only glimpse of the river itself. Sometimes filled bank to bank with a roiling red torrent, the Little Colorado is more often a slow-moving meandering stream or a mosaic of dried mud.

The shallow rivercourse and the level, seemingly unbroken roll of the land to the south are deceptive, for this plain is actually cut by narrow deep canyons. The freeway bridges one of the longest and deepest of these, Canyon Diablo; early explorers were forced to detour many miles to cross this canyon. Intermittent streams, which run mostly during summer thunderstorms, heavy winter rains, or when snow is melting, flow north through these rocky gorges and drain into the Little Colorado. Carved through limestone and sandstone, some are sheer-walled clefts; wider canyons often enclose brush-choked stream beds. White sand and water-worn bedrock pave some canyon floors, and sylvan stretches provide an amazing contrast to the arid tableland above.

Prominent landmarks along the interstate are few and diminished by distance. The highest point, briefly visible to the traveler, is Pilot Rock, in the northwest corner of Petrified Forest National Park. At 6,236 feet, this dark peak is not towering, for the elevation is fairly uniform, between 5,000 and 6,000 feet. To the south, a line of flat-topped mesas marks the Twin Butte area. Farther west near Holbrook, the conical outline of Woodruff Butte punctuates the horizon. If the air is clear, the monolithic Hopi Buttes far north of Winslow can be seen, while to the south the twin mounds of the Sunset Mountains stand like a gateway to the Mogollon Rim.

But on the whole, the unheeding motorist speeding along the interstate sees only an inhospitable wasteland with little to arouse interest. A detour through Petrified Forest National Park, however, reveals the hidden beauty of this area. Less than a mile north of the interstate, the park's Rim Drive overlooks the panorama of the Painted Desert, a splendor of colorful earth and rocks eroded out of the dun land surface. Constant carving by wind and water has exposed layers of the Chinle Formation. Mostly sandstones and mudstones, the Chinle comes in a startling array of colors—from reds, pinks, and purples, to grays, greens, and blues. The colors result from concentrations and combinations of minerals and the manner in which the sediments were deposited millions of years ago.[2] The vista changes with light throughout the day and with weather throughout the year; it is never the same and is always a wonder. Although the Painted Desert extends many miles to the west, paralleling Interstate 40, it is rarely visible to travelers. It can be seen along the roads to Keam's Canyon, Second Mesa, and Cameron; but the park overlook provides the most accessible and sweeping view possible of this dramatic landscape.

The Painted Desert is not the only scenic marvel in the park. Blue Mesa is an unearthly moonscape of jagged blue clay hills laced with cracks and furrows, knobs and mounds eroding into gullies and sandy washes. On the crests of these ridges, balanced on pedestals of hardened silt, lie the trunks of petrified trees—the reason for the creation of this national park.

Even more exciting fossils are found in the park. Remains of the reptiles and amphibians known as thecodonts, which preceded the dinosaurs, have been found embedded in Chinle exposures. The late Triassic Period saw the dawn of the age of dinosaurs, and the fossilized bones of the earliest known specimens have recently been discovered here. The Petrified Forest has proven to be one of the richest areas in the world for the study of this little-known period. Each year, paleontologists are finding and identifying a growing number of ancient vertebrates. Fossils can't be viewed in situ by the casual tourist, but the park's Visitor Center displays replicas of some and provides information about the yearly progress of park paleontology.

THE PEOPLE AND THEIR ART

Petrified Forest National Park is one of the few easily accessible places for the unacquainted to be introduced to Indian rock art. From the "Newspaper Rock" overlook in the central part of the park, people can view a fine example of this art form. A huge boulder, resting on a talus slope below the mesa, is adorned with hundreds of intricate petroglyphs probably produced from 650 to 1,000 years ago.[3]

The people who created much of the rock art here and along the scarp of the mesa might have lived at Puerco Pueblo, less than a mile to the north. This large pueblo of over 100 rooms was occupied from about A.D. 1250 to 1380.[4] The pueblo is situated on a low rise just

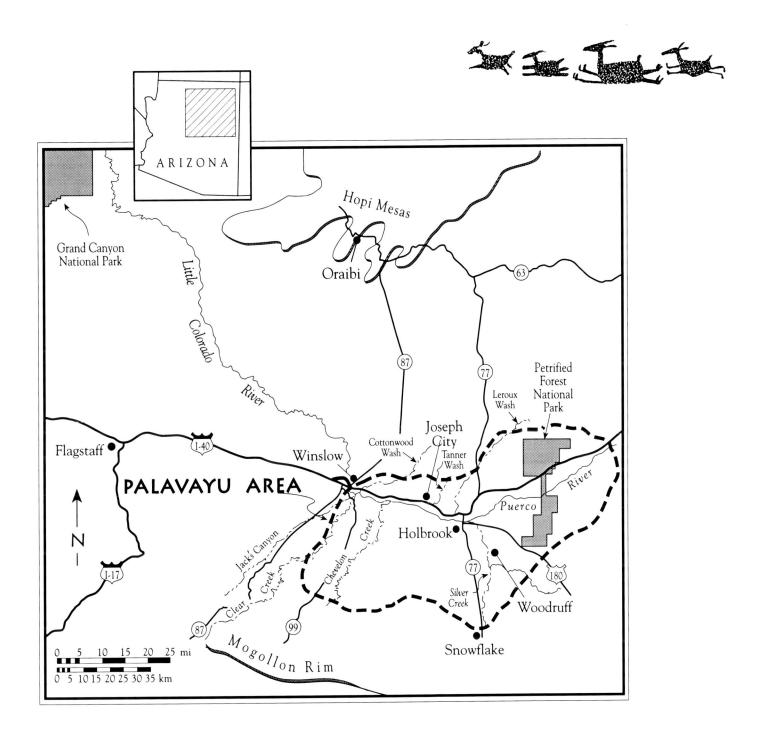

Figure 1.2. The Palavayu rock art area in Northeast Arizona

south of the Puerco River. Here, too, the visitor can see many petroglyphs on the sandstone boulders which ring the base of the hill. Puerco Ruin is the largest village in the park, but is only one of hundreds of habitation sites of different sizes and time periods documented there. East and west of the Petrified Forest, through the Puerco River Valley to the Little Colorado River near Winslow, scores of archaeological sites attest to a long history of human presence.

Throughout the region and through the centuries people left their engravings and paintings, which we call petroglyphs and pictographs, on the walls of the narrow canyons, in caves and shelters, on mesa cliffs, boulders and bedrock. This artistic tradition combined the symbolic imagery of their religious beliefs with depictions of secular pursuits. Rock art is therefore not only a creative art form, but also a valuable source of information about a people who left no written record. Portrayed in the petroglyphs and pictographs are details of dress and adornment, ritual objects, weaponry, hunting methods, and scenes of ceremony. Apparent in the art of all the time periods is the preternatural concern with animal life. Mammals, reptiles, insects, and birds obviously possessed more than biological importance in the world view of these ancient people. And although a gulf of understanding separates us from these early artists, we feel, through their art, the mystery and power of their spiritual world.

Who were the people who left this art on stone? To the Hopi they were the *Hisatsinom*,[5] or "ancient people." More commonly used is the Navajo word *Anasazi* meaning "enemy ancestors." This term refers to the enmity between the Navajos, who arrived later in the Southwest, and the Pueblo people whom they encountered here. A more general designation is "prehistoric Pueblos," a term that better describes the widely scattered populations which at different times occupied much of the Colorado Plateau. Their common range of traits is manifest in the remains of their architecture, settlement patterns, material culture, and burial customs.

But there were regional variations, and thus the Pueblo people can be divided into subgroups. Briefly, these include the Kayenta people of the Four Corners area, San Juan or Mesa Verde people of southern Utah and Colorado, Chacoans of northwestern New Mexico, the Cibola of eastern Arizona, the Virgin people in southern Nevada, and Rio Grande people of central New Mexico. The culture of the central Little Colorado River drainage is generally termed Western Anasazi, and more narrowly defined, after A.D. 1000, as the Winslow Branch of the Western Pueblos.[6] Geographically centered between the Kayenta, Sinagua, Cibola, and Mogollon culture areas, the Palavayu region displays a mix of patterns which shifted in emphasis throughout prehistory; influences from each are evident in certain areas at different times. Semipermanent settlements of the Pueblos appeared in this region in the Basketmaker II period, usually dated A.D. 300 to 500. Excavations in Petrified Forest National Park, however, have established an even earlier beginning date for this cultural stage, at around A.D. 1.[7] Over the centuries a fluctuating population peaked in the Petrified Forest area during the Pueblo II–III period (ca. A.D. 950 to 1300), and in the central Little Colorado region in the late Pueblo III–IV period (ca. A.D. 1275 to 1400).[8]

Most of the rock art in the Petrified Forest area likely derives from the PII–III period of expansion.[9] Earlier and later art is certainly present, but not in great quantity. Only one site within the park boundaries exhibits the characteristic style of the early Basketmaker artists. Rock art attributed to the PIV period (A.D. 1300 to 1450), infrequent in the park, is primarily found near Puerco Ruin; it is sparsely represented at a few sites outside the park.

To the west, in the central Little Colorado River area, much of the rock art found near Cottonwood Creek, Chevelon Creek, and at Homol'ovi ruins is of late PIII or PIV periods. South of these pueblos, however, along the many canyon creeks which drain into the Little Colorado, there is an abundance of petroglyphs of the Archaic and Basketmaker styles. The paucity of archaeological investigation in this broken and difficult terrain leaves unanswered many questions about these early nomadic people. Where did they come from, and where did they go? So far, only the rock art records their passing.

The rock art tradition declined after A.D. 1400, when the entire region along the Puerco and Little Colorado rivers was abandoned, the populations presumably dispersing to the Hopi Mesas and to the Zuni River Valley, where their descendants survive to the present day.

PALEO-INDIAN PERIOD	9500 B.C. TO 6000 B.C.
ARCHAIC PERIOD	6000 B.C. TO CA. A.D.1
BASKETMAKER II - III PERIOD	EARLY CA. A.D. 1 TO A.D. 300
	LATE CA. A.D. 300 TO A.D. 700
BASKETMAKER III - PUEBLO I PERIOD	A.D. 700 TO A.D. 950
PUEBLO II - PUEBLO III PERIOD	EARLY A.D. 950 TO A.D. 1100
	LATE A.D. 1100 TO A.D. 1300
PUEBLO IV	A.D. 1300 TO A.D. 1450

Sources: Wells (1989) and Burton (1993).

Figure 1.3. Chronology of Culture Stages for Palavayu

THE ART: STYLES AND TECHNIQUES

"Style" refers to the characteristic manner of expression or design in certain types of rock art. Subject matter and technological attributes are components of style. Differences in style can help date rock art and suggest the makers. How rock art was made, its "freshness" on the rock surface, its association with datable ceramics, and comparison with pottery, kiva mural, and other designs are all part of style.[10]

Petroglyphs were made by pecking, incising, abrading, or scratching the surface of rock. Pecking, the most common technique, was accomplished by direct percussion with a blunt hammerstone, direct percussion with a sharpened rock, or indirect percussion with a chisel-like rock struck by a hammerstone. Incising was done by cutting into the rock with a sharpened stone. Abrading, or grinding the surface of rock with another stone, smoothed the interior of a pecked petroglyph. Scratching seems to have been used to plan or sketch in the design of a petroglyph, but also sometimes to make a finished image.

In the Southwest, ancient artists preferred sandstone coated with rock varnish (or "desert" varnish), commonly called patina. Abundant in the Palavayu, this varnish is the dark discoloration on rock surfaces exposed to the elements. When petroglyphs are pecked or incised through this veneer of manganese oxide, the lighter rock beneath is revealed. Where very dark varnish approaches a bluish-black color, the contrast of the lighter petroglyph creates a dramatic, pleasing effect. Over time, the petroglyph itself becomes covered with varnish. Thus, generally the darker the glyph, the older it is. If one element is superimposed by another, this too will indicate a different age, particularly if there is a marked contrast in the varnish.

Another clue to the antiquity of rock art is vertical placement of elements on cliff faces. Petroglyphs which are high above others and out of reach today probably were made before ground level was lowered by erosion.

A possible key to the age of rock art is its association with datable archaeological sites: habitations, camps, or tool-making or food-processing areas. There is no way of knowing for sure, however, if these sites are contemporaneous with the rock art.

Sometimes artifacts identifiable with a particular time period are pictured in rock art. The atlatl, a hunting weapon, was superseded by the bow and arrow, which came into use in this part of the Southwest sometime after A.D. 500.[11] Although both may have been used at the same time, atlatl depiction in rock art generally indicates considerable age. The S-shaped fending stick, an artifact found in Basketmaker II habitation sites, may be pictured in rock art thought to be of Basketmaker origin.[12] Pottery designs have long been a reliable tool for dating. Some subject matter obviously dates from the historic era: the Spanish introduced the horse and other domesticated animals into the Southwest after A.D. 1540. Guns and wheeled vehicles also arrived in the region during this historic period.

Except for patina, all of these analytical considerations also apply to pictographs, or painted rock art. Among the thousands of rock art sites in Palavayu, only twenty-one feature pictographs, perhaps because they are not as durable. The few paintings found are in caves, rock shelters, and under cliff overhangs (Figures 1.10-1.12). Several petroglyphs have been found which were painted. Other painted glyphs and pictograph sites likely existed, but they have not survived time and weather.

Techniques used to produce petroglyphs are valuable in determining time relationships.[13] Glyph-making methods seem to have been as subject to custom and tradition as pottery or stone tool production were. Although some techniques of petroglyph manufacture were employed throughout prehistory, certain methods consistently appear in particular styles or time periods.

Figure 1.4. A rock art boulder blends harmoniously with the Petrified Forest landscape. The prominent stick figure with extended extremities is reminiscent of a water skate, an insect generally associated with moisture in the Zuni world view. Height of stick figure 38 cm.

Figure 1.5. The destructive forces of erosion that are slowly consuming many of the rock art treasures in Palavayu are clearly evident on this sandstone sliver at the "Jitterbug" site in Petrified Forest. Prominent among the geometric and representational icons are several dot-centered circles whose functions remain obscure. Speculative interpretations range from solar/lunar symbols to representations of the "center of concentrated life power." Length of snake on left 65 cm.

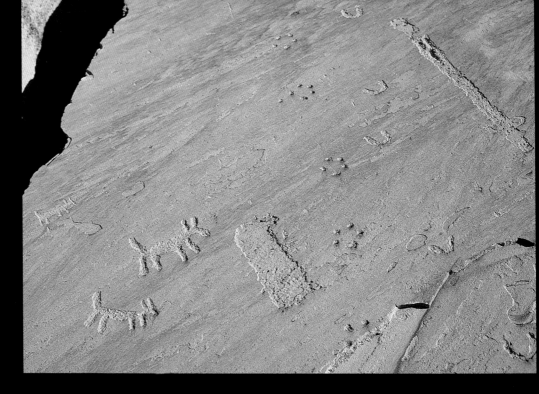

Figure 1.6. This realistic rendition of an atlatl or spear-thrower at a site west of Petrified Forest is one of only a handful discovered to date in Palavayu. The weapon is the prime diagnostic tool of the hunting and gathering lifeway of the Archaic Tradition, whose beginning is dated to approximately 6000 B.C. The atlatl apparently survived into the early Pueblo period in this area, for the animals and tracks of pronghorn and cougar associated with its depiction do not match those of the Basketmaker style. Note that there is the same degree of revarnishing on all the incised elements. Length of spear-thrower 39 cm.

Figure 1.7. This panel at the "No Name Mesa" site is an example of the frequently stunning unison of rock art location and natural scenery. That certain rock piles, cliff walls, or boulder formations were inherently endowed with religious and magical powers was a belief probably held by humans since time immemorial. Small wonder then that shaman artists and other religious specialists complemented such power-charged places with their own symbols to create veritable sacred zones. These zones were probably taboo to children and other ordinary mortals. This may explain the fact that rock art sites, even when found near habitation sites, show no apparent traces of prehistoric vandalism.
Height of largest figure 71 cm.

Figure 1.8. Engraved sandstone boulders form the "Picnic Gallery" in Petrified Forest. It is located amid colorful badlands, the gray siltstones and purple claystones that are part of the Chinle formation. Height of figure in foreground 84 cm.

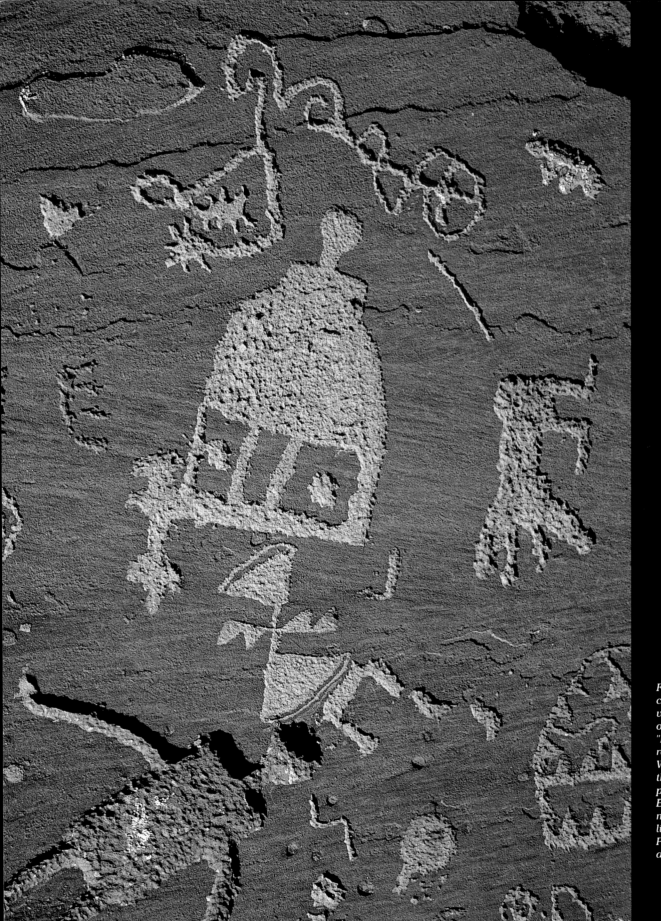

Figure 1.9. Both the stylistic characteristics and differential varnishing of the pictured elements on this sandstone slab at "Benchmark Mesa" indicate a wide range of manufacturing episodes. While the stylized bear paw and the deeply gouged human figure probably belong to the Palavayu Basketmaker periods, the central masklike object and the other lightly pecked glyphs appear to be Pueblo IV in age. Length of anthropomorph 41 cm.

1.10

1.11

1.12

Figures 1.10.-1.12. Pictographs or rock paintings, executed in red, white, black, yellow, brown, and green are extremely rare in Palavayu. To date, twenty-one pictograph sites have been discovered. While the "Bric-a-brac" site only has one green anthropomorph, the panel at the "Arabesque" site consists of an array of figurative and nonfigurative elements. Among the former are several flute players, birds, and a hunting scene. "Dot's Spot," the most extensive of all the painted sites, features dozens of handprints and numerous geometric, human and animal designs. Nearly all of them show paint removal by intentional pecking. Whether this surface alteration signifies spiritual exorcism of malevolent powers suspected to reside in the images or an attempt by later people to share or intensify their power, we will never know. Approximate length of snake in Figure 1.10, 80 cm; height of white anthropomorph in Figure 1.11, 25 cm; height of green anthropomorph in Figure 1.12, 27 cm.

Figure 2.1. These knob-headed serpents at "Benchmark Mesa" are executed in the gridded fashion so typical of Palavayu Archaic and Basketmaker art. Betraying shamanic origin, the antiquity of the snake motifs is underlined by the complete revarnishing of the designs to the original hues of the rock veneer. Length of serpent on left 52 cm.

Roving bands of Paleo-Indian big-game hunters first entered the Puerco and Little Colorado River valleys more than 8,000 years ago. Their presence is confirmed by scattered surface finds of their distinctive fluted points.[1] However, archaeological evidence from the ensuing Archaic period (6000 B.C. to A.D. 1) marks this era as the true beginning of human occupation of this region. Small groups of people, probably kin-related, followed the movements of game and the seasonal growth of wild food-plants. Bounded and determined by these patterns and by the cycles of weather, their nomadic lives revolved around hunting and gathering camps. Repeatedly visited on a seasonal basis, these camps eventually may have become the pithouse settlements of the early Basketmakers. Maize (corn) appeared in the late Archaic period, and with it the beginnings of agriculture. The Basketmaker II and III periods (A.D.1 to 800) saw a growing population that was settling down. Villages began to be occupied year-round.

A study by Peter Pilles found that "although Paleo-Indian and Archaic cultures are known for the Little Colorado River Valley, no rock art has been found that is assignable to these groups."[2] Since then, however, petroglyphs have been discovered in the Little Colorado River drainage that convincingly extend the time range of this art back into the Archaic period. The earliest rock art tradition presently recognized in the Colorado Plateau region of the Southwest is termed the Basketmaker Style, although its time of origin cannot be dated with certainty.[3] Christy Turner's research in Glen Canyon, Arizona[4] (done before inundation by Lake Powell), first defined the style horizon and time period for this type of art. On the basis of patina, positioning, and associated archaeological sites, this rock art is assigned to the oldest category of the study, Style 5 (of five style horizons), with a beginning date estimated around 100 B.C. Pottery associations established the ending date for this type of art in the Glen Canyon area (circa A.D. 1050), bringing it into Pueblo II times. Turner later proposed an Archaic beginning for the style (between 8000 and 4000 B.C.), based upon radiocarbon dating of artifacts recovered in the canyons of the Colorado River and geological evidence of cliff erosion beneath the petroglyph panels.[5] Polly Schaafsma changed the Style 5 designation to a more descriptive one, the Glen Canyon Linear Petroglyph Style (which will be the term used here),[6] and added a later phase, the San Juan Anthropomorphic Style.[7]

In the Glen Canyon Linear Petroglyph Style of the Colorado River region, human figures are depicted frontally, with outlined rectilinear or oval bodies. Torsos are often filled with vertical or parallel hatching, and solidly pecked figures are rare (Figure 2.2a). Although usually armless, the figures do have legs that are single lines and heads that are small. Sometimes they have headdresses or vertical horns or feathers.[8] Animals, mainly mountain sheep, are also executed in outline with rectangular, sometimes oval bodies often filled with interior hatching, and with single line legs and small heads. Snakelike forms are common. Abstract elements include the "squiggle maze," lines of dots, joined circles, concentric circles, and rakes. Schaafsma further defined this style and added animal tracks, plantlike forms, and a variety of abstract elements including ticked lines, grids, zigzag lines, ladders,

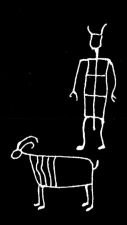

ARCHAIC

AND

BASKETMAKER

STYLES

and sunbursts.[9] The manufacturing method described by Turner is direct percussion by blunt or sharpened hammerstone, with the glyph often deeply pecked.

The San Juan Anthropomorphic Style of Basketmaker rock art is characterized by large frontal broad-shouldered human figures, with drooping hands and feet, often embellished with necklaces, earrings, exotic headgear, and body decorations (Figure 2.2b).[10] Centered in the drainage area of the San Juan River, the style is thought to be somewhat later than the Glen Canyon Linear Petroglyph Style, because at several sites Glen Canyon Linear figures are clearly superimposed by San Juan figures. Although much of the San Juan Style of rock art is painted, especially in the Cedar Mesa, Marsh Pass, and Canyon de Chelly areas, some of the most dramatic examples are found in petroglyph panels along the upper San Juan River. Here, the large human figures are adorned with jewelry, fringed sashes, and elaborate headdresses. Strange cross-barred devices protrude from the ears of some figures, and vertical stacks of arcs and lines hover above the heads of some, seeming to symbolize movement or power. Several figures are phallic, and a few—whose bodies enclose small anthropomorphs—may be female. Sally Cole suggests that other decorative features may indicate that the female is represented: possible depictions of breasts and of menstrual aprons.[11] The figures are accompanied by apparent ceremonial objects such as pouches which may be medicine bags, basketlike items, isolated stacks of crescents resembling staffs (but also used as headdresses), and outlined circles with tabs similar in shape to wood artifacts from Basketmaker III burials.[12] Also present are hand and footprints, spirals, concentric circles, rakes, lines of dots, snakes, and mountain sheep. Several images resembling heads topped with loops or handles are found in the upper San Juan River area (Figure 2.2b), as well as in the Cedar Mesa and Canyon de Chelly regions. Cole theorizes that these may represent trophy heads, like the whole face and hair scalp which Kidder and Guernsey excavated from a Basketmaker II site in northeastern Arizona.[13]

Schaafsma proposes that the typical San Juan anthropomorph represents either a shaman or a supernatural being.[14] The symbolism and otherworldly character of these figures strongly suggest this art derives from shamanistic ideology believed to have been shared by Southwestern hunter-gatherer peoples.[15] It is also possible that ancestral spirits or deities are portrayed.

Archaic and Basketmaker rock art sites in the Palavayu region are primarily confined to canyons which drain north into the Little Colorado River. Remote, difficult of access, often on private land requiring the owner's permission to enter, few of the canyon sites are known. Only a small number of Basketmaker petroglyph sites along Silver Creek and near the Puerco and Little Colorado rivers are accessible, and only a handful of researchers has studied them.[16] With such a limited number of Basketmaker rock art examples, a definable regional style has heretofore been difficult to perceive. Only recently has a systematic exploration of the remote canyon drainages been made by Ekkehart Malotki, with the landowners' permission. At their request, the exact locations of sites are not published. To date, Malotki has discovered more than seventy new Basketmaker rock art sites. From his

14

Figure 2.2a. Examples of the Glen Canyon Linear Style (not to scale)

Figure 2.2b. Examples of the San Juan Anthropomorphic Style (not to scale)

compilation of more than thirteen hundred human petroglyph figures, in association with scores of animal figures and abstract elements, it has been possible to discern a discrete style of art in the Palavayu region. The many examples afford comparisons of varnish, style, and associated images which seem to follow a broad chronological sequence.

The earliest Palavayu rock art probably originated sometime during, or possibly preceding, the Archaic period. Infrequent and thinly scattered in the region, the glyphs assumed to be oldest are usually completely revarnished, and, comparable to Archaic rock art in other areas of the Southwest, are comprised mainly of abstract forms. Human and animal figures, if present, are simple and crudely portrayed. Curvilinear meanders, random straight and wavy lines, circles, spirals, grids, and rakes occur most often. Snakes with knobs for heads are common; of particular interest are the snake images seen in Figure 2.1. The black varnish of the deeply pecked elements may indicate extreme age.

One design, the rake, seems to have been transmuted over time from the abstract to the representational. Malotki speculates that this would account for the genesis of the rake-bodied anthropomorph.[17] Perhaps the most commonly depicted of abstract images, the rake first acquires a head, then arms (Figure 2.3). Initially there is a plain, solidly pecked head and neck; later heads are bi-, tri-, or quadrisected, assuming the appearance of facial features. The rake changes from vertical straight or wavy lines descending from an increasingly emphasized "shoulder," to a recognizably human shape. Although the interior designs of vertical lines (or dots, in several examples) are retained, bisecting horizontal lines are added. Progression of this petroglyph image from abstract to anthropomorphic appears to go from older to younger. The rake with unmodified human head is darkest in color, and has a markedly older appearance. The addition of arms and facial features was obviously later. However, the metamorphosis of the rake into the Linear and Majestic styles of human figure, while plausible and attractive, is conjectural at this time. Ken Hedges offers yet another interpretation for this symbol: the possibility that the winglike rake signifies shamanic flight.[18] Whatever its meaning, the unaltered rake image continued to be depicted throughout the time span assigned to the Basketmaker Style.

Snake and rake motifs are two nonhuman images most often seen in Palavayu Basketmaker rock art. Interestingly, each has an implied association with rain. This affinity is well documented in the case of the snake and best demonstrated in ethnographic accounts of the Hopi Snake dance. At the close of the ceremony snakes are released at shrines of the four directions, and prayerfully urged to carry pleas to the spirits to send rain. It is easy to understand how the snake became affiliated with water and the control of weather. Its sinuous flow of movement resembles a stream's fluid motion. The snake's undulations also suggest the pattern of lightning, and the snake strikes swiftly, as lightning strikes. Snakes dwell underground and have access to subsurface springs and, no less importantly, to the supernatural beings who inhabit the underworld. These associations would be apparent to the earliest people, and the snake's relationship to water may be one of the most ancient concepts.

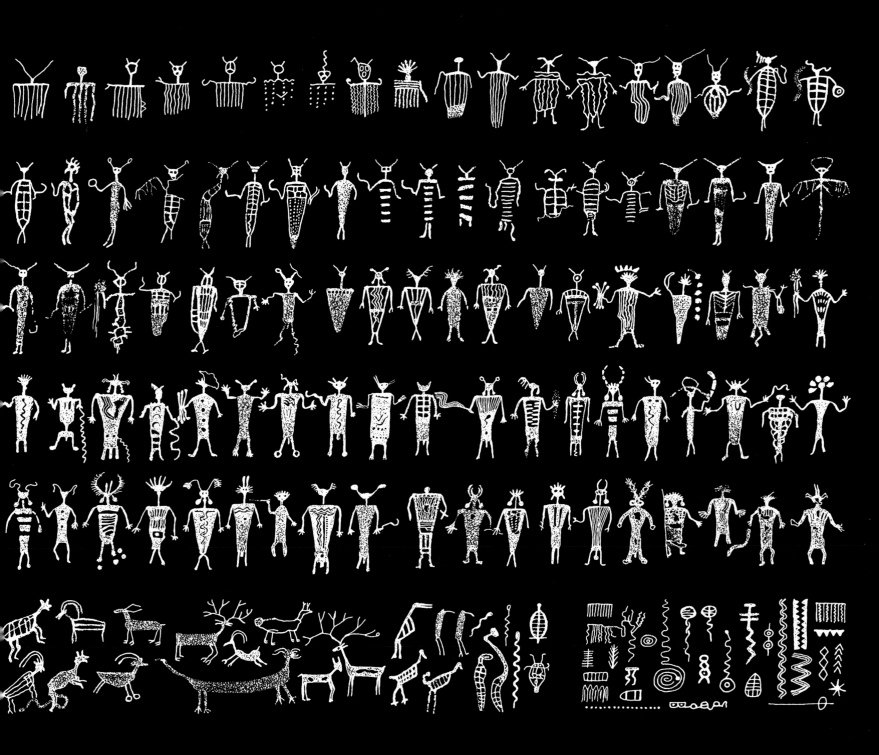

Figure 2.3. Examples of the Palavayu Linear and Majestic Basketmaker Styles (not to scale).

Although lacking ethnographic verification, the rake is often described as a rain symbol because it resembles a cloud and rain curtain: straight or wavy lines "showering" from a horizontal bar. This image could be a visual observation reduced to the abstract. Considering how frequently it is represented in Basketmaker rock art, it must have symbolized something of importance. This raises the question: if the rake and snake symbolize rain, how important was rain to the Archaic hunters and gatherers?

Although it is well known that rainfall, or the lack of it, posed a major concern for the farmers of the later Pueblo periods, it does not seem likely that a nomadic people would share this preoccupation. These small, mobile groups could seek out greener pastures in a particularly dry year. However, as the larger part of the diet sustaining these foraging people consisted of wild seeds, herbs, berries, nuts, fruits, tubers, roots, and mushrooms, the need for sufficient rain is obvious. Game animals, too, are vitally dependent on water sources. The appearance of maize in the Southwest sometime in the latter half of the Archaic period[19] implies the introduction of a deliberate seeding in some areas. Perhaps in addition to the seeding of wild plants, these peoples also cultivated maize in places they visited recurrently. Planted casually without continuing care, and regarded as a supplementary resource, these "crops" depended solely upon rainfall. Even before the practice of agriculture became established, the importance of seasonal rain and the link between supernatural spirits and weather control may have been a concern to Archaic people.

Turner defines Style 5 (or Glen Canyon Linear Style) as consisting almost exclusively of rectilinear anthropomorphic forms; triangular forms are "rare" and are thought to be a later innovation.[20] In the Palavayu region, Basketmaker human figures are not only rectilinear but also oval, trapezoidal, or triangular. These shapes all appear to be contemporaneous but with differing elaborations which may denote changes through time. The outlined trapezoidal and elongated oval figures with interior vertical or horizontal lines or dots may represent the earliest types, perhaps originating in the Archaic period. They most resemble the Glen Canyon Linear Style figures, and so shall be designated the Palavayu Linear Basketmaker Style here. Almost all of these beings display horns, although they are longer, more diagonal, and more insectlike in appearance than are those of the Glen Canyon Linear Style. Although some heads are minute knobs, many are larger, with staring eyes and open mouths. Most carry S-curved objects which may be fending or throwing sticks. Other straight line objects have been tentatively identified as atlatls.[21] Some figures hold circular elements and at several sites others grip wavy forms which unmistakably are snakes. Torsos of at least three individuals are decorated with snakes (Figure 2.5). Human figures at five different sites carry something which can best be described as a bouquet of flowers or plants (Figures 2.10 and 2.11 show two examples). Far to the north, in Utah, pictographs of the Barrier Canyon Style (thought to date from the late Archaic and possibly earlier[22]) also depict anthropomorphs holding snakes and bundles of grasses or plants. These two motifs seemingly were significant to the people in both of these places. Some Palavayu figures are phallic, most are not. Arms and legs are simple lines, and stick fingers, usually three or four in number, are depicted often. Solidly pecked elements seldom appear in the Glen Canyon Linear Style, according to Turner, but many Palavayu Linear Basketmaker figures are partially or completely pecked. This technique is frequently used for triangular or sub-triangular forms and may indicate an innovative development. Both outlined rectangular and solid triangular shapes occur together on many panels.

Animals vary in form and treatment. Mountain sheep and deer with outlined bodies and interior decoration similar to those of the Glen Canyon Linear Style are sometimes found. They are usually accompanied by simple, solidly pecked animals difficult to identify. The two types are apparently contemporaneous. All are often depicted with cloven hoofs, a feature previously considered a characteristic of the late PIII period.[23] In a few instances, circles represent the feet. Solidly pecked deer and elk with elaborate antlers are also seen. In addition to these mammals, centipedes, owls and other birds, dragonflies, a turtle, and an insect have been found.

Snakes are common, and they are often depicted as wavy lines or coiled spirals with heads. Several appear to be horned, much like the horned serpents seen in rock art of the later PIV period. One snake image, unlike any other seen in Basketmaker art, has been found at two widely separated rock art sites. It is the representation of a snake with face, arms, and hands. Both glyphs are so similar in concept, even though obviously made by different artists, that this being obviously conforms to some established belief.[24] At a site on a Silver Creek tributary, the figure is one element of a typical group of Palavayu Linear Basketmaker figures superimposed by glyphs of a later period. The snake has large eyes in negative relief, two arms with hands and stick fingers, a patterned body, and a faintly pecked tail rattle. The other example, on a panel near Holbrook, is not directly associated with Basketmaker art, but the snake glyph duplicates aspects of the other snake. It has the same large negative eyes, arms, hands with stick fingers, and a tail rattle (Figure 2.7). It dominates the panel which is composed of abstract, plantlike forms, and it is flanked on both sides by two less distinct snakes with vertical straight bodies and the same negative facial features, arms, and hands. This anthropomorphized creature may represent a deified or mythic animal.

Many researchers believe that the religious beliefs of the Basketmaker people were based upon shamanism.[25] This magico-religious system centers around individuals with supernatural powers gained through visions, dreams, or the technique of ecstatic trance. The role of the shaman is to benefit and regulate the well-being of his people. He (or she) is capable of soul flight to the upper world or travel to nether realms to mediate with spirits and gods. The shaman combats evil, cures illness, promotes fertility, controls weather, and with the help of animal spirit helpers, ensures success of the hunt. Certain conventions in the rock art portrayal of the shaman are believed to identify these magical capabilities. Rays emanating from the head[26] and "power lines," long wavy lines projecting from the hands or body of a figure,[27] may indicate a supernatural status. Horns are considered a universal symbol of shamanic power[28] and are perhaps the most common attribute utilized. Birds, bird-

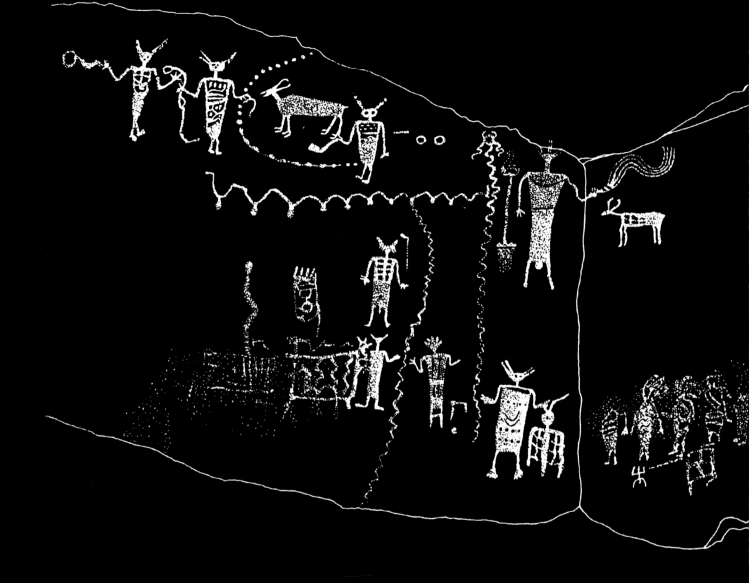

Figure 2.4. The "Biface Site." Tucked away in the nearly inaccessible canyon depths of a tributary to the Little Colorado, the "Biface" site is estimated to be between 1,500 and 2,500 years old. Unmarred by vandalism, it is executed in the Palavayu Linear Basketmaker Style, and the Palavayu Majestic Basketmaker Style. Of the 115 pictorial elements that make up the motif inventory of the panel, 45 are anthropomorphic, 46 zoomorphic, and the rest abstract or nonfigurative.

"Biface" may once have served as a shaman's retreat or sacred place. Evidence for this assumption can be seen not only in the site's isolated location, but also in its mix of entoptic and iconic images. Among the entoptic phenomena, rakes, undulating lines, spirals, filigrees, and amoebalike configurations can be discerned. Of the iconic elements, patterned-body anthropomorphs with supernatural head attachments, hand-held power objects, and associated animal spirit helpers are prominent. Shamanistic imagery of this kind is characteristically produced by the human nervous system in altered states of consciousness. Overall width of site 8 meters.

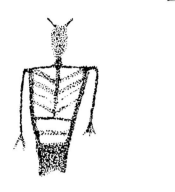

headed figures, and winged figures may refer to the shamanic spiritual flight.[29] Interior cross-hatching in the Basketmaker Linear Style figure is sometimes described as the "x-ray" style, referring to its skeletonized appearance; one of the powers a shaman has is the ability to reduce to a skeletal state, "a passing beyond the profane human condition."[30]

In addition to the horns, which appear on the majority of Palavayu Linear Basketmaker anthropomorphs, the other diagnostics are also present. A few figures at different sites have diagonal cross-hatching on the upper body which resembles skeletal rib cages, perhaps representing the particular ability of shamanic transformation. Figures on a rock art panel at a site along the Little Colorado River suggest another trait of the shaman. A curious individual appears in a group of typical Basketmaker human figures. Displaying horns and the same type of head and large eyes as the others, outstretched wings replace arms, and the legless body seems to be rising. It is a convincing suggestion of shamanic flight.

An alternative interpretation of the Basketmaker anthropomorph as supernatural spirit or deity is reinforced by a rock art depiction (Figure 2.13) at the same site on the Little Colorado River. A large horned figure is portrayed in the typical formal attitude. But to one side a human figure is shown in profile, arms raised as if in awe, body bent forward in a naturalistic stance that is in striking contrast to the other stationary image. The two figures are clearly part of the same composition, alike in style and manufacturing technique, but the lifelike human is unusual in Basketmaker art.[31] The difference between the two figures likely illustrates the artist's conception of the human and the superhuman, further suggesting the possibility that a deity is being portrayed.

At a Chevelon Creek site, figures of a slightly different style are found which may represent an evolutionary sequence. Anthropomorphs there are reminiscent of Schaafsma's San Juan Anthropomorphic Style, with tapered trapezoidal bodies; earrings, hairbobs, or both; solidly pecked areas in torso interiors; and featureless faces (Figure 2.3). Many human figures are wholly pecked. Most are phallic. A few fainter (or more heavily revarnished) Linear Style figures are found at the site and in the near vicinity, providing a contrast which argues for a difference in age. Many animals, mostly deer, accompany both types of human figures.

A peculiarity of this site is that almost every glyph has a small repecked area, usually centered within each figure. The repecking is somewhat lighter in color and does not suggest an attempt at obliteration or vandalism. Rather, it seems to indicate a purposeful attempt to touch each human and animal in a vital spot. Perhaps later people did this to derive magical power from these images (or perhaps to negate that power). Other examples of renewal are evident in different locations, none better illustrated than that in Figure 2.19. Here, the repecking is only partially done on a Basketmaker figure; the two adjacent figures, showing the same light color as the repecking, are adorned with sashes characteristic of the apparel seen in PIV rock art. Obviously, later people attempted to rejuvenate the older glyph. A few Basketmaker petroglyphs which exhibit a coarseness or irregularity of line, sometimes uncommonly fresh-looking, may have been retraced by individuals of a later period for some unknown purpose.

Manufacturing techniques for the Palavayu Basketmaker Style are diverse. Turner describes deeply pecked, mostly broad lines for his Style 5.[32] Many of the Palavayu Linear Basketmaker glyphs have narrow lines which are lightly pecked with widely spaced dints; some have deeper, more closely spaced dints in solid areas. In his study of rock art in the Little Colorado basin, Pilles proposes that a blunt hammerstone was normally used to produce Basketmaker petroglyphs, with a sharpened hammerstone used directly for fine patterns.[33] For the rock art in Petrified Forest that he considers Basketmaker in age, Richard Martynec suggests that direct percussion with a sharpened stone was primarily used.[34] It is difficult to imagine that either of these techniques could produce some of the intricate, finely executed images found at many sites. Some of the more complex petroglyph figures composed of fine lines or carefully defined negative patterns indicate the controlled use of a sharpened stone (or chisel) and hammerstone. This too may imply a development over time. The Palavayu Basketmaker figure seems to become more complex in design, which would account for this change in technique. Added to the linear rectangular and oval-bodied figures, at first simply decorated with lines, bars, and dots, are added triangular and trapezoidal bodies with increasingly intricate designs. Horns become minimal and are replaced by varied headdresses. The S-shaped object becomes infrequent. Heads are adorned with feathers, hairbobs, and earrings, and facial features are eliminated. Patterns in negative relief become more common. This distinctive change in the assemblage of images is termed here the Palavayu Majestic Basketmaker Style.

In the absence of archaeological investigation, it is premature to theorize a time frame for Palavayu Basketmaker art. Little cultural material is associated with the Basketmaker rock art sites in the Palavayu region, a distinct difference from the situation found during the intensive archaeological survey of Glen Canyon. No Basketmaker habitation sites have been noted in the Little Colorado River drainages, nor have such sites or diagnostic artifacts been found at the five known Basketmaker rock art sites along Silver Creek and the Puerco and Little Colorado rivers. There is a convincing argument for assigning the major span of the rock art termed "Basketmaker" to the earlier Archaic period: although numerous pithouse dwellings and villages dating from the Basketmaker II and III eras dot the ridges and mesas of Petrified Forest and the surrounding lands, there is no Basketmaker art nearby, even though rock art of a later period is present. This can only mean that the Basketmaker style of rock art either had an exclusive function or tradition linked with hunting and gathering, seasonal migratory movement, or esoteric ritual confined to specific locations, or that the rock art predates the semisedentary Basketmaker II period.

Undoubtedly, Basketmaker rock art spanned many centuries and has an undetermined beginning. The transition to the style of art which followed, that of the PII–PIII time period, may reflect a major change in the life style of the people, from seminomadic hunters and gatherers to settled farmers.

23

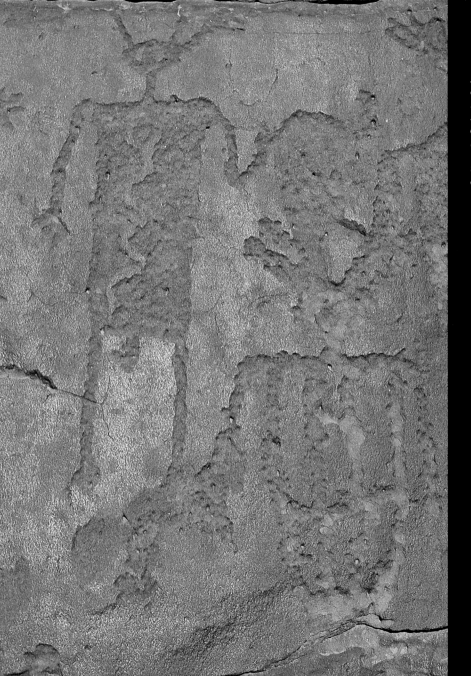

Figures 2.5 and 2.6. Fascination with water and rain, evident in much of Palavayu Basketmaker iconography, is frequently reinforced by recurring associations of Basketmaker anthropomorphs with serpent imagery. While in Figure 2.5 a human's torso is ornamented directly with the reptile, in Figure 2.6 the anthropomorphs seem to be handling highly schematized snakes. These depictions suggest that the snake was part of the shamanistic spirit helper complex. Both images are from the "Biface" site. Length of snake-decorated anthropomorph in Figure 2.5, 34 cm; of pronghorn in Figure 2.6, 35 cm.

Figure 2.7. The partly anthropomorphized serpent, executed in typical Palavayu Linear Basketmaker Style, indicates that the reptile was probably considered a highly numinous creature even in pre-Puebloan times. The tail rattle clearly identifies this as a rattlesnake. The age-old veneration accorded to the serpent, amply reflected in Palavayu rock art imagery, seems to attest to the prevalence of an ancient snake cult which may still survive in the Hopi Snake dance. Length of serpent 105 cm.

Figure 2.8. The geometric elements filling this panel are essentially late Archaic in character. Deeply darkened from revarnishing, the entoptic motifs of circles, spirals, chain arrangements, wavy lines and rakes belong to the visionary imagery that is typically derived from trance experiences. Early Linear Basketmaker Style is detectable in the bisected body of the bighorn sheep near the tail end of the bizarre "raptor" to its right. The solidly pecked bison that superimposes the "raptor"-headed zoomorph is the only portrayal of this animal in Palavayu. Length of "raptor" 123 cm.

Figure 2.9. Reminiscent of the "snake with arms" seen in Figure 2.7, this partially anthropomorphized creature is accompanied by a human figure and an animal drawn in the Palavayu Linear Basketmaker Style. The antennae, rays, and antlers projecting from the heads, as well as their skeletal appearance, strongly suggest a shamanistic origin of the art. Length of "snake-creature" 86 cm.

2.11

◄ 2.10

Figures 2.10 and 2.11. At five sites, Basketmaker figures are pictured
holding what appear to be bunches of flowers or seed grass. However,
these objects may equally represent wands or emblems of shamanic
authority. Height of Figure 2.10 at "Bellbottom" 37 cm; of Figure 2.11 at
"Scarface" 96 cm.

Figure 2.12. Elements such as simple undulations, curvilinear meanders, zigzags, sawtooth lines, rakes, chevrons, and splash dots are frequently found in Palavayu Basketmaker rock art. In this panel at a site southeast of Winslow, such elements surround the solidly pecked bodies of the human figures in a veritable symphony of water and serpent symbols, underpinning those images' roles as rain shamans or deities. Height of horned figure in center 83 cm.

Figure 2.13. In the lower left-hand section of this early Basketmaker panel the human figure depicted in profile seems to raise his hands in supplication to the towering immobile images he faces—perhaps the shaman-artist's conception of mortal man entreating the immortal gods or of his own encounter with the supernatural spirits. Height of supplicant 30 cm.

Figure 2.15. These early, Linear Style Basketmaker figures from "Helmsway" exude a spectral aura characteristic of shamanic art. The otherworldly character of their transparent, skeletonized bodies is further emphasized by the disembodied heads hovering between them like balloons on a string, which may actually represent serpents. Height of anthropomorph on left with fending stick 59 cm.

Figure 2.14. Squiggle mazes, consisting of erratically wandering lines and a profusion of irregularly dissected elements, are part of the Palavayu Archaic and Basketmaker traditions. Complex filigree patterns of this nature may have been "received" by the artist during vision quests or trance states induced by the ingestion of hallucinogens. Among the Western interpretations suggested for the squiggle maze are trapping devices for evil spirits and maps of the underworld. While intriguing, these inferences are totally speculative and not borne out by any ethnographic evidence. Width 152 cm.

Figure 2.16. An elk with elaborate, branching antlers is deliberately superimposed on a male figure in this example of the Palavayu Majestic Basketmaker Style. The animal probably represents the spirit or dream helper "received" by the shaman in a vision during his altered state of consciousness. Length of elk 34 cm.

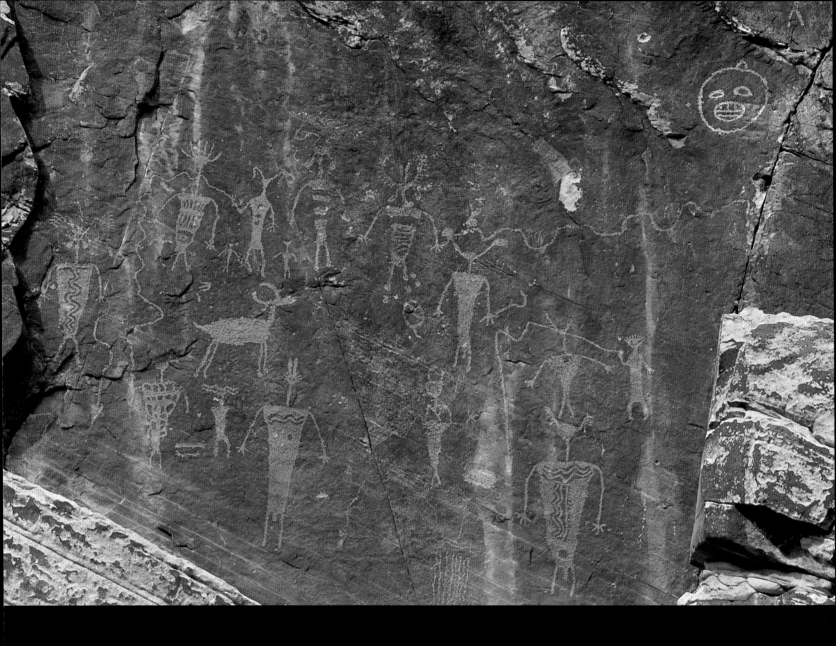

Figure 2.17. A number of patterned-body anthropomorphs surround a pronghorn at a Basketmaker panel of the Palavayu Majestic Style. Curvilinear lines terminating in arrowheadlike tips emanate from four of the figures, configurations that seem to combine serpent and lightning symbolism.

The masklike image in the top right-hand corner of the panel apparently was added later, as is evidenced by its different style and the lighter varnish. The loop at the top of the head and distortion of the mouth, resembling the result of mummification, may actually represent a "trophy head." Height of pronghorn 41 cm.

Figure 2.18. Both anthropomorphic and zoomorphic Basketmaker figures in this panel at the "Steps" site are pockmarked with multiple indentations. The depressions, apparently made by a blunt hammerstone, are strategically placed in "vital" spots such as chest and head areas. They are likely the work of more recent people, as indicated by the lighter revarnishing of the scars. The motivation for this alteration is speculative: Ritual obliteration cannot be ruled out, but the selective placement of the indentations seems to point to a desire for renewing or sharing the power of the original rock images. Height of figure in lower right-hand corner 61 cm.

Figure 2.19. While the revarnishing of the lower portion of the Basketmaker torso on the left nearly equals that of the cliff surface, its upper section is freshly repecked and matches the Puebloan human figures on its right. Note the careful execution of the repecking. It may stem from the later artist's desire to reactivate the spiritual power of the figure, to heighten its power by superimposing his own work, or simply to share the power. Height of center figure 52 cm.

Figure 3.1. Stylistically, the images crowding this sandstone face at the "Bobby D." site may represent a transition from the Basketmaker into the Pueblo period. Note the human figure at top center with the stacked-crescent headdress reminiscent of the San Juan Style of Basketmaker rock art. The sawtooth, zigzag, and ticked lines typically are part of the Palavayu Basketmaker motif repertoire. Length of sawtooth line 50 cm.

Pueblo II was a period of great expansion in the Petrified Forest region and in the middle Little Colorado River Valley to the west. Population increased, more land was cultivated, and small above-ground habitation sites were regularly spaced across the countryside. This period also marked a change in the rock art style in the Palavayu area, a change which probably began during the Basketmaker III stage but did not become wholly evident until late in Pueblo II times. A rock art style cannot be identified for Pueblo I.[1] This is a period which has also been difficult to define archaeologically within Petrified Forest National Park, as few sites are "pure" PI, most having earlier Basketmaker or later PII components. The transition of the Basketmaker rock art style to that of late PII and PIII is equally hard to recognize.

Pilles, in his survey of Little Colorado River Valley rock art, tentatively identified a possible early and middle PII style on several panels of petroglyphs in which some elements contrast in patina, form, and manufacturing technique with surrounding glyphs. Designs presumed to be PII in age include a variety of geometric patterns: circular and rectangular scrolls, outlined circles, solidly pecked circles joined by lines, and so on. There are both outline and solid zoomorphic figures including quadrupeds, mountain sheep, a horned toad, and a snake with triangular coils. Also associated with these images, the bird-bodied quadruped with ball-shaped feet is usually considered typical of the PIV style but may have originated in this earlier period. Produced by poorly controlled indirect percussion, these glyphs exhibit a somewhat sketchy or crude appearance.

Lichen growth on petroglyphs is considered a possible age determinant by Pilles, who noted in his survey that although lichen is found on petroglyphs of the PII period, it is rarely seen on glyphs of the following PIII and PIV periods.[2] There are many lichen-covered petroglyphs in Petrified Forest National Park and surrounding lands, but because of variations at the different rock art sites in the exposure of the parent rock to sun, weather, or humidity, lichen may not be a reliable dating factor in this large area.

The low frequency of rock art which might represent the PI–early PII span may be due either to a smaller population before the late Pueblo II period,[3] or to a decline of interest in making rock art, with a consequent loss of skill. Toward the end of this unproductive stage, rock art began to be produced in quantity. A diverse proliferation of human and animal forms, geometric and abstract designs, and secular and ceremonial subjects is seen. Formal and stylized in the Basketmaker era, petroglyphic art now displayed a flowering of creative expression. Basketmaker rock art is thought to have been made by, or under, the direction of a shaman.[4] The consistent mode of imagery, narrowly limited in design and content, suggests this art was constrained (either by ritual concerns or by tradition) to stay within certain boundaries. Succeeding late PII–PIII art, on the other hand, encompasses a wide variety of subjects and ideas executed by artists of varying abilities, whose motives for making rock art may have ranged from religious purposes to recording mundane matters. The sheer abundance of petroglyphs produced in this area between A.D. 1050 and 1300 may reflect the growth of the population and establishment of an agricultural society with a reliable food source and a more settled life style.

PUEBLO II–

PUEBLO III

STYLES

Human figures in rock art varied greatly throughout the late PII and PIII periods (Figure 3.2). Both the outlined form and the solidly pecked type are common, but the outlined human figure seems more typical of late PIII. The frontal figure is most frequently depicted, but banner and staff bearers, flute players, and hunters with bows and arrows are shown in profile. There is a progression from the static imagery of the early stage of this style toward animation and movement in the PIII period, when some anthropomorphs are shown walking, running, or dancing. Stick figures are also prevalent, early and late. Stick-bodied and "normal" flute players outnumber the humpbacked, phallic type, which appears later in this area, toward the end of Pueblo III or early Pueblo IV, and in much smaller numbers.

Women, indistinguishable in Palavayu Basketmaker art, are not depicted in PII–PIII art as frequently as are men. When represented, females are usually portrayed in special contexts. Three methods of imagery identify females. The most common is the presence of hair whorls, the typical hair style of Pueblo maidens. Although this custom of hair dressing is ancient in origin,[5] it seems to have been pictured most often in the rock art of the PIII and PIV periods. The presence of female genitalia is a second method of portrayal, and considering the subtlety of female anatomy, genitals are delineated in surprisingly diverse ways. These diagnostic features are employed when motherhood is indicated, for the female half of a couple, and when females are shown in scenes suggesting fertility ritual. A third convention used to portray the female, not always consistent but often a clue to gender, is the extension of the torso, rounded or squared, below the hips. This method was first recognized when seen in combination with genitalia, hair whorls, or both, but sometimes it is the sole characteristic. Some female anthropomorphs are probably supernatural entities, as discussed in later chapters. Rarely, women are shown giving birth, or engaging in sexual intercourse.

Snakes, lizards, lizard men, and animals are profuse in Palavayu rock art. The animals, not always identifiable, are usually horned, and most resemble pronghorn. Mountain sheep and deer are seldom pictured at sites in the park area. They are more often depicted just east and west, or in the canyon drainages of the Little Colorado River. Mountain lions and small animals resembling dogs are numerous. Animal tracks are common, with both stylized and realistic bear tracks being the most plentiful, followed by feline or canine paw prints. Deer and pronghorn tracks are sometimes represented as u-shaped hoof prints, more often as tapered "quotation mark" shapes. When the latter prints are dotted at the base (like exclamation marks), dew claws are being depicted, which identifies them as deer tracks (pronghorn lack dew claws).

Bird tracks are also common, as well as bird images. Long-legged water birds pictured near the Puerco River in Petrified Forest National Park appear, on the basis of similar patina, to be contemporary with the PIII-early PIV rock art around Puerco Ruin.[6] Other birds can be identified by certain characteristics. The eagle, usually with widespread wings in the "thunderbird" mode, is represented at many sites and in several stylistic forms. Quail, recognizable by the distinctive topknot, are depicted at a site near Silver Creek and at one east of the park. Macaws or turkeys, both with curved beaks and long tail feathers, are seen in association with late PIII and PIV images. Owls, rarely seen in rock art, are unmistakably represented at seven Palavayu petroglyph sites. Bats, the winged mammals, are also realistically portrayed at a rock shelter outside the park.

Shown fairly often are various insects and like species including moths, butterflies, caterpillars, beetles, centipedes, and scorpions. The centipede may be one of the earliest creatures pictured and is certainly one of the most numerous. It is consistently shown as a many-legged, sticklike body with pincers or antennae at one or both ends.

Simple abstract designs appeared in Basketmaker times. Two of the most common geometric glyphs are pictured throughout the Basketmaker, PII, and PIII periods. They are the spiral, one of the earliest to appear, and the concentric circle, of equal age and ubiquity. The outlined cross, an enigmatic symbol widespread in Southwestern rock art and numerous in the Palavayu region, is also known to be an early design on Basketmaker sandals.[7] It is not common in Basketmaker rock art, however, and only one example can be reliably dated to the Basketmaker III period. Designs on late PI and PII ceramics are reproduced in rock art, and many of these petroglyphs may correspond to those periods; but the same design elements continue to be incorporated in pottery-patterned glyphs associated with later PIII rock art, which confuses temporal sequence. Beautifully executed geometric compositions occur often in Palavayu rock art, and increasingly intricate patterns probably paralleled the development of ceramic design.

Pilles sees certain stylistic features developing in the early and middle PIII period. Anthropomorphs are frequently portrayed with oversized hands and feet, and often with genitalia. He finds portions of anatomy and partial human figures typical of this period. On human footprints the first toe is often at a right angle to the foot.[8]

In the PIII era an array of cultural material is depicted. Men, and in one instance women (Chapter Nine), carry or display staffs, banners, and dance wands. Although the bow and arrow probably appeared in rock art soon after its arrival in the Southwest, other weapons such as clubs and spears are pictured less often and cannot be assigned to a time period. The atlatl may have continued to be a part of the hunter's weaponry for an unknown length of time after the advent of the bow and arrow. Associated with Basketmaker rock art, it is also sometimes present in rock art of a seemingly later style and age.

From the earliest period to the latest, symbolism was employed by the rock artists of Palavayu. Lines of animal tracks or human footprints may indicate movement or trails, or perhaps illustrate narratives. Animals pierced with shafts or arrows may show (or promote) success in the hunt, and human or animal sexual scenes may represent (or induce) fertility. Numerous abstract images are present which modern Native Americans say are symbolic of wind, water, or migration (the spiral), clouds (terraces and triangles), the sun (concentric and rayed circles), the sipapu (squares within squares), and friendship (interlocking half-circles).[9] Figurative as well as nonfigurative elements have been identified as clan insignia. Symbolism may reside in any glyph, and the intent of the artist cannot now be known. An image which appears simple and straightforward to us now may have had entirely different connotations to the artisan who made it.

Some motifs are considered characteristic of Palavayu rock art. Lizards with round bellies are most commonly associated with the PII–PIII style of this region, as are lizard men, which are ambiguous figures indefinable as either lizard or man. Mountain lions with tails curved over their backs are important and are seen often. Human footprints far outnumber handprints, but bird and animal tracks are even more profuse. In particular the bear track is seen in such overwhelming numbers that it apparently was a meaningful symbol (paradoxically, the bear itself was seldom portrayed, being identified at only ten sites). Geometrics and pottery/textile designs are also so plentiful that they could be described as hallmarks of the area's style.

Certain images seem to appear exclusively in Palavayu rock art. Dance wands, cross-barred staffs, crescent-topped staffs, and banners carried by human figures are all ceremonial objects which, to date, have not been found in the rock art of other areas. An unusual type of anthropomorph is found primarily in the park region. Reminiscent of Linear Basketmaker figures and yet obviously of more recent date, this type is an outlined human figure with interior decoration, and often with facial features. In contrast to the triangular or trapezoidal Linear Basketmaker variety with interior fine line or dot patterns, this figure is usually rectangular in shape with bold angular lines, scrolls, and sawtooth designs decorating the torso (Figure 7.2). Facial features are not usual in the rock art of this period and region, but have been found on both human and animal figures, concentrated primarily in an area east of the park.

The bird-headed, or bird-topped man, is a representation common in the rock art of Canyon de Chelly and the San Juan River drainage. Only a few examples have been previously reported in this southern area of the Colorado Plateau,[10] but recently the bird-head motif has been discovered at a number of petroglyph sites near Petrified Forest National Park and in remote areas of the Little Colorado River drainage (Figure 9.6).

Some Palavayu petroglyph scenes suggest narrative or ritual enactment. Bowmen threaten flute players, staff bearers, or men in ceremonial headdress. Several scenes depict a staff bearer balanced on the shoulders of another man, a puzzling acrobatic display. A well-known group of petroglyphs in the "Cave of Life," a rock shelter in Petrified Forest National Park, pictures a priestly figure presiding over a copulating couple who are linked to a chain of other animate forms. Possibly this is a portrayal of the life force, or, as one researcher has proposed, a drama of ritual marriage "to re-create the world and renovate Life."[11] Such scenes imply these were repeated ceremonial events familiar and significant to the people.

Some complex rock art panels illustrate specific activities. Several show lines of pronghorn or deer being herded into enclosures, a hunting ploy which survived into historic times. One such panel is composed of hunters who flourish objects that resemble snares or lassos (Figure 5.5). The capture of eagles is also depicted, a custom related to ceremonial purposes that is still practiced by the Hopi Indians (Figure 5.32).

Methods employed to produce rock art in the PII–PIII period were varied. Indirect percussion, a manufacturing technique in which a hammerstone is used to strike a chisel-like

Figure 3.2. Variations on the human figure in Palavayu rock art of the Pueblo periods (not to scale)

rock, already employed in the Basketmaker period, is frequently used in the initial stage of the PII rock art style. The PII artists did not have as good control of this method as did those of PIII times. Rock artists of this later period used it to great effect in producing finely executed and complex figures such as the geometric designs so abundant in this region. Direct percussion with a blunt or sharpened hammerstone was also employed in the PIII period, and even this method demonstrates fine workmanship. Negativism was a technique used occasionally. In this method, interior designs were left unpecked and were outlined by solidly pecked areas, a reverse of the usual procedure. Glyphs so produced were usually carefully made, with decorative, pleasing results. A light grinding over the surface of the petroglyph is first discernable in early PIII rock art, and this technique became more popular in late PIII and early PIV periods, when a pronounced smoothing appears on many glyphs. Incising with a sharpened stone also became common in this later time period, used primarily to delineate legs, fingers, toes, and open mouths.

An additional type of manufacture is found at almost every rock art site in the Puerco/Little Colorado River region, although it is revealed only on close examination. This type of glyph is scratched rather than pecked, and the scratches, if done lightly, or if revarnished, can be nearly invisible. Many are long, random lines which seem unrelated to surrounding petroglyphs. Some form geometric patterns appearing to overlay the pecked images. Don Christensen has discussed the debate concerning the purpose and age of these scratched elements;[12] he notes that while some scratches appear fresh and recent, others appear to be as old as the petroglyphs they accompany or sometimes seem to superimpose. A number of examples seem to be attempts to deface older glyphs, but others are isolated designs complete in themselves. Scratched elements such as fingers, toes, and lines radiating from the head are seen on some pecked human figures, and it is sometimes difficult to tell if these were made by the original artist or are later (even modern) augmentations. "Unfinished" glyphs sometimes show scratched guide lines which for unknown reasons the artists left unpecked; many scratched images may simply be preforms which were never finished. Several examples, however, defy this theory: there are geometric designs so minute that it is seemingly impossible to peck the fine-line patterns.

In a rock art survey of Great Basin petroglyphs in Nevada and eastern California, Robert Heizer and Martin Baumhoff noted scratched glyphs and labeled them the Great Basin Scratched Style.[13] In a later study, this style was attributed to historic Shoshonean tribes.[14] Eric Ritter and Brian Hatoff contest this in their study of rock art sites in western Nevada.[15] In their opinion, scratching co-occurs with petroglyphs that date to the late prehistoric period. Also, as Stephen Stoney points out, a scratched rock art "style" connotes production by a distinct cultural group in a specific time period, which is probably not the case.[16] Scratched elements recorded in the Mt. Trumbull area of northern Arizona are incorporated with Virgin Anasazi glyphs of the PII–PIII periods,[17] and in Snake Gulch, also on the Arizona Strip, scratched motifs are apparently contemporaneous with pictographs of Basketmaker age.[18] Although controversial as to time period and origin, the scratched style is included in this chapter on

PII–PIII rock art because some scratched images seen in the Puerco–Little Colorado area seem (on the basis of patina) to be contemporary with the petroglyphs of that era.

The Puerco and Little Colorado rivers served as avenues of travel for prehistoric people. Hunting parties, interpueblo travelers, migrants, and traders followed these waterways for centuries, bringing an ever-changing baggage of new ideas. Because the Palavayu region lies between four cultural areas—the Kayenta, the Mogollon, the Cibola, and the Sinagua—it would seem likely that influences from these and other subgroups should be evident in Palavayu rock art, as there are some distinct differences in the style and designs of rock art in each area. Such influences are rarely apparent. In Petrified Forest National Park, the earliest cultural influences seen archaeologically are thought to be from the Mogollon area,[19] and this contact continued, to a lesser degree, through the PIII period. Ties to the Cibola Branch of the Anasazi predominate in Pueblo I, and continue into PIII.[20] The Sinagua shared similar pottery-making techniques with the earliest potters in the Petrified Forest area and left evidence of contact in later periods, probably communicating by way of the Little Colorado River.[21] Although never dominant, the Kayenta Branch nevertheless became a part of the cultural blending seen throughout the Pueblo period of occupation in the park. Despite these influences, the manifestation of them in the region's rock art is scarce.

Although the Cibola Branch seems preeminent in Petrified Forest archaeology, as indicated in analyses of ceramic assemblages, Susan Wells sees a closer affinity to the Winslow Branch Anasazi (c. A.D. 1000 to 1250).[22] Focused primarily in the Hopi Buttes District, the southern boundary of this cultural area follows the Little Colorado River from Holbrook to Winslow and north past Leupp.[23] The rock art along this tentatively determined border is termed the Little Colorado River Valley Style by Pilles. Just as there are basic similarities in the late archaeology of the Petrified Forest area and the Winslow Branch of the middle Little Colorado River area, the same holds true for the rock art of these regions. But there are also differences in the rock art of the two areas. The Palavayu region is larger and encompasses a more profuse array of Basketmaker and PII–PIII rock art than does the area surveyed by Pilles. The Palavayu includes the canyon drainages south of the Little Colorado River which abound in rock art dating from the Basketmaker era, the Archaic, or both, in a style distinctive from the art of those traditions found in other regions. It is also defined by the presence of petroglyph images rarely found in rock art outside its boundaries. The images, discussed and illustrated in later chapters, include bird-topped staffs, cross-barred staffs, banners or devices on poles, and the slab paho. Absence of these images in the Winslow area may indicate a difference in religious practices, or a difference in time period. Prevalence of the PIV style of rock art in the Winslow area reflects the huge population increase taking place there during that period, while concurrently the Petrified Forest area was being slowly abandoned, and PIV rock art is much more infrequent. This seems to indicate the uncommon petroglyph images so numerous in the Petrified Forest were probably produced in an earlier time period. The ritual objects these images represent would therefore be associated with an ideology preceding the kachina religion, which appeared in the PIV period at about the time the large Winslow area pueblos expanded in size and population.[24]

PII–PIII rock art of the Palavayu region is most akin to the widespread rock art tradition of the Plateau Anasazi, although enough differences exist to constitute a regional style of its own. Mountain Mogollon petroglyph art (designated the Reserve Petroglyph Style by Schaafsma[25]) and Palavayu rock art share an inventory of subject images. Animal tracks (the bear track considered a diagnostic in both areas), human footprints, long-tailed animals resembling mountain lions, fringed-winged eagles, reclining and upright flute players, stick figures with legs pointing forward or up, and the outlined cross frequently appear in both traditions. The Reserve Petroglyph style dates after A.D. 1000, when the Mogollon and Pueblo groups were interacting. Thus, it is uncertain who was influenced by whom.

Another contact zone between the Plateau Anasazi and the Mogollon people appears in the Quemado district of western New Mexico. There, human figures of rectilinear outline, with interior decorative design and with facial features, suggest an origin for the similar examples found in and near Petrified Forest National Park. Schaafsma believes "faces" to be a Mimbres feature,[26] and the Mimbres region in southwestern New Mexico may be a possible source of influence for the Palavayu petroglyph images by way of the Quemado area.

Comparisons between Palavayu and Sinagua rock art usually center upon the many geometric designs in both regions. Schaafsma considers these designs to be related to the Sinagua textile tradition, particularly the numerous overall "limitless" pattern typical of Sinagua weavings.[27] Salado and Hohokam, along with some Anasazi ceramic and textile designs, may also have influenced them. In the Palavayu area the limitless patterns are lacking. Geometric images include enclosed squares, rectangles, and circles with interior design elements, and open or unbounded patterns, most with various motifs derived from local or imported ceramics. Although geometric designs in the Palavayu and Sinagua areas share many ceramic motifs, there is a significant difference in concept between the two.

The PIII period was a time of stress for much of the Pueblo world. Although the reasons for this have not been fully determined, it may have stemmed from climate change, environmental degradation, resource depletion, pressure from hostile tribes, or other causes. Much of the northern Colorado Plateau was abandoned; some peoples moved south and some east to the Rio Grande Valley, where populations aggregated into large towns. The Homol'ovi area near Winslow experienced rapid expansion at the end of PIII and into PIV times, when six large pueblos were established along the Little Colorado River. Conversely, in the Petrified Forest area settlements remained small, numerous, and dispersed until the end of the PIII period, when these sites began to be abandoned. During that time, Puerco Ruin, and Canyon Butte and Stone Ax ruins (just west and east of the park) comprised the only significant populations. Puerco, Stone Ax, and a few small sites were inhabited into PIV times, but the entire Petrified Forest region was apparently vacated by the end of the PIV period.

Pilles[28] and Martynec[29] see rock art skills degenerating in both the Puerco and Little Colorado regions beginning in the late PIII period. Petroglyphs exhibit a carelessness in execution, and much of the art loses aesthetic quality. Manufacturing techniques employed both the sharpened hammerstone and indirect percussion. Incising and grinding were often used, and are considered diagnostic for this period. Design elements include bird-bodied animals with cloven hoofs and open mouths, which Pilles believes are also present in PII rock art. Other identifying elements he mentions are animals with knee joints, pecked balls for feet, extra long legs, and horns joined to the neck rather than to the head. Blocky feet, on both animal and human figures, are common. These stylistic features continue into the PIV period, when a new imagery emerges. Rock art once more appears to be dominated by a single religious belief system just as Basketmaker art was apparently governed by shamanic ideology. A sweeping change in the socioreligious structure of the Pueblo world manifests itself in the rock art of Pueblo IV.

▲ 3.3

▲ 3.4

Figures 3.3 and 3.4. Interpreted either as phallic human or humanized lizard, the symbolic or metaphorical meaning of "lizard-men" is uncertain. Various roles have been suggested for the image—assistant totem of the shaman, a frog or lizard god, or emblem of sexual potency. But without ethnographic foundation, these must be treated as pure speculation. It may be noteworthy in this context that the Hopi kachina pantheon contains one lizard deity. This is Manangya, the "Collared Lizard." The relationship between the three lizard-men flanking an armless anthropomorph with beautifully radiant aureole in Figure 3.3 is not apparent. The lizard-man image in Figure 3.4, from one of the rock art panels at the Flattops in Petrified Forest, is accompanied by a spiral, bear paw print, cross-staff bearer, and slab paho, underscoring the sacred importance of the site. Height of rayed figure in Figure 3.3, 95 cm; height of slab paho in Figure 3.4, 28 cm.

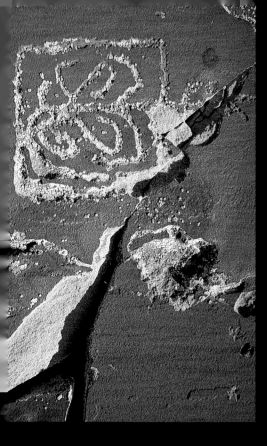

Figure 3.5. Adding a distinct aesthetic dimension to the petroglyph, the lichen growth encrusting this butterfly at "Daisy Spur" will eventually obliterate it. The butterfly motif, while only sparsely occurring in Palavayu rock art, still plays a significant ceremonial role in Hopi culture. Width 16.5 cm.

Figure 3.6. Squared spirals, interlocking rectangular scrolls, and rectilinear meanders in many variations were among the most popular geometric design motifs of the Palavayu rock artist. The juxtaposition of representational and nonrepresentational elements in this panel at "Kim's Peak" along Dead Wash creates an aesthetically pleasing counterpoint. Width of nonfigurative design 28 cm.

Figure 3.7. The "Golden Disk" site in Petrified Forest commands instantaneous "aesthetic arrest." However, the beauty of the panel has no bearing on the meaning of the art. The unidentifiable bipedal zoomorph in the center suggests a composite of pronghorn (horns) and mountain lion (paws). Hybridized creatures of this sort occur occasionally in Palavayu rock art and may be the pictorial result of shamanic vision quests. Diameter of disk 60 cm.

Figure 3.8. These three standing "decobods," patterned-body anthropomorphs, may illustrate a one-time custom of decorating the body with paint or tattoos. The most prominent figure can clearly be identified as female. All three may represent divine personages worshipped long ago at this shrine at the "Coyote Den" site. Height of figure on right 41 cm.

Figure 3.9. Dynamic energy emanates from this kinesthetic, massive concentration of circles and spirals—both simple and rayed—that flank a single human with upraised hands on this boulder in "Roller Canyon." While we cannot fathom the significance of these abstract motifs to the prehistoric artist, coils may be symbolically linked to the power of the serpent, circular and radiant designs to that of the sun. Diameter of rayed concentric circle on right end of panel 44 cm.

Figure 3.10. This horned figure at "Moingail" with fringed winged arms and big drooping feet exudes a strong shamanic aura. The "shaman" is carrying a rattle in his right hand, and the left hand seems to be holding or touching a snake. Four additional serpents, one coiled and displaying its bifid tongue, complement the potent scene. The coyotelike animal underneath the coiled snake may represent one of the spirit helpers the "shaman" calls upon in this apparent act of magic transformation. Height of tallest figure 70 cm.

Figure 3.11. This lively line of arm-waving dancers may be involved in a rainmaking ritual. Evidence for this speculation can be seen in the associated image of the stylized toad. Length of line dance 66 cm.

Figure 3.12. At first sight, this curious geometric design from "Daisy Spur" appears to be a mask. Featuring terraced cloud motifs on the forehead, rectilinear spiral eyes, and a feathered beard, the configuration resembles a Hopi Longhair kachina. This illusion of a masklike image shifts into something entirely different when the human head and arms attached to its right are taken into account. The set of parallel vertical zigzags now suggests a dance formation. Whatever the meaning of the arresting emblem, mystifying motifs of this kind are not infrequent occurrences in Palavayu rock art. Height 35 cm.

Figures 3.13-3.15. In each of these photographs lichen, by encroachment or invasion, has added color, emphasis, or texture to the underlying glyphs. In Figure 3.13 the geometric design is partly obscured by the advancing mosslike layer. In Figure 3.14 two human figures are embossed with colorful lichen. A white crust fills the pecked areas of the images in Figure 3.15. Slow-growing lichen may be centuries old, and while beautiful in itself is extremely destructive to rock surfaces and the petroglyphic art upon them. Height of geometric design in Figure 3.13; 16 cm; height of black anthropomorph in Figure 3.14, 40 cm, and width of human group in Figure 3.15, 33 cm.

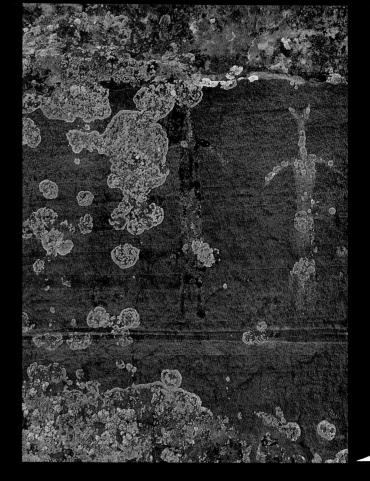

◢ 3.14

◢ 3.13

◢ 3.15

Figure 3.16. At this panel of the "Second Flume" site, two human figures, distinguished by erect phalli and long switchlike extensions from their heads, are seen grasping what looks like the overlong tail of a horned lizard and a rope tied to the head of a fowl resembling a turkey. While the artist's intent must remain unknowable, the scenes are extremely unusual in that they exhibit a certain amount of humor, if not mischief. Height of figure on right 31 cm.

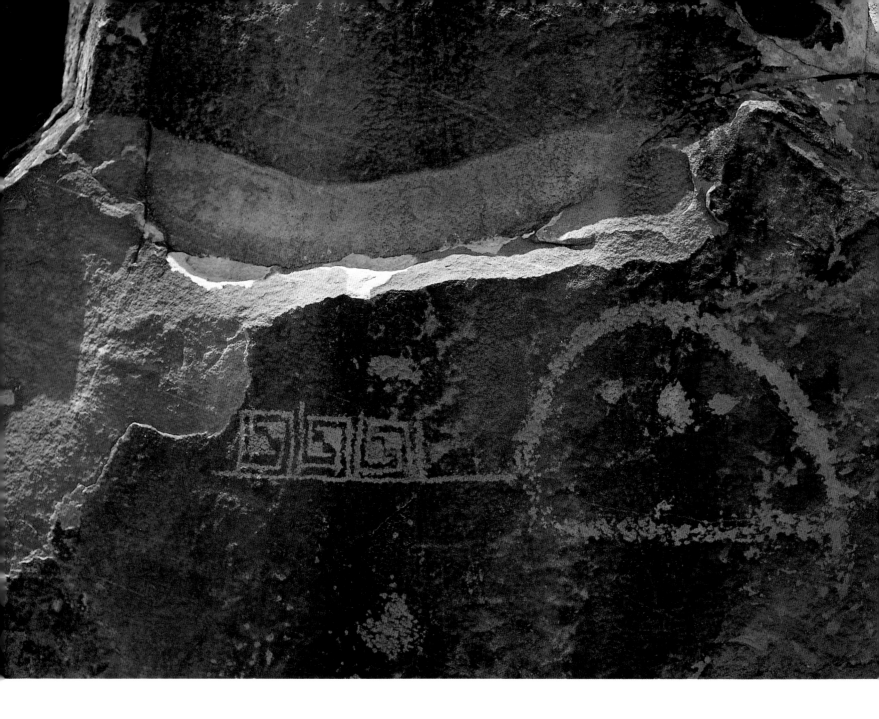

Figure 4.1. As a symbol of awe-inspiring power, the mask has been part of humankind's religious and artistic devices for millennia. When "faces" in Palavayu rock art first begin to be "masks" is difficult to say. Solitary, disembodied heads already appear in the Palavayu Linear Basketmaker Style, and many countenances of Pueblo II and Pueblo III figures are masklike rather than mimetic of human facial features. A massive influx of definite masks starts in the early fourteenth century with the introduction of the kachina religion, and they become diagnostic emblems of the Pueblo IV period. Width of geometric band 16 cm.

Early in the fourteenth century, new images appeared in the rock art of the Palavayu region, signaling a profound change in the social and ceremonial structure of Pueblo society. Portrayal of masks and masked beings announced the arrival of the kachina religion, a belief system which seems to have swept the Pueblo world with astonishing speed. Its most basic expression, the mask, is depicted in pottery decoration, kiva murals, and rock art. Through ceramic analysis and archaeological excavation, reasonably accurate dates can be assigned to the religion's appearance in different areas.

The origin of the kachina religion is not known. There are parallels and similar icons in Pueblo period and Mesoamerican art, and a proto-kachina ideology from Mexico may have diffused into the Pueblo world along a widespread trade network. Schaafsma asserts that beginning around A.D. 1000 in the Mogollon region of southern New Mexico, the mask tradition is first discerned in ceramic designs of the Mimbres culture and in the Jornada Style of rock art.[1] An image widely represented in the rock art is a figure similar to the Mexican rain god *Tlaloc*, and may imply that religious practices of the Jornada and Mimbres people were largely concerned with the bringing of rain. The kachina religion of the Pueblo people shares this concern, and Schaafsma points out parallels in rock art imagery of the Rio Grande and Jornada regions suggesting a logical cultural connection between the Pueblo kachina sect and the Jornada religious complex, from a probable Mexican origin.[2] Cloud imagery, highly stylized life-forms portrayed with facial features, and isolated faces and masks are important components of both Rio Grande and Jornada Styles of rock art. Another oft-seen image is the horned serpent, a symbol of the Mexican god *Quetzalcoatl*, also an indication of origin to the south.

The great population increase in the northern Rio Grande Valley after A.D. 1300 spawned the florescence of a new style of rock art. Termed the Rio Grande Style, Schaafsma believes it is derived from the Jornada Style. In this new tradition, kachina symbolism is fully evolved, and it also appears early in the fourteenth century in the middle Little Colorado River region, ostensibly having spread from the east. Kachina iconography is present in rock art at Homol'ovi pueblos, at Puerco Ruin in Petrified Forest, and at Nuvakwewtaqa at Chavez Pass, south of Homol'ovi. It is also occasionally seen in designs on pottery excavated from Chevelon Ruin and the Homol'ovi sites.[3]

The kachina religion possibly developed indigenously in the Western Pueblo region, influenced by ideas from Mexican and Mogollon sources.[4] This theory is persuasive, because the PIV rock art of the Western Pueblo area seems to represent a stylistic tradition distinct from the Rio Grande Style.

Despite uncertainty regarding the origin and antecedents of the kachina religion, there is agreement over the reasons for its rapid assimilation into Pueblo society. When major areas of the northern Colorado Plateau were abandoned during the late PIII and PIV periods, the Anasazi populations migrated into the Rio Grande River Valley, the middle and upper Little Colorado River Valley, and into some areas below the Mogollon Rim. Pueblos expanded in size as diverse groups of people were accepted into local populations. A need

grew to unify these villagers of differing backgrounds into a cooperative and integrated community. The kachina religion draws members from the entire village and would have fulfilled this role. Kachina ceremonial structure in Pueblo societies differs from east to west,[5] and according to the way it fits into each social organization it may be controlled by clan, society, or moiety. Since these organizations endured relatively unchanged throughout the historic era, it is assumed they also operated in basically the same manner during prehistoric times.

Kachina religion, a pan-Pueblo phenomenon, adapted early to the requirements for communal harmony and to the needs of the people. These necessities were addressed by different rites that had specific functions: to cure ills, foster proper behavior, bring success in war and the hunt, promote fertility, inspire discipline and punish offenders, redistribute food, perpetuate traditions and religious tenets, and bring rain. In the arid land of the Western Pueblos, the bringing of rain posed the major concern. In the Eastern Pueblos, with their access to the water of the Rio Grande River and its tributaries, rainmaking did not loom foremost in importance. Medicine, hunt, and warrior societies of historic times indicate these pursuits were of greater consequence to them. At the eastern Keresan villages, prominently developed medicine societies emphasized curing.

What is a kachina? The word "kachina" is a popular anglicized version of what is correctly spelled "katsina" in Hopi. As Malotki has shown,[6] this word is untranslatable and nonindigenous to the Hopi culture. All linguistic evidence points to the term's origin from the Keres-speaking culture of New Mexico.[7] In the ethnographic literature concerning Hopi beliefs, kachinas are described as "beneficent supernaturals,"[8] "spiritual beings," and "gods."[9] They dwell in lakes, springs, and mountains. During the first half of the year they visit the Hopi villages, bringing many benefits to the people including much-needed rain. The kachinas arrive in the form of masked impersonators: Hopi men who assume a great responsibility in performing these roles, for the mask embodies the actual transfer of personal identity to kachina spirit. This belief is well illustrated in a Hopi origin myth recounted in Mischa Titiev's study of Oraibi. One of several versions, this story stated that kachinas accompanied the Hopi when they emerged from the Underworld. They traveled with the people in their early wanderings and brought them many blessings with their songs and dances. An attack by enemies killed the kachinas, and they returned to their homes in the Underworld. To retain contact with their benefactors, the Hopi developed the custom of using masks and sacred garments in their dances "in order to impersonate the gods." It is the donning of the mask that symbolizes the nature and purpose of this impersonation, for—as Titiev goes on to say—"it is the mask...that transmutes the man into a god in Hopi belief." Although Titiev does not further refer to kachinas as gods, some scholars and historians of religion prefer that designation.[10] In an investigation of the relationship of language and cultural concepts, Malotki reasons:

Figure 4.2a. Examples of the Rio Grande Style (not to scale)

Figure 4.2b. Examples of the Palavayu PIV Style (not to scale)

The term "spirit" evokes the traditional Indo-European dualism of spirit and matter, a dichotomy which is generally alien to American Indians. Hopi kachinas, however, can take on both visible and invisible shapes, they are at once material/visible and immaterial/invisible. Kachinas are endowed with the whole spectrum of human and personal characteristics. Hopi mythology abounds with situations in which kachinas mingle with the Hopi people and even marry Hopi girls. In a non-mythological or ceremonial context they visit the Hopi villages, entertain them with dances and bestow gifts on them. As kachinas can be very concrete and physical beings, this rules out using the concept of "spirit." Moreover, spirits usually do not intermarry with humans; kachinas do. Nor is the term "supernatural being" really applicable because kachinas appear also as natural phenomena. Hopi kachinas in their phenomenology resemble the Greek gods and, of course, gods come in many sizes.[11]

Some of the most ancient kachinas are the *wu'ya*, or clan ancestor of individual clans, impersonated only at certain times by men chosen by the proprietary clan. Their masks are permanent; they may be refurbished but never changed in design. They are powerful entities and therefore associated with the major Hopi ceremonies. They are abiding figures in the assemblage of kachinas; lesser kachinas disappear and reappear, new ones are borrowed from other Pueblos or are developed from outside influences and events. The roster of supporting players may change, but the leading characters are unchanging.

That some kachinas were connected with the initial naming of the owning clan and "brought" to Hopi suggests these deities existed long before incorporation into the kachina religion. It is likely that deities representing the same entity but possessing different traits were imported from several directions. This might account for the many-sided and often contradictory aspects of these beings.

Schaafsma sees the Rio Grande Style as a continuity of the Jornada Style of rock art, sharing a similar element inventory and stylistic affinities, but decreasing in complexity of design from southern to northern areas.[12] Masks and ceremonial figures are abundant, some masks resembling those of modern kachinas (Figure 4.2a). Other images include humpbacked flute players, decorative shields and shield figures, stars and star faces, corn plants, birds (eagles, cranes, parrots, turkeys) and bird motifs (thunderbirds, mirrored bird pairs, birds in profile with raised wings), one- and two-horned snakes, fish, mountain lions, badgers, skunks, and bears.

The Rio Grande Style has also been used to describe rock art in the Western Pueblo region thought to date after A.D. 1300. In the Palavayu area, rock art of this style differs from the eastern expression in both subject matter and manner of portrayal (Figure 4.2b). Missing are the stars and star faces, intricately patterned masks and headgear, one-horned snakes, fish, badgers, and skunks. Although depictions of the same birds occur, the mirrored pairs and birds with raised wings are lacking. Humpbacked flute players are few, corn plants rare,

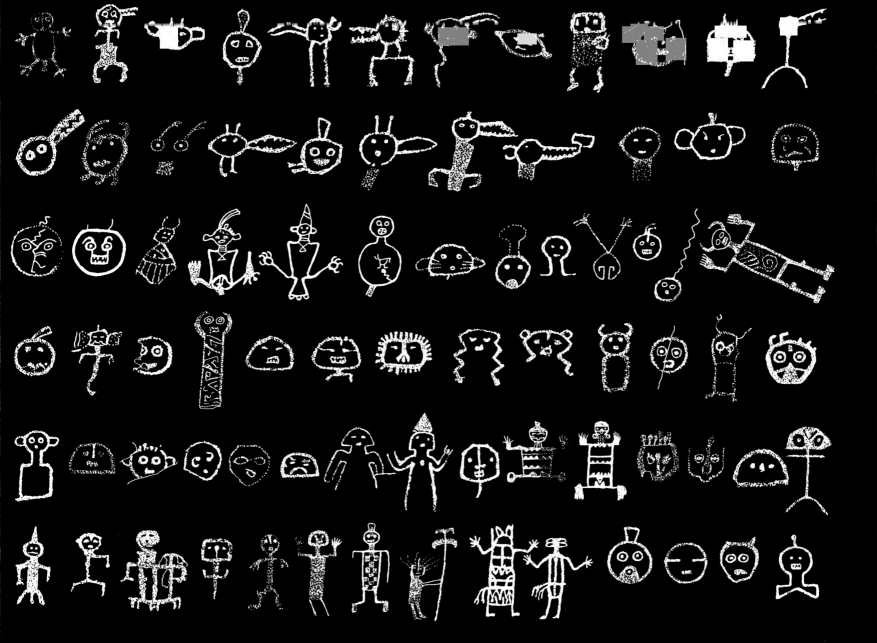

Figure 4.3. Masks and masked figures, Palavayu PIV Style (not to scale)

and only six examples of shields or shield-bodied figures have been found. The "cloud terrace," a stepped pyramid, is occasionally seen. Masks are usually simple in design with three dots or circles often representing eyes and mouth (Figure 4.3). Variations picture rectangular and toothy mouths, round eyes with pupils, and elongated eyes. Heads are usually round, but squares, triangular shapes, and flat-bottomed or flat-topped circles are sometimes found. One mask is framed by curving horns, and a single example has no outline at all. This feature is common in Jornada and the eastern Rio Grande Style, but not often seen in the west. Some masks are partially bisected with lines descending from the forehead, perhaps representing noses. Ears are sometimes pictured, and occasionally, horns. A number of mask images near Puerco Ruin have snouts or birdlike beaks. A few full-bodied masked figures are found, but only two at the same site (Figure 2.19) are adorned with the sash and ceremonial attire seen on such eastern figures. When depicted, bodies in Palavayu rock art are usually rectangular, legs may have knobby knees, and feet often turn outward or to one side. While it is impossible to identify specific kachinas among the masks portrayed, some with bared teeth and goggle eyes are reminiscent of Hopi Ogre kachinas, and two petroglyph examples resemble the Hopi god *Maasaw*. In general, the masks seen in the western area are simpler in design and accompanied by fewer of the motifs and elaborate images of the eastern area.

In his study of rock art between Winslow and Holbrook, Pilles prefers to designate the PIV style of rock art there as a part of the Little Colorado River Valley tradition, rather than of the Rio Grande Style.[13] The characteristics he lists, in addition to possible masks, are human figures with round or rectangular bodies and simple lines for limbs, hair whorls on females, stick figures, human footprints (sometimes with bunionlike protrusions), geometric patterns, and life forms resembling dogs, parrots, and rabbits. Pilles sees a relationship between certain elements and their depiction in solid or outline form. Human faces and bodies, masks, and geometric designs are usually executed in outline; animals, footprints, and some stylized anthropomorphs are solidly pecked. Occasionally, composite animal forms are in evidence. A bird-bodied animal with cloven hoofs is a part of this inventory, a portrayal also noted in Palavayu Basketmaker rock art. Blocky feet on animals are a diagnostic element. The manufacturing techniques Pilles mentions include both the blunt and sharpened hammerstone, usually producing a glyph of shallow depth.

Rock art with kachina iconography is thinly scattered in the Palavayu region, and concentrated primarily in areas near ruins dating from the PIII and PIV periods. The PIV ruins within Petrified Forest National Park include Puerco Ruin and a few smaller pueblos in the southeast area. Just outside the southeast boundary of the park lies Wallace Tank (or Stone Ax) Ruin and a large unnamed ruin east of Wallace Tank. The PIII sites include the Canyon Butte Ruins outside the western border, and within the park, a multiroom site atop Mountain Lion Mesa. It may be coincidental that rock art with kachina imagery appears near those sites which date earlier than A.D. 1300, but other possibilities exist for this circumstance. The land west of the park border is privately owned, and aside from a limited

survey and excavation at the Canyon Butte Ruins in 1901 by anthropologist Walter Hough, the area has not been systematically investigated. There may be other sites in this area that were occupied in the PIV period. The small number of PIV images at neighboring rock art galleries, which are otherwise typical of the PII–PIII period, may possibly represent visitation by later people. Throughout the Pueblo region, abandoned ancestral villages were considered shrines and were regularly revisited.[14] The group of masks and masked figures on boulders below the northern tip of Mountain Lion Mesa lie about halfway between the Canyon Butte and Wallace Tank ruins along a natural route between the two areas. The Mountain Lion Mesa petroglyphs of PIV vintage are also small in number compared to the many glyphs of the PII–PIII period which crowd the nearby cliff faces. Kachina images may have been deliberately located on the mesa because it is a highly visible point along a well-traveled trail.

Wallace Tank Pueblo and the unnamed PIV ruin lie in an area bereft of rock or cliff. Significantly, the only other assemblages of PIV rock art, apart from those at Mountain Lion Mesa and Puerco Ruin, are found on either side of Crystal Ridge. This mesa is located within the park between Wallace Tank and Mountain Lion Mesa, providing the only rock suitable for petroglyphs within a reasonable distance from Wallace Tank.

Kachina iconography at rock art sites near the Homol'ovi group of ruins has been researched by Cole[15] and will not be discussed here, as it occurs just outside the northern perimeter of the area designated the Palavayu. Other examples of kachina imagery are found at a few sites east of the park, along the banks of the Little Colorado River near the town of Woodruff, and on the rock faces along Clear Creek and Jack's Canyon south of Winslow.

Certain masked images in the Palavayu region are of special interest. On one face of the massive boulder below Mountain Lion Mesa, upon which the majority of PIV glyphs appears, is the horizontal full-length figure seen in Figure 4.13. The head is horned, and the face, with large round eyes and bared teeth, resembles masks of Hopi Ogre kachinas. Its rectangular body, knobby knees, and feet turned to one side are elements which typify anthropomorphs of this time period. An unusual feature of this image is the x-ray effect, which shows a skeletal rib cage and viscera. Combined with the recumbent attitude of the figure, the impression is of death. Basketmaker figures occasionally suggest such skeletal patterns, theorized to be related to shamanistic beliefs, but the concept of kachina doesn't include such symbolism. This masked figure, as far as is known, is unique.

Two full-length figures at "Slab Crest" display design elements similar to those on PIV ceramics and kiva murals (Figure 4.4). Faces on both petroglyph figures are bisected horizontally by lines which may represent masks or painted facial decorations. The bisecting line in petroglyph image Figure 4.4b particularly resembles that of the Pottery Mound kiva mural Figure 4.4c. Distinctive treatment of the hands on the Jeddito bowl in Figure 4.4d is similar to that of the petroglyph image in Figure 4.4a. Both petroglyph figures can be identified as female by the conventionalized depiction of genitalia. The kiva mural figure is unmistakably female, with hair whorls and Pueblo-style dress, and the figure on the Fourmile polychrome bowl (Figure 4.4e) may be depicted with a "vulva" pattern. The petroglyph individuals are situated on fairly level rock faces. Close to one figure is a hollowed-out pit, and the right foot of the other figure is itself a cuplike depression. The pits may have been made to receive offerings, and these figures represent female deities, as the figure on the pottery bowl may also personify. Location of this rock art site on the highest crest of a ridge, along with the many ritual "slab pahos" pictured there (Chapter Nine), suggest this was indeed a shrine or sacred place.

A second example of a petroglyph site which may have been considered a shrine "owned," or at least visited, by nonlocal people is found east of the park. This rock art site centers on a large isolated boulder surrounded by smaller rocks on which most of the petroglyphs appear. The nearest settlement found in the area is on a low mesa about a quarter-mile distant. Surface sherds there indicate the small village dates to the PI period. Although many glyphs on the rock faces of the mesa and at the boulder site could also date from that time period, there are a number of human figures with masks, or images depicted in a typical PIV style. These full-length figures seem to be engaged in ceremony, and carry unusual ceremonial staffs: rods topped with inverted crescents. One such isolated staff is placed on the highest face of the large boulder, a circumstance also noted at "Slab Crest," where a slab paho prominently adorns a rock at the apex of the ridge. From all evidence, people of a different time and place than those from the nearby village apparently visited this site for ritual purposes.

In the rock art survey conducted by Pilles in the Little Colorado River area, he notes that much of the rock art attributed to the PIV period compares unfavorably, on the whole, with the rock art of the preceding PII–PIII periods. As Turner found with the PIV rock art of the Glen Canyon area, it appears to be a "degenerate" form, and often seems to be carelessly made. This is not always true of PIV rock art in the Palavayu region, which is sometimes intricate in design and carefully executed. Such panels admittedly are rare. Although plentiful in the area Pilles surveyed, PIV rock art is much less frequent in the Petrified Forest locale, and in the canyon drainages south of the Little Colorado River. This is probably due to the earlier withdrawal of populations to the Homol'ovi pueblos, Zuni, and the Hopi mesas. Around A.D. 1400, the lower Puerco and the middle Little Colorado River Valley were completely abandoned, and the prehistoric rock art traditions end.

a.

b.

c.

d.

e.

Figure 4.4. Ceramic, mural, and petroglyph females

    a. & b. Petroglyph, "Slab Crest"
    c. Kiva 9, Layer 2, south wall, Pottery Mound (after Hibben)
    d. Jeddito Black-on-Yellow bowl, Homol'ovi (after Hays)
    e. Fourmile Polychrome bowl, Homol'ovi (after Hays)

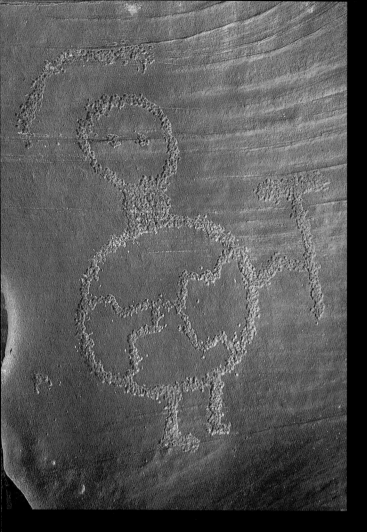

Figure 4.5. Anthropomorphs whose torsos consist of shieldlike images are generally known as shield figures or shield bearers. This example from the "Flintstone" site in Jack's Canyon carries a weapon, possibly a stone-ax. Common in the Rio Grande Style rock art of New Mexico, shield figures are extremely rare in the Palavayu. Height 57 cm.

Figure 4.6. According to Hopi belief, a mask becomes alive the instant it is donned by the impersonator—and the person is transformed into the god the mask portrays. Attempts to identify masks with certain kachinas of the various Pueblo pantheons are notoriously futile. The artist of this gigantic mask at "Puerco Ridge" in Petrified Forest has designed the mask's facial features in such a way that they convey the illusion of a walking stick-man. Height 98 cm.

Figure 4.8. Unlike Paalölöqangw, the mythic "Water Serpent" of the Hopis that is endowed with one backward- or forward-reaching horn, both of the examples from Palavayu are equipped with two horns. In this side view of the reptile on a rock art panel near Joseph City, the horns go forward; at a site near Carr Lake Draw they are curved backward. Length of serpent 180 cm.

Figure 4.9. Composite animals, blending portions of several different creatures, are occasionally found in Pueblo IV Palavayu rock art. At the "Golden Fleece" site, we see what appears to be a large cougar, with feline features, birdlike beak, and paws that resemble human hands and feet. Defying specific identification, the resulting hybrid creature may represent an imaginary deity whose extraordinary power rests in the attributes of the combined animals. Height of anthropomorph in a squat position 60 cm.

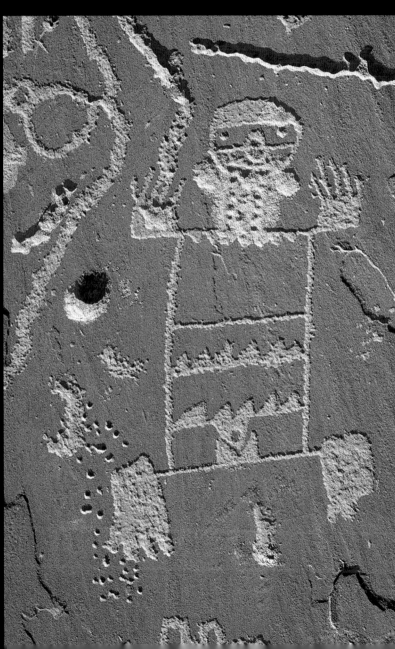

Figure 4.10. This scene from "Valley of the Flutes" seems to depict a human with outstretched arms supplicating a strange cloudlike entity. Terraced forms of this type are still emblematic of clouds in modern Pueblo iconography. Compare also the supplicant of the Basketmaker scene in Figure 2.13, more than a thousand years older than the present PIV figure. Height of cloud image 68 cm.

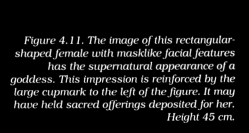

Figure 4.11. The image of this rectangular-shaped female with masklike facial features has the supernatural appearance of a goddess. This impression is reinforced by the large cupmark to the left of the figure. It may have held sacred offerings deposited for her. Height 45 cm.

Figure 4.12. The juxtaposition of these two figures, whose facial features strongly resemble kachina masks, conveys a vivid sense of ritual. They seem to portray the enactment of a mythic drama, perhaps the hieros gamos or "sacred marriage" between a male sky god (note the bird-shaped, feather-tipped body and the taloned hands) and a female earth goddess. Note the pendant necklaces in the form of an hourglass. Identically drawn strands adorn anthropomorphs on mural frescoes from Pottery Mound, a prehistoric Pueblo community dating to about A.D. 1350. Height of female figure 34 cm.

Figure 4.13. The horns, large round eyes, and toothy mouth of this full length figure are reminiscent of Hopi Ogre kachinas, but the exposed ribs and viscera detailed on the image are unprecedented in Palavayu rock art. Length of figure 92 cm.

Figure 4.14. The entire configuration of this contoured bird, including its solidly pecked head, suggests an eagle. The depicted heart line, symbolic of the vital power center of the creature, and probably also an indicator of supernatural power, is the only one found in Palavayu to date. Height 44 cm.

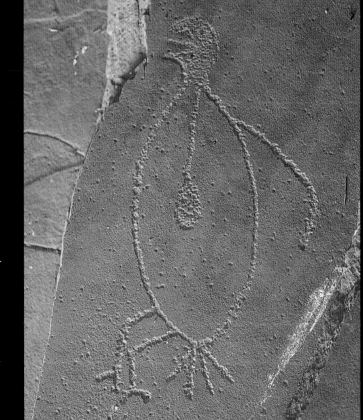

Figure 5.1. The archer portrayed at this rock art site west of Petrified Forest National Park is equipped with a "nodule club" in addition to his bow and arrow. The club, a weapon of warfare, was apparently carried by hunters as well as warriors. Height 31 cm.

Throughout the long span of time from the Basketmaker era to the late Pueblo period, animals are among the most frequently pictured subjects in rock art of the Palavayu region. An overriding interest to depict game animals by hunter-gatherers is understandable, but continued major concern with animals through the centuries when farming provided the primary food source is less so. Two rock art surveys conducted in Petrified Forest National Park in recent years at twenty-two petroglyph sites dated generally from the PII through PIII periods, produced an almost equal number of human images and animal images.[1] This ratio, though not tested in a survey of the total number of Palavayu sites, is probably representative. Although certainly involved in large part with hunting, the obvious concern with animal life may also involve more complex associations.

Human figures of the Palavayu Basketmaker Style are often surrounded by animal images, but there are no examples which show hunters actually engaged in hunting. At two Basketmaker rock art sites south of Winslow, a different kind of interaction is implied. At the "Biface" site, animals are deliberately superimposed onto human figures; on panels at the other site, the "Steps," human figures overlay animals. All elements appear to be contemporary in age. A study using ethnographic records to interpret hunter-gatherer rock art in the American West contends the origin of such rock art follows an almost universal pattern, representing images seen by shamans in altered states of consciousness.[2] This trancelike state, induced by physical exertion, fatigue, fasting, or by ingestion of hallucinogens, was employed to receive visions and gain supernatural power through the acquisition of a spirit helper. The animals superimposing or underlying human figures at Palavayu rock art sites may symbolize the bond between shaman and spirit animal helper, whose assistance could not only bring success to the hunt and increase the supply of game, but also aid in healing disease and in bringing rain and other benefits to the shaman's people. Most of the animals appear to be deer and elk, many portrayed with greatly exaggerated racks of antlers. One panel at the "Steps" site pictures rows of animals flanking and facing a central human figure. At the "Biface" site, an elk with elaborately branching antlers has been pecked over the horned head of a human being. A panel at "Trophy Head," a third site in the area, pictures anthropomorphs with ornate headdresses encircling a lone horned animal. All these images suggest both man and animal are represented in contexts transcending reality. As horns are universal symbols of shamanic power, unrealistically large antlers of the deer and elk may indicate these animals are spirit helpers, rather than prey.

The concept of the spirit familiar or guardian spirit is a belief held by the later Pueblo people as well.[3] Stone images of animals are always prominent on the altars used in many Pueblo ceremonies, and are kept as guardians in family dwellings. The bear is the curer animal in Keresan, Tewan, and Zuni medicine societies, and the badger serves in that role at Hopi. Supreme predator, the mountain lion is the patron of most Pueblo hunting societies, and its powers are invoked by hunt shamans. Animals are also the totems, or clan ancestors, of some Pueblo clans; because of the spiritual relationship, clan members could ask the animal for help. Animals have always been regarded by Indians as more than a food source, and their depictions in rock art must be considered in other possible contexts as well as the hunting association.

Animal images appear as clan symbols. A notable example is the hundreds of petroglyph clan "signatures" pecked on the rocks at Willow Springs, Arizona, by Hopis on pilgrimage to the salt deposits in the Grand Canyon. Coyote and rabbit, along with many from the bird, reptile, and insect families, are among the images that represent specific clans. Animal tracks represent the bear and badger clans, which may be significant to those petroglyph tracks found in such large numbers in the Petrified Forest area. In addition to the clan symbols portrayed at Willow Springs, many can be found on the cliff faces and boulders around the Hopi mesas. Some petroglyphs near Wupatki and Homol'ovi II have been identified as clan signatures by Hopi, but few other authenticated examples exist elsewhere. Many of the animals pictured in the rock art of the Palavayu region may record clan affiliation, for the custom of marking clan symbols on stone is an ancient one.

Deified animals may also be represented in rock art. Mythical creatures who frequently appear in Pueblo legend, such as the dread *Kwaatoko*, a monster eagle who "sorely troubled the Hopi people" of long ago,[4] Knife-Wing, Zuni Beast God of the Zenith, and the Horned or Plumed Water Serpent (known in its different manifestations as *Paalölöqangw* at Hopi, *Kolowisi* at Zuni, and *Avanyu* among the Rio Grande Tewa) have been identified in rock art. Other animals, the mountain lion and the bear in particular, have supernatural aspects in Pueblo beliefs but are not distinguished by special imagery. It would be difficult to positively separate depictions of animals of the natural world from those which symbolize animal spirits, for even those pictured in hunting scenes probably represent symbolic prey, rather than actual kills. It is still debatable whether rock art depicts hunts or kills that already occurred, or whether successful hunts or kills were pictured to evoke sympathetic magic to accomplish this goal. The second view operates on the principle that the picturing of a hoped-for result will magically produce a like effect, especially in controlling the chase, bagging game, and promoting the increase and abundance of animals. Rock art researchers have long considered this the motive for picturing hunting scenes. It is also possible that some animals or hunting scenes are metaphors for entirely different beings, activities, or rituals known only to the artisan and his people.

Much of the lore regarding Hopi hunting and hunting ritual has been preserved in a study made by Ernest Beaglehole in the early 1930s, drawing upon the knowledge and remembrances of elderly Hopi informants.[5] At that time, these traditional hunting practices were disappearing with the encroachment of the modern world and the dwindling of the animal population. The study is invaluable for its record of customs and beliefs which undoubtedly endured from the prehistoric past. Prominent in these accounts are precise descriptions of the ritual necessary to lure and propitiate game. Preparation for the hunt was initiated by the hunt chief, a role probably derived from the more ancient hunt shaman, for the chief is responsible for calling the animals by special songs, and seeing that homage is paid to the deities. After the kill, hunters carefully followed certain procedures for

68

butchering and dividing the animal, and they made offerings to appease the animal's soul and prevent it from warning away its living relatives. The attitude of Pueblo people toward animals has always been one of respect. With the possible exception of coyotes,[6] animals have never been hunted for sport, and their conservation has been a concern evident in Pueblo hunting methods and the rites surrounding them. Deer and pronghorn antelope, according to one of Beaglehole's Hopi informants, have a physical rebirth if killed by a method employed in early years: "to smother them enables their spirits to go to their home and so to live again on earth."[7] The increase of animals is important to all Pueblo people, and this interest can be perceived in prehistoric rock art as well; it may be expressed in the portrayal of obviously pregnant animals, and those accompanied by young. A ceremony seeming to involve the fertility of the pronghorn appears in the petroglyph panel in Figure 9.18. Another panel shows a female entity believed to be the Pueblo goddess known as the "Mother of Game" encircled by the animals to which she has given birth (Figure 9.1). She permits hunters to kill them (if the proper rites have been performed), and is responsible for the increase of her "children."

Though diminished in necessity after the establishment of agriculture, hunting continued to play an important role well into the twentieth century. Indeed, if one relied on rock art alone to gain an understanding of Pueblo societies, it might seem animals and hunting held primacy over agriculture. Many petroglyph scenes suggest that the local cultures perceived animals on levels other than the mundane or "natural" state. The function of much of this rock art—other than hunting magic—may have been to venerate the special status of animals, or to call upon their powers and cooperation. It was particularly desirable that game consented to be killed (game animals that "give themselves" are kachinas[8]), and the making of petroglyphs may have been a part of hunting ritual, to honor them and ask their help in making the hunt successful.

WEAPONS AND HUNTING

Human figures with bows and arrows are often seen in Palavayu rock art, usually shown in the act of aiming arrows at animals. Other weapons are pictured as isolated glyphs or, in the case of the spear, held by men in warlike attitudes. A weapon used exclusively against human enemies was the nodule club, a stone tied with a flexible attachment to the end of a club; its use by Hopi warriors long ago is described by Alexander Stephen in his *Hopi Journal*.[9] Interestingly, this weapon is sometimes shown as part of prehistoric hunting equipment as well, for in several rock art examples archers shooting deer are shown girded with this implement (Figure 5.1). It may have been necessary to be so armed, as a hunter searching alone for game could have been vulnerable to enemy attack. A fascinating panel of petroglyphs along the Little Colorado River portrays men not only wearing the nodule club, but also carrying what seem to be snares or lassoes (Figure 5.5). The presence of a deer (or pronghorn), and a mountain lion implies this is a hunting scene, but the hunters aren't carrying bows and arrows. One man holds a curved object, perhaps a throwing stick, while

69

the others wave arms and carry loops and crooks. Jesse Walter Fewkes mentions that the crook was the prayer offering of a warrior society, made in the form of an ancient weapon "allied to the bow."[10] No further reference has been found relating to such a weapon, but it may be pictured in this rock art panel. To one side of this petroglyph group stands a human figure with raised hands and elaborate headdress, adding a ceremonial flavor to the scene. Is it a hunt or a ritual?

Methods of hunting in the Western Pueblo region varied little from pueblo to pueblo; all were sacred activities accompanied by ceremonial rites and offerings. Animal drives were communal affairs, requiring the help of men and boys drawn from the whole village. As described by Stephen,[11] deer, pronghorn, and rabbit hunts employed two long lines of people who surrounded a large area and then drove the animals toward the hunters. He also indicated a more ambitious undertaking practiced in early historical times for hunting pronghorn. This required the construction of brush fences that converged toward a stockade of tree boles and limbs around which the hunters stationed themselves. The brush fences, wing-shaped, were built for a distance of 800 to 1,000 yards. Extending from those were piles of brush and boughs spaced apart at intervals for several miles (sometimes for ten or twelve, usually for not more than four or five, he notes). Boys were sent to frighten and divert pronghorn herds toward the brush piles, where hiding villagers kept them on a course toward the stockade. If the drive was successful, the hunters then dispatched the milling animals.

This technique, known as the chute and pound method, is considered by Beaglehole to be a Navajo method subsequently borrowed by the Pueblo people.[12] But evidence seen in rock art confirms its use in prehistoric periods before the Navajo's estimated arrival in the Palavayu region.[13] In eight different rock art panels, enclosures are pictured with wing-shaped openings into which lines of animals move. The largest and most complex panel, at the "Royal Flush" site (Figure 5.4), shows four men with waving hands, two within and two outside the enclosure, appearing to direct the movement of the animals. One man waves a much exaggerated hand, as if to emphasize the urgency of the drive. The tableau includes a bow and arrow and human footprints, among many other elements. Panels at three other sites, "Triptych" (Figure 5.6), "Daisy Spur," and "Locket," picture animals entering the same type of enclosure; a man with bow and arrow is associated with the latter group. The most exciting expression of this theme appears on a petroglyph panel along the Little Colorado River (Figure 5.7). Reduced to the abstract, only animal tracks and human footprints portray the action of the hunt. Hoofprints enter and circle the enclosure; at the center, a bow and arrow is depicted next to a human footprint, while outside, other human footprints surround the corral. The story is told by symbol alone.

Archaeological finds also substantiate the driving and corralling of numbers of animals in the prehistoric periods. Large hunting nets have been found, of a length and size that could have been used to construct a chute or barrier. These might have been employed in capturing a wide range of large and small animals by communal hunting activity. One such

net was found in the Palavayu area in a cave near Chevelon Creek;[14] association with Pueblo II sherds dates it between A.D. 900 and 1100. Other large nets recovered, dating from A.D. 350 to 1450, indicate this type of hunting was common, prehistorically, for many centuries.

In the historical period, especially before the acquisition of horses, deer and pronghorn were hunted and run down on foot by hunters who worked in pairs—for protection from enemies and "to help each other."[15] Groups of men also participated in extended hunting expeditions, and on some of these forays Pueblo hunters wore animal disguises. The reminiscence of an Acoma Indian of a hunting trip made in 1887 mentions "a stuffed antelope head worn on the head, the face painted, and maybe some kind of shirt to make them look like antelope."[16] The Zuni are also said to have used such disguises.[17]

The Hopi hunted large game in early spring, late summer, in the fall when the animals were fattest, and in December when tracking in the snow was easier.[18] Other Pueblo people also generally preferred these times. They all hunted small animals throughout the year, often trapping them by deadfall or snare. Rabbits are perhaps the most widely hunted of Pueblo game animals, and the communal rabbit hunt, as laden with ritual as those for deer or pronghorn, was often held in connection with ceremonies to provide meat for feasting. Methods included the beating of large areas, and "surrounds," or converging circles of hunters. When rabbits threatened damage to crops, all clans hunted them. Occasionally, lone hunters also supplemented a usually meatless diet with a bag of these plentiful rodents. The main weapon was a rabbit stick, a club shaped somewhat like a boomerang, that could be thrown for a good distance with force and accuracy. Believed to be an ancient weapon, the rabbit stick is perhaps older than the bow and arrow;[19] examples have been excavated from Basketmaker sites, and it is considered one interpretation for the S-shaped object held by Basketmaker petroglyph figures.

MAMMALS

The animals pictured in the rock art of the region represent only a small proportion of those common to the area in prehistoric times. It is assumed these mammals, birds, reptiles, and insects had a special meaning for the prehistoric people who depicted them. The importance of game is undeniable, and this importance is reflected in the large numbers of sheep, deer, and pronghorn appearing in rock art. But game animals, predators, and life forms of other species also had supernatural status, and this may explain why some animal life is repeatedly pictured while others are excluded entirely.

MOUNTAIN SHEEP

Bighorn and mountain sheep are described as the preeminent motif in western rock art.[20] The largest concentrations of sheep petroglyphs are found in the desert and mountain ranges of southeast California and southern Nevada, but they are represented in the rock art of every western state. The abundance and wide distribution of sheep images have generated much debate about the meaning these glyphs held for the people who made them. The diverse ways in which sheep are pictured, and the often unrealistic or fanciful distortions (such as backward-facing feet, nose elongations, heads at both ends of the body) all indicate symbolism was inherent in this animal's portrayal. Theories suggest the use of sheep images as directional markers or as records of stories in which sheep represent people.[21] One-horn and two-horn sheep images have been theorized to have been the protoform for the One and Two-horn Societies of the Hopi ceremonial structure.[22] Sheep have also been seen as representing supernatural beings "who may be deities, ancestors, the souls of deceased humans, or transformed shamans."[23] In Great Basin rock art, ethnographic data collected early in the century from descendants of the Numic culture indicate that mountain sheep were spirit helpers of the rain shaman, and were powerful aids to weather control.[24]

Sheep petroglyphs are abundant in the Palavayu region. Perhaps most prolifically depicted prior to the PIII period, they continue to be represented occasionally until the PIV abandonment of the area. Not as numerous in Petrified Forest rock art sites as in those of the canyon drainages of the Little Colorado River, this contrast may be due to the differences in habitat. The rock art images here do not differ greatly from those of other western areas, except that the profiled body with single horn seen in the Jornada Style of New Mexico and the Fremont Style of Utah is lacking. There are several examples of the two-headed sheep (one prominently visible on "Newspaper Rock"), one sheep with elongated nose, and some with feet turned backwards. Petroglyphs along a wash which drains into the Little Colorado River show some sheep figures impaled by arrows or darts remarkably like those found in the rock art of the Coso Range in California. A bird-headed human figure pictured nearby carries an object resembling the stylized image of an atlatl.

Pilles[25] suggests that over time pronghorn figures appear to replace sheep in the Little Colorado region. This may indicate a change in hunting practices, or perhaps a climatic change resulting in a decrease in sheep populations and an increase in pronghorn populations. Even as late as the nineteenth century, however, the Hopi hunted mountain sheep.[26] Anglo settlement of the West late in that century began the final depletion of the sheep populations in the Palavayu.

DEER, ELK, AND PRONGHORN

Animals pictured in Palavayu rock art are not always easy to identify. In particular, deer and pronghorn are easily confused. Pronghorn are not true antelopes; they are more closely related to the goat and other bovids, and the difference, crucial to their portrayal in rock art, lies in the fact that pronghorn have horns, not antlers. Even this distinction cannot always be relied on, for immature deer lack the branching antlers of adults. If important to distinguish one animal from the other when depicting them in rock art, however, horns or antlers were the determining factor. So far, only two petroglyph examples have been found picturing another of the pronghorn's unique attributes: the contrasting white rump. One such example is a large petroglyph image associated with Basketmaker figures at the "Trophy Head" site. The other, of a different style and time period, is located in the Little Colorado River drainage (Figure 5.10)

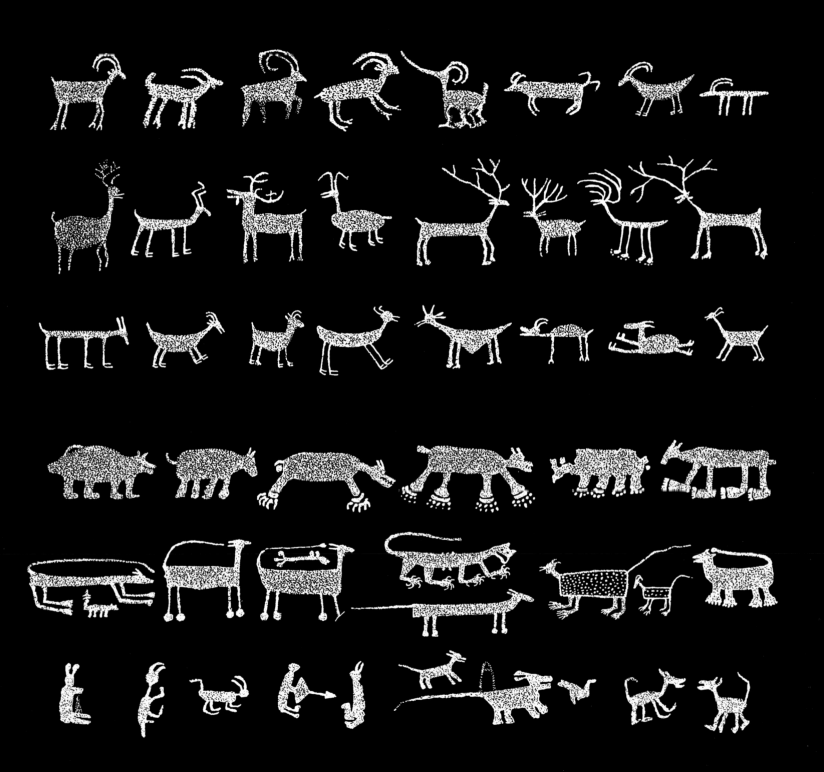

Figure 5.2 Examples of mammal depictions in Palawuuu rock art (not to scale)

Among those that can be identified, pronghorn far outnumber deer as preferred subjects in rock art. This may reflect the actual situation in the prehistoric Palavayu region, which is seen in microcosm today. Pronghorn prefer the open grassy lands that extend from the Petrified Forest to wooded areas south of the Little Colorado River. Deer are more common in brushy canyons and hilly forests. Pronghorn dominate the rock art panels of Petrified Forest National Park and the lands reaching to the Little Colorado River. Petroglyphs attributed to Basketmaker folk, in the Chevelon Creek and other canyons, picture many deer and elk. All three types of animals still exist in the Palavayu, although their numbers are probably a fraction of those in former times.

BEAR

Of all the animals held in special regard by the Pueblo people, none is as feared and venerated as the bear. Strong, fierce, and dangerous, bear were hunted with trepidation. Other aspects of its nature, as well as temperament, gave the bear unequaled status in the animal world. Physically, bears are much like men, and this anthropomorphic quality separated them from the other animals. Bears can stand or walk on their hind legs in a humanlike manner, or sit "against a tree with paws, like arms, at their sides and perhaps one leg drawn up under the body."[27] Their plantigrade tracks (walking on the whole sole of the foot) resemble human footprints, in that heel, arch, and toes are distinguishable. Facial and bodily expressions are very human: bears, when attacked, can whine in a pleading way, and tears may even appear in their eyes.[28] Their dispositions, like man's, can range unpredictably from playful to sullen. It is understandable that bears would be given an ambivalent standing in Pueblo belief. On the one hand, they were sometimes hunted and their meat eaten, while skins, paws, skulls, and claws were taken for ceremonial uses. On the other hand, they were considered the most important of animal supernaturals, the object of propitiation in war and the hunt, and—at Zuni and in the Keresan pueblos—the principal patron of medicine societies. In those villages, bears were known to possess great curing powers. Shamans "become bears when they draw on their bear paws."[29]

Never the object of organized hunts by the Hopi, bears were occasionally killed in chance encounters.[30] Although Hopis consumed the meat when kills occurred, they never considered the bear a food animal. During his excavations at Awat'ovi in 1892, Fewkes found a large bear skeleton in one of the rooms and surmised it had probably been awaiting consumption. In spite of this practical attitude, the bear's special status required that after being killed (and before becoming nourishment) he be treated like a dead human enemy and accorded the appropriate ceremonial tributes.[31]

If the ethnological record hadn't confirmed the bear's presence in Western Pueblo territory, rock art would certainly establish it. Both the bear and its tracks are pictured in the Palavayu region. Bear tracks are often found rendered in a naturalistic way, series of them carefully defining alternate front and back paws. The front-paw track is also depicted in variations of abstract form. This motif is so profuse in the Petrified Forest area that it arouses

74

curiosity. Is it a schematization, a part (the paw) representative of the whole (bear)? Is it a clan insignia? Is it meant to honor the bear, or to evoke his power? Its meaning remains obscure, but its prevalence suggests a symbolic portrayal rather than the mere imitation of a familiar trail sign. In medicine societies of the Keres, Zuni, and Tewa, the bear paw is the equivalent of the mask in transforming man into animal spirit.[32] It may have represented a similar form of power for the Pueblo people of the Palavayu.

In great contrast to the many tracks found at the majority of rock art sites, only twelve images of the entire bear itself have been found in Palavayu rock art. Four of the bears are depicted in an unusual way: bear tracks replace the bear's feet. This may have been an artistic device to help identify the animal, but three of these bear images (Figure 5.2) are created with a skill which makes recognition unmistakable. Each has the stubby tail, short ears, and thick body of the bear. These three are ferocious in appearance, with the long claws, shoulder hump, and concave face that indicate they are grizzly bears. The addition of the track to these images may have signified the difference between black bear and grizzly, both former denizens of the region.

MOUNTAIN LIONS

This predator is also a spirit animal of great power, primarily associated with war at the Hopi mesas, and revered as the patron of hunting societies in the Keresan and Eastern Pueblos. Considered the most courageous and superior of hunters, the mountain lion was asked for help by Keres hunt shamans, and his stone fetish was carried by hunters on hunting expeditions from those villages and from Zuni.[33] Hopis depicted the lion in sand paintings and represented it in effigy on altars of the Snake-Antelope and War societies. The warlike Snakes called the lion War Chief, and impersonated it during the initiation of novices.[34] Also filling the role of guardian and protector, his stone effigy was called a "watcher."[35] Secretive and nocturnal, the mountain lion has an aura of mystery. It is easy to imagine the fascination and awe this creature inspired among the people who shared his hunting territories.

The Palavayu region is a natural habitat for this carnivore, with rocky, difficult terrain and an abundance of small and large game. It is apparent from the numerous depictions in rock art that the lion was a well-known resident. Displayed in the Petrified Forest National Park museum is a petroglyph slab adorned with the singularly artful image of a female mountain lion. This petroglyph figure has been reproduced so often as a pleasing motif that it has almost become synonymous with the park. Recovered from the Blue Mesa area in the thirties, the petroglyph slab is only one of many rock art examples of the lion found at sites in the Petrified Forest area. It is equally well represented throughout the Palavayu region.

The mountain lion is portrayed in rock art in a fairly consistent manner. A long tail is the diagnostic feature, usually curving back over the body (but sometimes straight), body long and feline, feet often ball-shaped but sometimes pictured with toes and claws. Size of the lion image varies greatly, from a few centimeters in length to the 180-centimeter-long

animal seen in Figure 5.23. Often depicted accompanying deer, pronghorn, or sheep, the lion may have been considered a protector or Master of Animals. As befitting a major supernatural, the petroglyph lion is sometimes associated with other images of ceremonial import. Figure 5.24 shows the impressively executed image of a mountain lion facing a group of figures that include flute players and a possible slab paho, a ritual object. At two other rock art sites, lions are accompanied by human staff bearers. Very different imagery is seen in other rock art examples of female lions with young. Figure 5.26 is an affecting portrayal of a lioness with curving tail protectively encircling her cub.

RABBITS AND BADGERS

Unaccountably, two animals of great importance to Western Pueblo people are seldom— if ever, in the case of the badger—represented in rock art. Plentiful, and hunted with relative ease in all seasons, rabbits have been a prime food source since earliest times. The badger, not economically useful, nevertheless held a major place in the supernatural world of animal spirits. At Hopi, he was revered for his curing powers, comparable to those of the bear in other pueblo societies. On Second Mesa the Badger Clan controlled the hunt, because that clan "owns all the animals."[36] It may be assumed that the badger has always been accorded this high status, for he is featured in many Hopi legends as well as one of the origin myths of the Badger Clan.[37] The badger paw is possibly depicted in Petrified Forest rock art and may be a symbol of this clan, or of the badger's curing magic. Tracks similar to the bear paw glyph but having longer curving claws which toe in, may represent this animal. If so, it is the only recognizable indication of the badger in rock art.

Only four petroglyph images of the rabbit have been identified in the Palavayu region. Significantly, two of these appear on rock art panels that may also portray the Mother of Game, for the rabbit figures prominently in legends about this goddess (Chapter Nine). The other two petroglyph rabbits, not as well depicted but displaying the essential long upright ears, are shown in hunting contexts. One is near the panel described earlier (Figure 5.5), which features men with crooks and snarelike loops, perhaps hunting or engaged in ritual pertaining to the hunt. In the last example a hunter threatens the rabbit with bow and arrow (Figure 5.12). Because this petroglyph is associated with a female image that may represent a supernatural being (Figure 4.11), this scene may also be symbolic of hunting ritual.

Considering the importance of the rabbit historically and prehistorically as a nonfailing, self-renewing resource, hunted with both ceremonial and practical regularity, its sparsity as a rock art subject is mystifying.

DOGS

From evidence of bone recovered at archaeological sites within and adjacent to Petrified Forest National Park, the dog is a known companion of the prehistoric people of this area.[38] Its likeness in rock art is often disputed, for the dog (coyotes and wolves must also be included) has no special physical feature to distinguish it from other pictured animals, especially if the crucial elements on indeterminate animals—horns and tails—are indistinct or lacking. Martynec's study of rock art at eleven sites within the park lists a high percentage of dog representations, particularly at "Newspaper Rock."[39] When the American Rock Art Research Association recorded this site in 1991, none of the zoomorphs were recognized as dogs, primarily because of problematical identification. At a rock art site near Puerco Ruin, two animals are pictured in apparent pursuit of water birds. Ears flying and tails outstretched, these images resemble canine appearance and behavior more closely than any in that area. Although it is certain dogs are among the many indefinable types of animals portrayed in the Palavayu, only one example from a Little Colorado River site can unequivocally be labelled so. On a high rock face busy with figures, a walking man is pictured (Figure 5.27). He may be elderly, for he is stooped in appearance and carries a staff. Behind him at the end of the leash he holds is—without question—his dog.

BATS

Bats, the winged mammals, are pictured in the kiva murals of Kuaua, an excavated pueblo on the Rio Grande. At Zuni bats are believed to be bringers of rain, and these images are so interpreted in the study of Kuaua murals by Bertha Dutton.[40] The bats in Figure 5.28 are found, rather appropriately, on the underside of a large rock slab that forms a cave shelter. On one end of the slab, two bats are realistically depicted, at the other end are two images neither quite bat nor human (Figure 5.29). As the four images appear on the same rock slab, it seems reasonable to call the two ambiguous figures "batlike," although this description might not be apt if they were found in another setting. The people responsible for this rock art may have been allied with the bat in ceremony or clan. This site is east of the park; the only other bat petroglyph presently known is at Mountain Lion Mesa within the park.

BIRDS

From the Basketmaker to the PIV period, birds are pictured in Palavayu rock art. The earliest representations are generally of long-legged water birds; later in the Pueblo periods eagles, turkeys, and parrots became the most commonly portrayed, and less often, owls, herons or cranes, and quail. Many unidentifiable birds are also present in the rock art of Pueblo periods.

The importance of bird symbolism in historic Pueblo ceremony has been extensively documented. Bird feathers and bird skins have persisted as vital accessories to every kind of ritual, for the bird has magical affinities with sun and sky (both are equated with the gods), and with air, the breath of life. The feathers of birds are attached to prayer sticks and altars, used on masks and ceremonial attire, and are fashioned singly or in tufts as prayer feathers. Each kind of bird has a special significance in the Pueblo world. Colors, habits, and traits assign each to a particular role or influence. Some birds are related to war or hunting; some, like certain animals, represent the directions. Others are associated with the seasons, omen and death, or the forces of life and growth. All may be messengers to the gods, and almost all have some part in bringing rain.[41]

EAGLES

Of the birds pictured in Palavayu rock art, the eagle is most prevalent, indicating its importance in Pueblo belief. As directional spirit of the zenith, the eagle is equal in power to the lion and bear. Eagle's alliance with the sun involves him in ritual pertaining to war, because sun and war are sometimes linked. He is one of the "pets" of the War Brothers, sons of the sun. The eagle's connection with war is not emphasized as much at Hopi as in other Pueblo societies; at Hopi a different aspect is of greater concern. The eagle's power is inherent in its plumage and down, and these are potent offerings with which to entreat the gods. Eagle feathers are so prized that since prehistoric times both young and mature eagles are captured alive, tethered on village rooftops, and occasionally plucked for feathers needed for ceremonies. The capture of eagles is not indiscriminate, for they can only be taken from clan-owned land.[42] These buttes and canyons may be many miles from the Hopi mesas, but clan ownership was established during the ancient migrations of the various clans to Hopi, and these property rights are still strictly observed. Young eaglets are taken from the nest at a certain age, and it is considered wrong to take all the young from one nest; perpetuation of the species is essential. The capture is conducted by clan leaders, who make the proper offerings and prayers before careful removal of the eaglet from the nest. The bird will be a family member of the clan, fed and cared for until mature, and "sent home" by ritual killing after the Niman ceremony when the kachinas leave the village. Although eagles are now protected by law from being killed or captured, the practice is of such religious import to the Hopi that, since 1975, they have been granted this right by the federal government.[43]

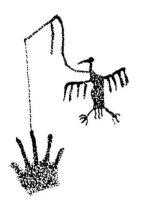

Eagle capture in the remote past is wonderfully recorded in Palavayu rock art. In a wilderness area studded with buttes and rocky mesas, nests of the golden eagle can be seen. It is their habit to return to the same nest in their breeding season, and some nests have been occupied by generations of eagles. An exciting find, made some years ago, is the petroglyph panel seen in Figure 5.32, located beneath an active eagle nest. The rock art pictures an eagle being lifted from its nest by rope and pole. This method is presently used to remove eaglets from canyon locations. A boy or young man is lowered to the nest, where he secures the eaglet by rope and it is hoisted to the canyon rim.[44] Another petroglyph motif of eagle capture is found in the same general area as the panel in Figure 5.32, but this one is depicted symbolically. The eaglet dangles from a rope and pole connected to what becomes the middle finger of a human hand. There are other petroglyph eagles tethered by rope to poles, but without human agency pictured; all rock art portrayals occur in the region in which the golden eagle nests.

MACAWS, PARROTS, AND TURKEYS

The Pueblo people of the Palavayu knew macaws, parrots, and turkeys. Probably starting in the middle of the eleventh century and most certainly by A.D. 1100, they imported macaws and parrots from Mexico.[45] Bones, feathers, and complete skeletons of parrots and macaws have been found in many ruins throughout the Southwest. In lands adjacent to the Palavayu

78

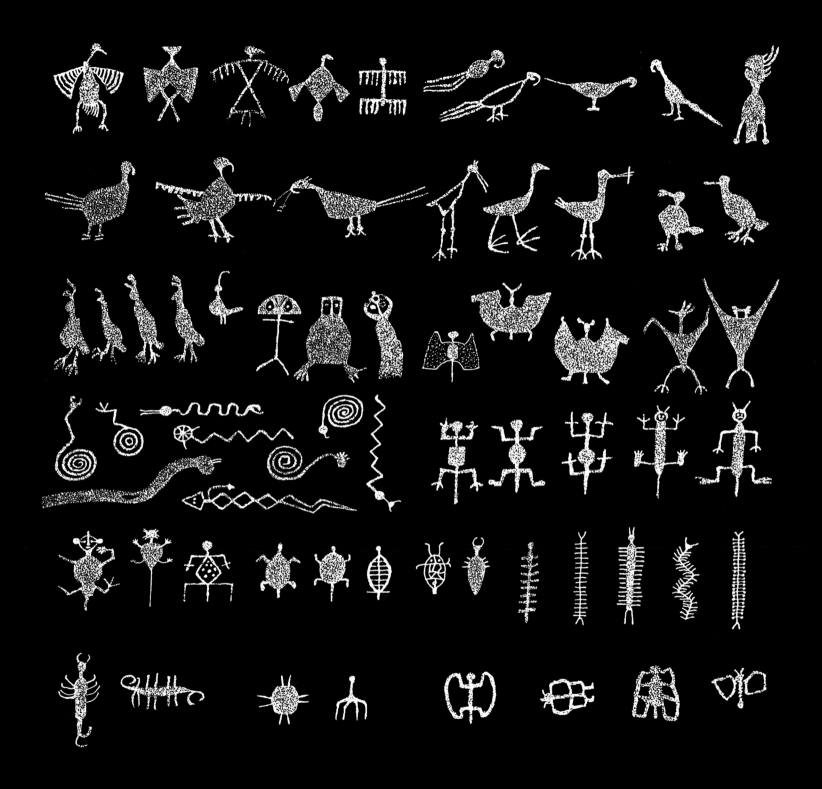

Figure 5.3. Depictions of birds, bats, reptiles, insects, and others in Palavayu rock art (not to scale)

region, the ruins of Grasshopper, Point of Pines, Kinishba, and Turkey Creek pueblos,[46] as well as ruins in Winona and Wupatki,[47] have yielded such remains. Portrayal of these birds in the rock art of the Palavayu also gives evidence of their familiarity to the local inhabitants. A primary reason for the importation of macaw feathers seems to be due to their high value as ceremonial and ritual offerings. This regard continues in present-day Pueblo villages. In prehistoric times, the birds themselves were kept captive, perhaps sequestered in subterranean rooms (as in Chaco Canyon), or tethered in protected areas. Tethering is graphically pictured at a site in Five Mile Draw where rock art depicts a human figure holding captive a macaw. Many such birds are portrayed singly, usually associated with petroglyphs thought to date from the late PIII, or PIV period. Only one petroglyph bird at a site near the Little Colorado River has conformations suggesting the thick bill and squared tail of the parrot.

Less easy to identify, the petroglyph turkey is apt to be confused with the macaw when depicted with clustered tail feathers and curving beak (this may actually represent the fleshy sac that hangs from the turkey's forehead). A likely turkey portrayal is found at "Dot's Spot," and is one of the rare instances of painted images (Figure 9.24). The style and painting technique is similar to pictographs in the Canyon de Chelly area, 150 miles to the northeast. There the turkey is commonly portrayed, often as a part of the "birdhead" motif, a human figure with a bird either resting on or replacing the figure's head. The Canyon de Chelly turkey is rounded and usually bicolored, with head and neck of one color, and body another. Such is the case of the "Dot's Spot" turkey, with white head and red body.

The turkey feathers were (and are) in great demand for ceremonial use, and according to Fewkes, they were used more than those of any other bird in the manufacture of prayer sticks.[48] Easy to domesticate, wild or mountain turkeys were kept by the Anasazi since early times. Whether they kept them only for their feathers or for food is a debatable question. The large amount of bone found in middens, and the number of awls, needles, and other tools made from turkey bone, may indicate that the turkey served not only practical need but also as food source. In any case, it is certain that turkey feathers were of paramount importance.

HERONS, CRANES, AND DUCKS

Wading birds, although not precisely identifiable, are pictured in Basketmaker art. These water birds, probably representing herons or cranes, are also portrayed in later Pueblo rock art. Long neck, long legs, and (usually) long bills serve as identifying features of these petroglyph birds. Predictably, many are pictured at rock art sites near the Puerco River in Petrified Forest National Park. Occasionally seen nowadays in this river area, wading birds were probably more abundant in prehistoric times, as their rock art portrayals indicate. Lines of birds are pictured, and from these realistic scenes it is easy to imagine that flocks were once common here. Ducks are also present in the region. They are important in Pueblo ceremonialism, and so it might be expected they would be portrayed in Palavayu rock art, as they are in other Western Pueblo areas. But although a few petroglyph images could represent ducks, few can be positively recognized.

QUAIL AND OWLS

Pueblo ethnographic literature says little about quail. Hamilton Tyler, quoting anthropologist Edmund Ladd's thesis on Zuni ornithology, mentions that it is taboo at that pueblo to use feathers of the quail in ceremony or as offering.[49] Quail are pictured at two widely separated rock art sites: one east of Petrified Forest National Park and one at the junction of Five Mile Draw and Silver Creek (Figure 5.43). The identifying element of these images is the distinctive topknot on the head. The Silver Creek example is especially typical of quail behavior, for it pictures five birds in a close single line, as quail run.

The owl plays a larger role in Pueblo belief and is featured in many folk tales from both eastern and western villages. While in the Rio Grande pueblos and at Zuni the owl may be associated with witchcraft, it is more apt to be connected with the god *Maasaw* at Hopi.[50] *Maasaw* is not only a god of death and darkness, forces with which the owl is often equated, but he is also a god of fertility, and the owl shares that relationship. There are several Hopi Owl kachinas, who appear in the *Powamuy* and Horned Water Serpent ceremonies, concerned with fertility and growth. Portrayal of the owl in the Palavayu region occurs as early as the Basketmaker period (Figure 5.34) and it is realistically depicted in later Pueblo periods as well (Figure 5.33). The petroglyph image seen in Figure 5.6, from a site east of the park, is apparently a human figure wearing an owl mask.

REPTILES

As Fewkes observed nearly a century ago, water animals are dominant symbols among people of arid regions whose rituals center around rainmaking.[51] Aquatic birds, reptiles, amphibians, and life forms linked to water are all included in this category. Snakes and lizards are seen in this light and are among the most numerously pictured creatures in the region. In particular, the snake seems to have been one of the first to be depicted in rock art, and continued unabated in all succeeding styles and time periods.

SNAKES

Earliest of the life forms represented in Archaic/Basketmaker rock art, the snake may often have been depicted as a shaman's spirit helper. Like the bird which can fly to worlds above, the snake can descend to the underworld, and both creatures are powerful helpers in shamanistic belief. The numerous images of the snake at the "Biface" site, close by, attached to, or placed upon the bodies of human figures reinforce this possibility.

The snake is linked with water and lightning, and in early times may also have evolved as a supernatural with control over weather and moisture. This power became of supreme importance when agriculture became man's lifeway. The Snake Dance ceremony still performed at Hopi may have developed from this belief. Once a ceremonial function at all three Hopi mesas and at Acoma,[52] the Snake Dance may have been a rite common throughout the ancient Pueblo world. In later times, from a concept derived from a Mesoamerican god *Quetzalcoatl*, the Horned Water Serpent emerged as an important deity

82

among all Pueblo people. A complex god associated with fertility, agriculture, and water, many considered *Quetzalcoatl* to be a beneficent god of wisdom and life. An antithetical aspect in Aztec belief was his demand for human sacrifice, a side of his nature which may have been expressed in the punitive and dangerous side of the Pueblo Horned Serpent who could cause floods and earthquakes. The Toltec and Aztec people perceived this deity as both feathered serpent and human being. Petroglyph figures believed to represent this being in Jornada Style rock art appear as both anthropomorph and snake, sometimes in composite form.[53] Iconography of the Jornada region in southern New Mexico demonstrates a close cultural affiliation with Mesoamerica, and it is here that representations and symbols of *Quetzalcoatl* are most elaborately expressed in rock art. In the Rio Grande area, the Horned Serpent, known as *Avanyu,* is a simpler derivation from the Jornada images, sometimes with two horns and occasionally shown in profile with one horn. Far to the west, the horned serpent appears in its simplest form in rock art that usually dates to the PIII, or early PIV period. It is deified at Zuni, where it is called *Kolowisi,* known as *Paalölöqangw* at Hopi, and figures prominently in myth and ceremony at both pueblos. In defiance of the generally accepted theory that the motif is a late arrival in the Western Pueblo region is the depiction of three serpents with clearly defined horns appearing on the "Biface" panels (Figure 2.4). This entire rock art site is indisputably of Basketmaker or Archaic origin, and the horned snake images are anomalies which cannot be explained. Other horned serpents are depicted in only moderate numbers in the Palavayu region. All, with the exception of two petroglyph examples, are of the frontal two-horned variety. One thick snake shown in profile dominates a large panel at a rock art site near Holbrook (Figure 4.8), another near Carr Lake Draw. This snake also displays two horns; as far as is known, there are no one-horned varieties in this region.

LIZARDS

Occurring as often as the snake glyph, the lizard is almost a hallmark of Palavayu rock art. It is particularly numerous in Petrified Forest National Park, in the vicinity of Puerco Ruin and "Newspaper Rock." Fashioned in many diverse ways, these petroglyph creatures have oval, rectangular, diamond-shaped, or elongated bodies. They are often portrayed with globular bellies, a stylistic feature seen in Hohokam ceramic and petroglyph art. Many are anthropomorphic, almost indistinguishable from the arms-up, legs-down human figures so common in Anasazi and Pueblo rock art. The tail of the lizard could equally represent a human phallus, and for this reason the term "lizard man" was coined for these ambiguous figures. Schaafsma proposes they may portray a supernatural being, citing the excavation of a lizard-woman effigy from a kiva at Salmon Ruins in New Mexico.[54] This seems a good possibility, because the lizard petroglyph is often found associated with, or even the focus of, rock art of a ceremonial nature. The lizard may also be a clan symbol.

Salamander, toad, and frog glyphs share the indeterminate identity of the lizard glyph, as all have similar conformation. Controversy surrounds a well-known petroglyph on a boulder below Puerco Ruin that depicts a heron or crane with a small figure impaled on its bill. Some see a human figure, and the scene symbolizing a mythic event; others think it is more likely that a frog provided dinner for the bird.

INSECTS, ARACHNIDS, AND OTHERS

Save for a few beetle representations, recognizable petroglyph portrayals of insects and like creatures in the Palavayu region appear limited to moths, butterflies, caterpillars, centipedes, scorpions, and perhaps spiders. Elsie Clews Parsons states that insects are important medicine spirits to the Western Pueblos, perhaps to all Pueblo people.[55] This is confirmed by M. Jane Young's study of rock art in the Zuni area.[56] Abundantly pictured, insects are important in Zuni cultural symbolism and possess special powers which can be acquired through ritual activities (the act of making their petroglyph images may be one method). Young's Zuni informants contributed lore reflecting beliefs perhaps common in ancient times. According to several, insects which live near water are helpful in bringing rain, and their wisdom ("they travel great distances, but always find their way back") may be invoked by prayer. Medicine men may become invisible to enemies by ritual ingestion of insects camouflaged with protective coloring or shape. Poisonous insects may be depicted to "sting" the enemy, perhaps an explanation for some of those kinds prevalent in rock art of the Palavayu region.

CENTIPEDES, CATERPILLARS, SCORPIONS, AND SPIDERS

The centipede appears earliest and is common in all time periods. Its presence in Basketmaker rock art may signify its importance as shaman's spirit helper, for—like the serpent—it has access to the underground world and the supernaturals dwelling there. In all depictions, its form rarely differs from the one-pole ladder pattern with antennae at one or both ends (Figure 5.41). An impressive exception is the long, wiggly specimen seen in Figure 5.37. Caterpillars are represented at least twice at two rock art sites within the park. The scorpion is a much more infrequent but sometimes finely made image (Figure 5.41). Neither insect seems important in Pueblo myth or folk tale. Their petroglyph depictions may represent mysterious or dangerous creatures whose supernatural powers can be appeased, dispelled, or even invoked by carving their likenesses. It is possible, too, that these images represent a people, or clan.

The spider has been identified as a clan symbol at Willow Springs, where Hopi artists pecked hundreds of such petroglyph symbols. A circle with lines for legs, usually six in number, is the common portrayal. A second more realistic design possibly representing the insect is found on a panel near the Little Colorado River. Apart from a clan symbol, the spider has another connotation for the Pueblo people. Spider Woman is a revered and venerable personage in Pueblo belief. She is sometimes portrayed in effigy for certain Hopi ceremonies, but is not pictured in rock art, unless the occasional petroglyph spider is linked with some aspect of this personage.

BUTTERFLIES AND DRAGONFLIES

According to Fewkes, the insects that dominate ceramic decoration on prehistoric Hopi pottery are the butterfly and the dragonfly,[57] also commonly seen in petroglyph sites surrounding the Hopi mesas. The images appear in Sikyatki pottery decoration (ca. A.D. 1375), and although other animal figures similar to those in the pottery decorations are seen in some Palavayu rock art of the Pueblo IV period—near Puerco Ruin and in the vicinity of Nuvakwewtaqa at Chavez Pass—the dragonfly is lacking. Oddly, the stylized image of the dragonfly, which resembles a cross with double cross-arms, is present in the Archaic-Basketmaker period; two appear on the "Biface" panel in Figure 2.4. The butterfly or moth is sometimes seen in rock art of the Palavayu; one adorns a large boulder face near Puerco Ruin. It is also a prominent motif on Sikyatki ceramics, and its image occurs frequently on both prehistoric and historic artifacts and ceremonial paraphernalia. There is a Butterfly clan whose symbol is represented at Willow Springs, and Fewkes maintained that evidence of an ancient and once important Butterfly sect survived in the rites of the *Owaqöl* women's ceremony at Hopi.

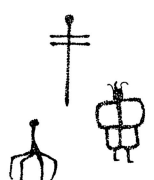

Figure 5.4. Remarkable for its outstanding workmanship and pleasing aesthetics, a communal game drive at the "Royal Flush" site is realistically portrayed. Note the two ushers with outstretched hands positioned inside the corral at top, while outside below another figure gestures with outsized hand. At bottom left another line of animals breaks away from the main string, heading into a second enclosure. Sympathetic magic is inherent in the scene, compelling the game animals to march into the corral as if under a spell. Diameter of corral 45 cm.

Figure 5.5. Men brandishing loops and crook staffs are grouped around a bighorn sheep and a mountain lion, while nearby a shamanic figure poses with upraised hands. Rather than portraying an ordinary hunting scene, the whole panel may depict a shaman's vision. The rays emanating from his head usually symbolize supernatural power, and the two quadrupeds may represent his animal familiars. Length of mountain lion 28 cm.

Figure 5.6. Sympathetic magic may have been the motivation for this game corral at the "Triptych Terrace" site. Although the corral is already filled to capacity, a long line of horned animals seems to be drawn to the trap's opening as if by magic. The masked stick figure at the lower left is more recent, by its less varnished appearance. Length of animal line 158 cm.

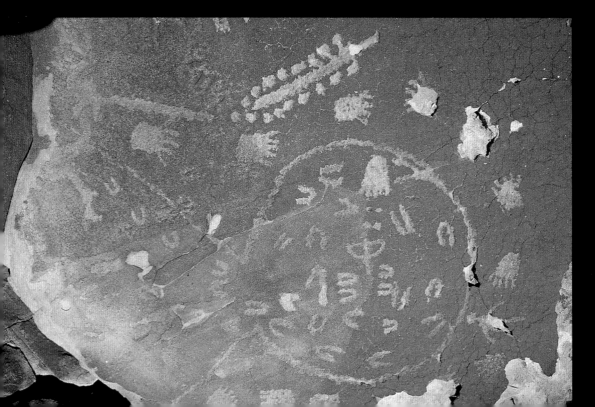

Figure 5.7. This game trap from the "Doggone Bay" site relies almost exclusively on abstract imagery. Entering into the funnel-shaped opening of the corral-like trap and milling inside are pronghorn hoofprints instead of the "real" animals. The bow and arrow, positioned in the center of the enclosure, stand for the hunter ready to shoot his prey at close range. The representational image of a human to the right of the corral perhaps portrays the sponsor of the communal hunt or the hunt shaman. Diameter of corral 49 cm.

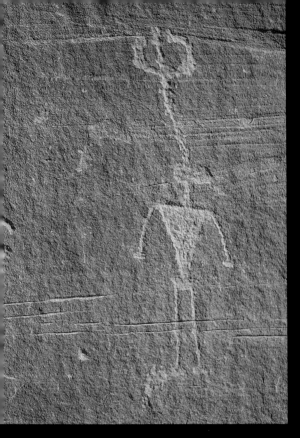

Figure 5.8. Scenes of human violence are extremely rare in Palavayu rock art, and the brutality here is unique. It is unclear if the image portrays an actual event—we may be looking at an example of sorcery magic. Killing an adversary ritually by drawing him with an arrow piercing his head is similar to the practice of sympathetic magic employed in securing hunting success. Here too the very act of executing the image, that is, killing the animal symbolically by penetrating it with arrow or spear, is expected to guarantee the outcome. In this sense, the pictured "headshot" figure is not unlike a voodoo doll that has pins sticking in its vital parts. Height of scene 43 cm.

Figure 5.9. Poses of bowmen aiming their arrows at human figures are rare and not necessarily literal portrayals of violence. The "victim" in this fight scene may actually be a participant in the enactment of a trance dance. Rather than his hair "standing on end," he may be wearing a feathered headdress. The long ribbon flowing from the head of the bowman may represent the potency activated and harnessed by the shaman. Height of archer 15 cm.

Figure 5.11. This panel from "Atlatl Butte" may have constituted a hunting or "increase" shrine for pronghorn, one of the prime game animals in Palavayu. The carnivore tracks mingling with the pronghorn in the top row symbolize the mountain lion, tutelary deity of hunters and game animals alike. The posture of the hunter with bow and arrow underscores the sympathetic or mimetic magic inherent in the panel. Height of archer 20 cm.

Figure 5.10. A rare occurrence in Palavayu rock art, the white rump of the pronghorn may be defined on this petroglyph animal. Length of pronghorn 43 cm.

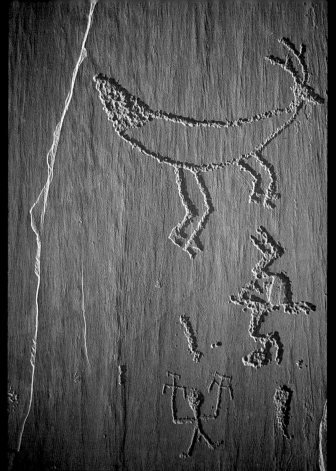

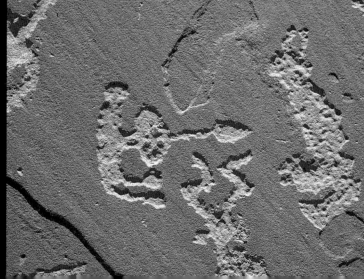

Figure 5.12. The rabbit, an edible species that is abundant and easily hunted, is only rarely portrayed in Palavayu rock art. This unique scene from "Slab Crest," with the rabbit sitting upright as if transfixed by the huntsman, appears raised in relief or appliqued rather than engraved. This embossing effect is an optical illusion caused by the interplay of light, shadow, and angle of the viewer's eye. Note the rabbit tracks to the right of the animal which occur more frequently than full-bodied rabbit images. Height of rabbit 19 cm.

Figures 5.13 and 5.14. Attested at several sites in Palavayu is this curious motif, an animal on "rockers," usually portrayed with zigzag legs, as in Figure 5.13. In Figure 5.14, one human figure appears to feed two deer or pronghorn, another leads an animal by a rope. These unlikely actions perhaps symbolize a hunt shaman's relationship with game animals: to derive supernatural power from them and propitiate them as well as to gain control over them. Width of left arc in Figure 5.13, 59 cm, length of human with quadruped in tow in Figure 5.14, 63 cm.

◢ 5.13

◢ 5.14

Figures 5.15-5.17. The horned "decobod" in Figure 5.15 from the "Boundary" site at Petrified Forest possibly represents a game deity evidenced by its intimate connection with the horned animal below it. Similar suggestions of a tutelary game spirit are evoked in Figures 5.16 and 5.17. Height of anthropomorph in Figure 5.15, 37 cm; in Figure 5.16, 60 cm; and in Figure 5.17, 30 cm.

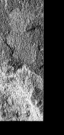

Figures 5.18 and 5.19. Pronghorn, deer, elk, and bighorn sheep make up the largest contingent of the Palavayu bestiary. Although attractive as food sources, their depictions must not be seen as a hunter's favorite pin-ups. Pueblo ethnographic evidence suggests that these game animals may have been regarded as symbols of shamanic power or worshipped as gods or spirit ancestors. Still, their increase was a constant concern, and this was often expressed in rock art by the depiction of pregnant animals, as seen in Figure 5.18. Length of sheep in Figure 5.18, 37 cm; of cartouche in Figure 5.19, 57 cm.

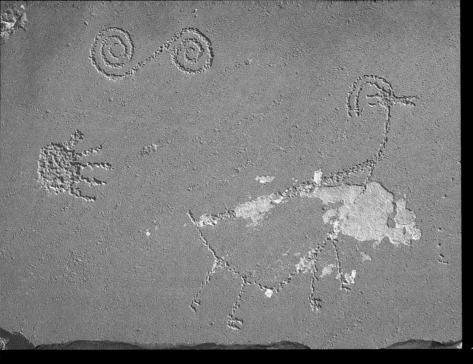

▲ 5.18

◄ 5.19

◢ 5.20

Figures 5.20 and 5.21. The
bear, power animal par
excellence in North American
Indian lore and religion, is
represented in full-bodied
shape no more than a dozen
times in the Palavayu rock art
bestiary. While the animal in
Figure 5.20 seems to depict a
black bear, the ferocious
portrayal of the animal in
Figure 5.21 may actually be
that of a grizzly. Deified
within the Hopi kachina
pantheon, the bear is
featured in a number of Hopi
folktales involving acts of
curing and shamanic
transformation. With
hundreds of stylized bear
paws and bear tracks
scattered throughout the
Palavayu, these icons may
have served as totemic
signatures of prehistoric clan
groups that recognized the
bear as their ancestor. Length
of bear in Figure 5.20, 48 cm;
in Figure 5.21, 63 cm.

◢ 5.21

Figures 5.22 and 5.23. Among the more than 100 depictions of full-sized cougars in Palavayu rock art, the one in Figure 5.22 from a location along the Little Colorado is unique in that its body is distinguished by elaborate interior decoration. At another location, the "Tiffany's Lion" site (Figure 5.23), the animal's special status seems to be underlined by its excessive size. Length of mountain lion in Figure 5.22, 40 cm; in Figure 5.23, 185 cm.

▲ 5.22

▲ 5.23

Figure 5.24. This composition along "Gangway East" portrays, from left to right, a pronghorn, a child-size human figure riding piggyback on a ithyphallic flute player, a large human figure, three nondescript elements, a possible ceremonial object like a prayer stick, and, most prominently, a solidly pecked mountain lion. Length of mountain lion 50 cm.

▲ 5.26

Figures 5.25 and 5.26. Portrayals of mountain lions, or cougars, abound in Palavayu. Drawn in complete outline with usually long recurving tail or represented by a mere paw imprint, the ubiquitous icons may attest to the one-time existence of a cougar cult. Depicted most often with the principal game animals of deer, pronghorn, and bighorn sheep, the cougar may have functioned as the helping spirit of a shaman, enjoyed the status of a tutelary game deity, or both. Its role as game deity is still apparent in the behavior of Toho, the Hopi "Mountain Lion" kachina, when he accompanies Deer and Antelope kachinas as a side dancer. Length of cougar in Figure 5.25, 93 cm; in Figure 5.26, 23 cm.

Figure 5.27. This cliff along the "Doggone Bay" site is adorned with an array of what appear to be ritual scenes. Most remarkable among them are the four "directional dancers" positioned around a large spiral. Equally fascinating is the armless figure, flanked by two bearers of spears or ceremonial staffs, directly underneath the hunting scene. Conversely, the human with a cane and a dog on a leash in the lower part of the panel appears rather mundane. Diameter of spiral 22 cm.

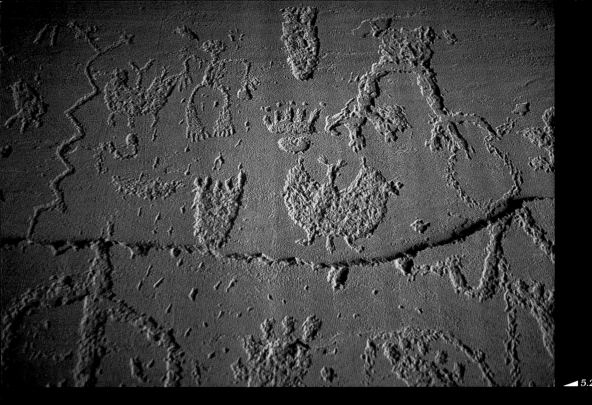

◄ 5.28

◄ 5.29

Figures 5.28 and 5.29. According to Zuni ideology, bats bring rain. In Hopi lore, the nocturnal mammal is associated with witchcraft. These panels from a site southeast of Petrified Forest are remarkable in that they feature two almost naturalistically drawn bats in one section, whereas the bat renditions in the adjacent section convey formidable supernatural quality. Width of big realistic bat 15 cm, height of taller stylized bat figure 84 cm.

Figure 5.32. This scene at a site east of Petrified Forest is reminiscent of Hopi eagle or hawk capturing practices still carried out today. During a capture, young birds are often retrieved on ropes from their nests. Wing span of bird 25 cm.

Figure 5.30. This panel at "Sentinel Butte" may depict the snaring of a bird, an interpretation based on the long, winding string that ends in an open noose next to the bird. Length of string 148 cm.

Figure 5.31. While much of the bird imagery found in Palavayu relates, metaphorically and symbolically, to shamanic events, some of the images are literal renditions of hunting scenes. The herons towering over the tiny archer may contain mythological or other meanings unfathomable to us; however, the huntsman's quest for a menu item appears to be the more obvious theme of this panel. Width of heron scene 106 cm.

Figure 5.33. Lichen enhances the images of an owl, a mountain lion, and a slab paho at a rock art site west of Petrified Forest National Park. Length of slab paho 53 cm.

Figure 5.34. These owl images, featuring spotted breasts and large round eyes, are executed in typical Basketmaker style as is evident from the antennae-like projections from their heads. Such antennae are often found on Palavayu Basketmaker anthropomorphs and are indicative of supernatural power. The birds may represent alter egos of the shaman who may have received them during a vision quest at this site. Height of owl on right 88 cm.

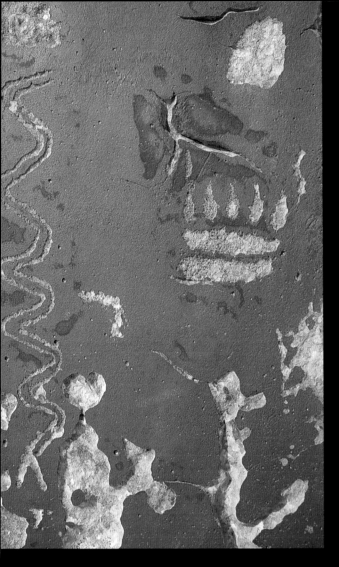

Figure 5.36. This powerful image, seemingly combining serpent and lightning symbolism, actually consists of two intertwined snake bodies. One terminates in a simple headlike thickening, and the other is endowed with a triangular face. The overall configuration approximates Hopi serpent depictions on altar sand mosaics constructed in conjunction with the biannual Hopi Snake dance. Approximate length 75 cm.

Figure 5.35. The impressive prominence of the serpent motif in Palavayu rock art clearly indicates that motivations other than food quest or economical usefulness commanded the portrayal of this animal. A frequently seen version of the serpent head is typically V-shaped. The "V" may symbolize the reptile's forked tongue or gaping mouth. It may also stand for a horned serpent or even a double-headed variety. Length of bear paw 16 cm.

Figure 5.37. The centipede, perhaps linked to the realm of the supernatural because of its subterranean abode, may have served the shaman as an important spirit helper. This wiggling depiction of the creature is complemented by an uncoiling snake and a hunting scene. Height of archer 11 cm.

Figures 5.39 and 5.40. The widely held view that the serpent was one of the earliest and most significant cult animals in the Americas seems to be borne out for the Palavayu region. Although serpent veneration was presumably linked primarily to water, moisture, and rain, human fecundity may also have played a role. The Basketmaker human in Figure 5.39, flanked on three sides by serpents, has a snake as a phallus. The anthropomorphized and horned serpents in Figure 5.40, on the other hand, are clearly associated with a female figure whose head, additionally, appears to be topped by a snake's bifurcated fangs. Height of anthropomorph in Figure 5.39, 62 cm; height of female in Figure 5.40, 60 cm.

◢ 5.39

◢ 5.40

Figure 5.41. The ideological motivation for creating the large number of centipedes that decorate rock art sites throughout Palavayu is not understood. Resembling a one-pole ladder, the centipede image with its multiple array of locomotive extremities perhaps belongs to the category of shamanic imagery. As such it might be symbolic of the shaman's vertical access to the world of souls and spirits.

The scorpion, on the other hand, a rare occurrence in Palavayu rock art, is still part of the Hopi kachina pantheon. Known as Putskoomoktaqa, "one who has a throwing stick in a bag," the Hopi word alludes to the tip of the scorpion's tail which is interpreted as a throwing stick. Carrying a rabbit stick when he appears, the kachina shows definite hunting associations. Length of scorpion 48 cm.

Figure 5.42. *These two creatures with large eyes and drooping wings may be eccentric representations of moths or butterflies. Height of larger image 32 cm.*

Figure 5.44. *Although not the conventional symbol seen in Pueblo IV kiva murals and on ceramics, this image may represent the dragonfly. Esteemed for its aqueous associations and frequently encountered in prehistoric Pueblo art, the dragonfly is extremely rare in Palavayu rock art. Height 81 cm.*

Figure 5.43. *The birds in this panel are easily identifiable as quail, and the two web-footed creatures beneath them may represent frogs or toads. While the symbolic significance of the quail is not immediately apparent from Pueblo ethnography, the frogs or toads are strongly linked with the realm of water and moisture. Height of bird on extreme right 21 cm.*

Figure 6.1. Lichen encroachment on this female anthropomorph prompted the designation "White Lady" for this petroglyph. The bisected head crowned with a three-pronged headdress bestows an aura of divine status. Perhaps this female figure represents Old Spider Woman, so prominent in Hopi mythology. Yet images of spiders are nearly absent in Palavayu rock art. Therefore, the earth goddess, Old Spider Woman, instead of being depicted as a spider, possibly is represented by this female portrayal. Height 98 cm.

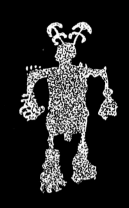

The male image predominates among human figures of Palavayu rock art. It is usually assumed, though debatable, that men were responsible for Southwestern rock art, an assumption supported by the themes of male activity which seem to prevail. Hunting, war, and ceremonial organization are pursuits and duties associated with men in historic Pueblo society, and presumably in prehistoric times also. Hunters, animals, and hunting scenes are the most commonly depicted subjects in Palavayu rock art, equalled by imagery of a religious or ritualistic nature. Discussing rock art in the Glen Canyon region, Turner includes geometric designs as evidence of male authorship, pointing out that men were the weavers in historic Hopi culture.[1] This would presume then that prehistoric pottery designs were derived from earlier textiles, and that pottery-making was woman's domain, as it has been in historic pueblo life.

Domestic and farming activities, collecting endeavors, women, birth, and death are infrequently pictured in the Glen Canyon area. Most of these motifs are also uncommon in the Palavayu area, but are not entirely lacking. A domestic theme is pictured at two widely separated petroglyph sites, at Puerco Ruin and in a side canyon southwest of Holbrook, where human figures balance pots on their heads, a way that Puebloan women transported food or water. Farming scenes are absent, and depiction of cultivated corn plants appears only in the Wupatki and Homol'ovi areas. But yucca plants—fibers, seeds, and fruit staples of historic and prehistoric Southwestern foraging people—are occasionally represented in Palavayu rock art. Thought to have been a female activity, food-plant gathering is implied at five different Basketmaker petroglyph sites where individuals are pictured holding what may be bunches of seed grasses or grain (Figure 2.3). But one human figure has a phallus, and gender of the other four is not sexually defined (so far women cannot be identified in Palavayu Basketmaker rock art). In later periods rock art depictions of women become significant, although still not as numerous as those of males. Women are generally portrayed in certain contexts, including the occasional birth scene (five examples are seen in Figure 6.2). Death may be symbolically indicated in a number of petroglyph depictions of upside-down or falling human figures, especially as these seem to appear most often on or near precipitous cliffs. The recumbent skeletal kachina figure pictured at Mountain Lion Mesa (Figure 4.13) may represent death, and it may also be symbolized in Palavayu rock art in ways foreign to modern perception. As Turner suggests, and this may be true in the Palavayu region, these motifs might all be uncommon either because their depiction in rock art was taboo, or because they are outside the province of male interests.

The division of labor between male and female in Basketmaker times is not clearly established. It is probable that males did heavy tasks such as cist or wall building, and made weapons and implements, and that women were responsible for child care, housekeeping, and production of household utensils. It is likely that men hunted, and women and children gathered seeds, nuts, berries, and other edible plants. Basket making among historic aboriginal people was usually a female activity, and generally is assumed to have been so in the distant past. Clothing in the earliest horizon of the hunters and gatherers was probably

MALE

AND

FEMALE

crafted from animal skins, and perhaps the most ancient of human weaving technology is the weft-twined fur robe used as a warm cloak, sleeping blanket, or burial shroud. Woven simply from strips of rabbit or other soft animal fur and plant fiber, these robes were probably traditionally a woman's responsibility.[2] Men may have shared in or had the exclusive duty of weaving snares, ropes, hunting nets, quivers, and sandals, and it is likely that women made skirts, aprons, tumplines, cradle bands, containers, and other items related to female needs.

Jewelry making, which involved skills related to stone working or flint knapping, probably began as a male activity (as it is today among the Pueblo Indians). Beads, pendants, and earrings are found in great quantity in excavations of Basketmaker sites, and they adorn human figures in Basketmaker pictographs and petroglyphs. Woven fabrics of yucca, other plant fibers, and human and animal hair have been found in early Basketmaker sites in the Glen Canyon area, and, as Turner suggests, may have been a male industry. Ceremonial duties are thought to have been a male responsibility in prehistoric Pueblo societies as in historic times. This was probably the situation in the Archaic and Basketmaker periods; only the male figure can be identified in the rock art of the Palavayu, and it appears to be solely concerned with religious matters.

106

Although males and females are unequally represented in rock art, women apparently enjoyed equal status in prehistoric Pueblo society, as in today's Pueblo culture. Social organization in the Western Pueblos of Zuni and Hopi is both matrilineal (descent reckoned through the female line) and matrilocal (married couples resident in or near the woman's family dwelling rather than the man's). The presence of this system in prehistoric periods has been inferred through the study of pueblo residence patterns, and in the distributions of pottery design-types and other female-associated items. The art of pottery making passed from mother to daughter, and certain similarities of ceramic design style or technique evident in pottery excavated from a localized area of a pueblo may indicate the maternal head of the clan and her daughters and their families resided in the same matrilocal unit.[3] Although generally excluded from participation in kachina ceremonies, women at Hopi are in charge of three female ceremonial societies and may be asked to fill certain offices in otherwise all-male rituals. As lineage heads, women own and occupy the family "house," usually own farm land, and often store the fetish and ceremonial equipment of their clans, a duty of prime importance. Such esteem was apparently accorded matriarchs in the Anasazi culture. According to Pilles, in the Sinagua and Hohokam areas high-status burials usually involved males; in the Anasazi territory they were often female.[4]

Human images in rock art which are larger and more impressive than surrounding figures could indicate individuals with special—even supernatural—powers. In Palavayu Basketmaker rock art, many petroglyph images suggest the portrayal of superhuman beings or deities, and these (if sexually defined) are always male. In later Pueblo rock art several female images also seem to be "larger than life" and display ceremonial features. In Figures 6.1 and 6.6 unusually large females are portrayed with three-pronged headdresses, and the woman in Figure 6.6 has a line descending from her forehead. Both of these characteristics

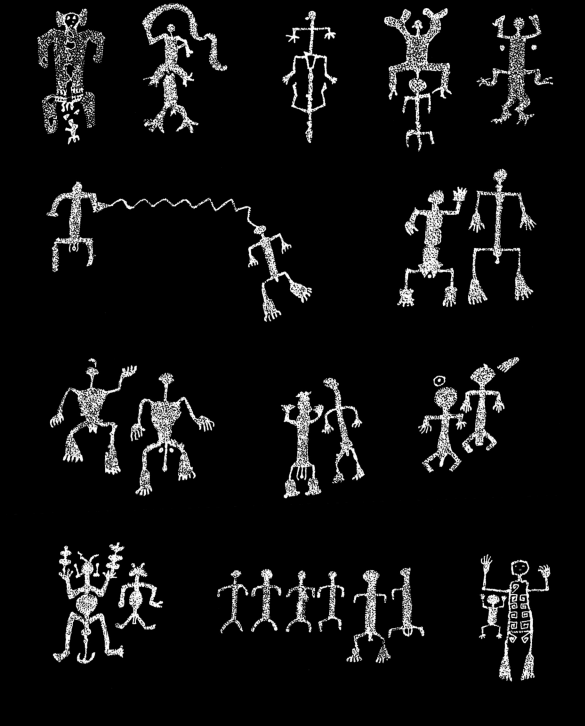

Figure 6.2. Birth scenes, male and female couples, and family scenes in Palavayu rock art (not to scale)

appear on present-day kachina representations.

In five rock art examples (four occurring within Petrified Forest National Park), men and women appear as couples. Each twosome stands close together facing the observer, and in three of the scenes the females raise a hand as if in greeting. Another example near "Newspaper Rock" portrays a man and woman joined by a lengthy zigzag line. At "Atlatl Butte," a couple is pictured with four children lined up beside them in proud array. A touching portrayal of motherhood appears at a rock art site in the Puerco River drainage where, on a lone boulder, a woman is depicted with a baby nestled close to her side. All are illustrated in Figure 6.2.

As noted by Schaafsma, sexual symbolism is more common in the rock art of Petrified Forest than in other Anasazi areas.[5] Only two examples, however, of graphic sexual intercourse have been found. A well-known instance occurs in the "Cave of Life" in the national park, and it best illustrates the true nature of such depictions (Figure 6.4). Far from being pornographic, this tableau clearly portrays a ritual of profound religious significance. A copulating couple is linked to a chain of animal figures and other elements surrounding an outlined cross, an ancient symbol of unknown meaning. Above them, a phallic male in commanding attitude elevates two staffs, one topped with the effigy of a bird, also an Archaic motif related to shamanic practice. This ceremonial depiction, involving two people chosen to symbolize the forces of life and creation, is a probable variant of the "sacred marriage" rite known to exist in historic North American Indian cultures.[6] A religious belief with shamanic overtones, it is designed to restore harmony and prosperity to the community and is regarded as a sacrament.

The second petroglyph example picturing a man and woman in sexual intercourse (Figure 6.3) is also within the park. Although not in a setting as obviously devoted to ceremonial matters as in the "Cave of Life," this one still hints at ritual. Reminiscent of the figures seen on Mimbres ceramics whose faces are bisected by light or dark bands resembling masks or face paint, the face of the female in the petroglyph scene is also divided into a solidly pecked lower half and unpecked upper area in which the eyes are elongated slits. The male figure has a birdlike beak, also suggesting a mask. These human figures seem to represent nonhuman participants in a rite, rather than participants in a sexual act.

Several symbolic portrayals of copulation have been found. In Figure 6.12 the petroglyph image of a male staff bearer appears with erect phallus pointed toward an abstract element generally interpreted as the female vulva. Figure 6.10 is an unusual representation, one of only two known examples in Palavayu rock art which clearly pictures the swollen belly of a pregnant woman. Below her and between her feet an erect male phallus is depicted.

Men dominate the scenes of dance and ceremony in Palavayu rock art. Only one panel has been found depicting women dancing and engaging in ritual (Figure 9.11). Apart from some kachina deities, few male petroglyph images in Pueblo period rock art have been specifically identified as gods, although many in Archaic and Basketmaker rock art strongly suggest this possibility. A few Pueblo period figures appear to be female deities related to the hunt and to human and animal reproduction (Chapter Nine). Elaborate delineation of the genitals suggests many female portrayals are passive symbols of fertility and procreation. Women are seldom depicted in mundane activities, whereas male figures hunt with bows and arrows, play flutes, and are pictured walking, running, and posturing—in addition to the ceremonial scenes in which they dance, carry staffs, placards, and banners. In general, evidence indicates the rock art artisans were male, who pictured the female as a life-generating icon.

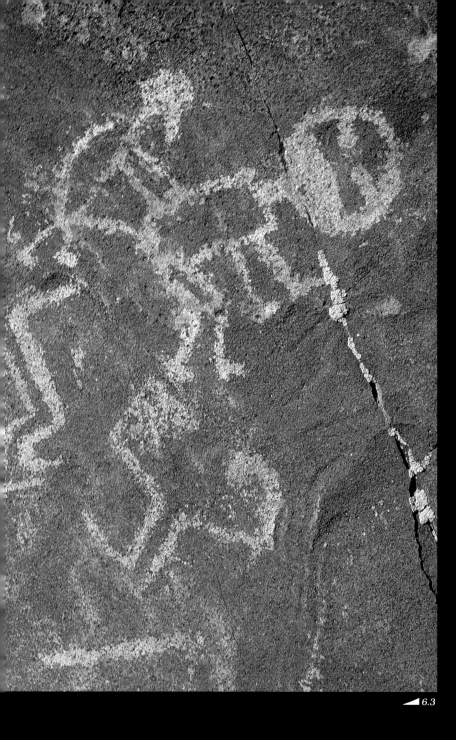

6.3

6.4

Figures 6.3 and 6.4. Among the thousands of rock art images in Palavayu, only two, Figure 6.3 at "Lone Juniper" and Figure 6.4 at the "Cave of Life," show explicit intercourse between anthropomorphic figures. Both sites are situated within Petrified Forest National Park. Width of larger anthropomorph in Figure 6.3, 20 cm; height of cross in Figure 6.4, 24 cm.

Figure 6.5. This cliff section from the extensive "Steps" site may have served as a fertility shrine. Evidence for this inference can be derived from the multiple abraded depressions or outright hollows which mark the arms, legs, and body of the woman giving birth in this scene. Women may have sought out this location to cure sterility or to assure an easy delivery. To this end, powder procured from a cupping may have been consumed by the women or pasted on their abdomen. Height of entire birthing scene 96 cm.

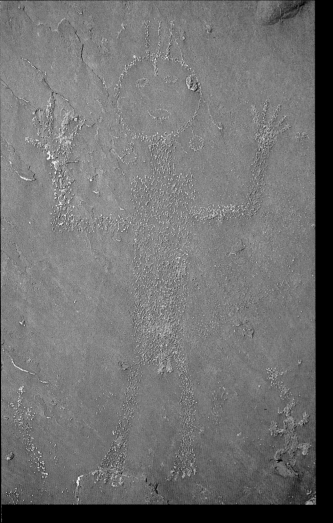

Figure 6.6. This stipple-pecked human figure of nearly life-size dimensions from "Black Anvil" may represent one of the many variant portraits of a tutelary game goddess that dot the Palavayu rock artscape. Note the three-pronged "crown" reminiscent of the one worn by the "White Lady" in Figure 6.1. The role of tutelary game mistress seems apparent from an associated mountain lion on the same slab not shown in the picture. The same association with a cougar suggests this semantic interpretation for the "White Lady" (see Figure 6.1). Height 128 cm.

Figure 6.7. Spirals and a stylized mountain lion accompany two women in what appears to be a childbirth scene. Length of lion 50 cm.

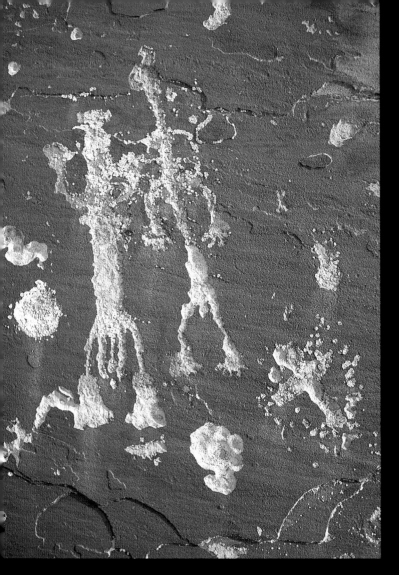

Figure 6.8. The sexual symbolism of this petroglyph couple probably represents the principles of procreativity and fertility, rather than any intent at pornography. Note the lateral bulges on the female figure which appear to signify her breasts. Such depictions are extremely rare in Palavayu rock art. Height of right figure 37 cm.

Figure 6.9. The male half of this couple is portrayed with imposing height and exaggerated genitalia, perhaps to symbolize the life force and underscore the magical power of the ceremonial staffs he carries. Height of left figure 42 cm.

Figure 6.10. Depictions of pregnant women are rarely seen in Palavayu rock art. This interpretation for the female image with ballooning abdomen seen in Figure 6.10 is reinforced by the simulation of an erect phallus between her feet. Height of figure 33 cm.

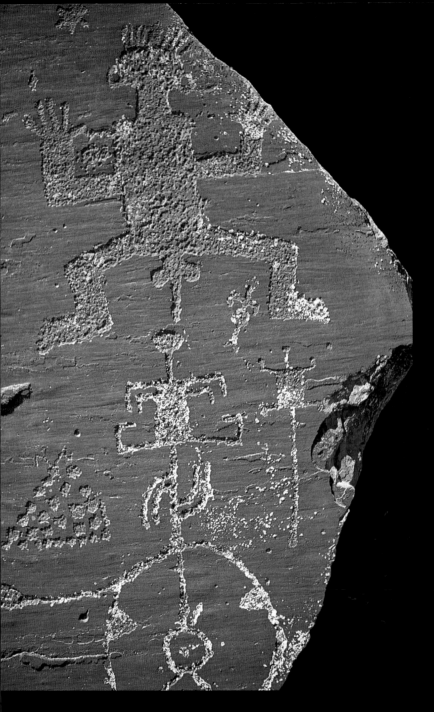

Figure 6.11. Among the many male anthropomorphs that can be identified because of their phallic attributes, only rarely is one depicted with such prominent genitals as this one from "Roller Canyon." The sexual potency that the figure exudes is further enhanced by the rays emanating from its head, generally an indicator of supernatural power. Height of male figure 56 cm.

Figure 6.12. This staff bearer from "Roller Canyon" strikes one as androgynous: the adornments on both sides of the head look like the hair whorls worn by Hopi girls of marriageable age, while the ithyphallic pose confirms male gender. The U-shaped element with a dot in its center to the left of the figure represents a female vulva. Thus, it is more likely that the hair bundles on the staff bearer depict side bobs typifying a man's hair fashion. (Compare Figure 5.40 which clearly defines the U-shaped element as a vulvaform). Height of staff bearer 37 cm.

Figure 6.13. Interpreting this scene as a simple "mother-child snapshot" is probably not compatible with the religious context in which most rock art was created. The careful decoration of the body may indicate the supernatural power and status of a goddess. Height of large figure 45 cm.

Figure 6.14. This "family portrait" at "Atlatl Butte" consists of six anthropomorphs. Note the gender of the "parents" is clearly marked, whereas the "children" are left neutral or asexual. The special potency and magic connected with the numeral four in Pueblo societies is well established. That the magic number four was selected for the offspring may be a clue that this scene belongs to a mythological context rather than the mundane sphere of daily life. Height of male figure 30 cm.

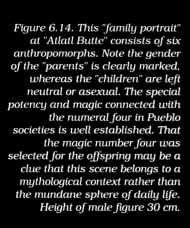

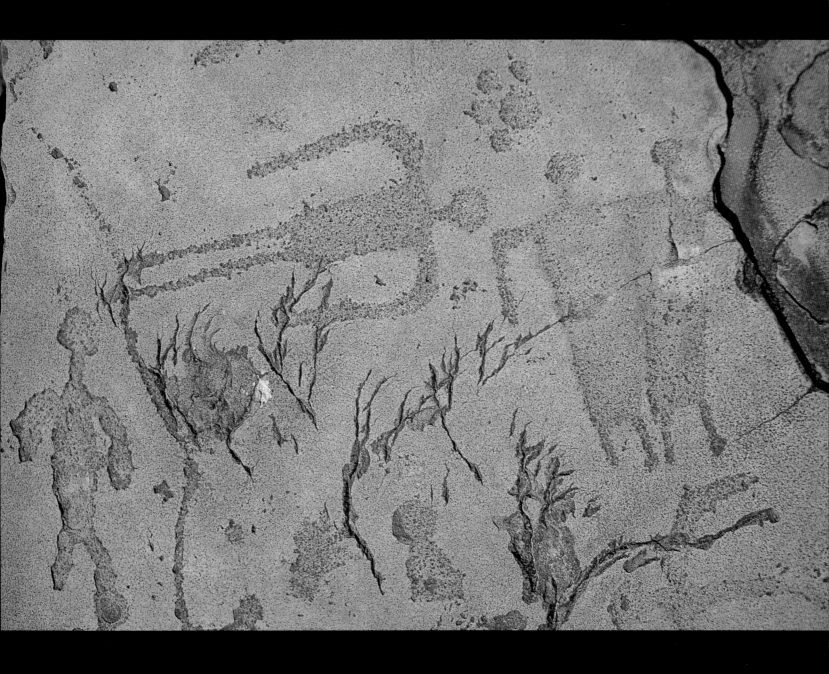

Figure 6.15. Although characterized by different body styles—trapezoidal, rectangular, and oval—these anthropomorphic figures at "Wheeler Dam" exhibit the same degree of revarnishing. It is thus safe to say that all of them were executed by the same artist. While it is tempting to theorize that the differing torso shapes possibly express gender differentiation (oval=female vs. angular=male) or some other classification (oval=human vs. angular=supernatural), there is no evidence to support any of these speculative assumptions. Height of "Siamese twins" 19 cm.

Figure 7.1. Meticulously incised, this single geometric block creation consists of twenty-seven squares of a ninefold repetition of three basic design elements. A masterpiece of engraving, it is reminiscent of the "limitless" designs seen in the rock art of the Sinagua region to the west of Palavayu. Width of geometric rectangle 65 cm.

Among the petroglyph images of Palavayu, the most pleasing and varied are the geometric designs that grace so many rock art panels. These motifs challenged the artisan's skill, and the results are often striking. Some of the more complex designs represent hours of careful work, and are good evidence the artisans did not merely while away leisure time.

"Art for art's sake" cannot be assumed as the primary motive for this type of decorative image; other unknown purposes were probably at work. But many of these motifs so favored by petroglyph artists clearly were executed with care and concern for aesthetic results. Although the originators may have regarded the motifs as purely ornamental, geometric designs may have carried important messages as well.

The elements comprising the designs often represented specific objects or ideas, their meanings evolved from sources within the artist's culture. Franz Boas determined that geometric patterns common in the art forms of all American Indians symbolize the animate and inanimate as well as abstract ideas; the designs often bear little resemblance to the tangible or living models they represent.[1] These meanings are decided either when a realistic form is gradually conventionalized into geometric "shorthand," or when an abstract form suggests certain real images. The former process is well illustrated by the conventionalized bird and feather designs on prehistoric Hopi pottery whereby wings are reduced to triangles, and feathers to parallel curved and rectangular lines; in some examples the designs are wholly abstract. Of the nonrepresentational patterns on earlier ceramics, the meaning attributed by the potters may never be known. This is also true of the geometric designs in rock art, which are most frequently derived from design motifs on ceramics and textiles.

Geometric patterns in Palavayu rock art thought to date from the Archaic period are consistent with those in hunter-gatherer rock art of other western areas of North America. The similarities of simple geometric designs in rock art of these widespread groups has suggested a shamanic origin for the designs, involving entoptic phenomena. A universal constant of the human nervous system, entoptic elements, or phosphenes, are images perceived by the brain which originate in the eye or nerves during an altered state of consciousness.[2] The images can result from pressure on the eyeball, flickering light, migraine headaches, fatigue, or other factors. More relevant to hunter-gatherer rock art, altered states may be induced by fasting, sensory deprivation, or use of hallucinogenic drugs, all known to be practices of the shaman to attain visions or to enter the spirit world. Images seen in the first stage of the hallucinatory state consist of changing geometric patterns, and these are thought to be remembered and reproduced in rock art by the shaman. Entoptic forms encompass a wide range of geometric designs. Prevalent in Palavayu Archaic-Basketmaker rock art, the most commonly seen are spirals, concentric circles, grids, rakes, parallel wavy lines, connected circles, dot patterns, and curvilinear meanders, sometimes superimposing each other and seemingly random in placement.

Beginning in the late Basketmaker or early Pueblo period, the arrangement of geometric elements begins to suggest a more deliberate composition, with increasing emphasis on rectilinear, angular, and stepped construction. This implies a direct link with the designs

GEOMETRIC

DESIGNS

appearing on the twined bags and baskets of the early Basketmakers; As Kate Peck Kent declares, "design is governed by structure," and weaving naturally limits design to horizontal, oblique, and perpendicular patterns.[3] Contrary to Turner's opinion that geometric designs are probably of male authorship as they are the traditional weavers in the Hopi culture, geometric designs were likely created in large part by female basket weavers, for that craft may even have preceded the weaving of fabrics. The Basketmaker III period marked the beginning of painted decoration on pottery, employing the same design elements used in basketry. These motifs also appeared in rock art, growing progressively more complex and virtually becoming an art tradition in themselves throughout the Palavayu region.

Geometric designs in Palavayu rock art of the Pueblo periods include open unbounded patterns; those bounded by squares, rectangles and circles; single abstract elements; and designs incorporated within human and animal figures, human footprints or sandal prints, and ceremonial objects. Christensen's study of 255 designs from eighty-eight sites in the Little Colorado and Puerco River valleys indicates that more than half of the geometric images are enclosed squares or rectangles.[4] Composed as a unit, the enclosed motif is usually the most diverse and "finished" in appearance. It contains stepped elements, keys, nested triangles, curved or rectangular scrolls, checkerboard patterns, or other decorative features arranged symmetrically, and sometimes asymmetrically. Bounded circular compositions are less common. Open designs are the second most numerous; scrolls, patterned bands, lines with pendant dots, ticks, or sawteeth, groups of dots, and combinations of these and various other elements present a meandering rather than integrated effect. Single geometric motifs such as swastikas, one-pole ladders, rakes, x's or simple crosses, outlined crosses, and other forms are occasionally seen. Apart from the many spirals and concentric circles in Palavayu rock art there are also "sunbursts," or rayed circles. Similar to the shield motifs seen in Rio Grande rock art, some circular designs appear to date from the PIV period. Prominent in the majority of geometric petroglyph images are designs borrowed from pottery produced or imported into the area, principally those dating to the PII–PIII periods. These time periods correspond to the highest population levels in the Petrified Forest area.

"Limitless" patterns typical of those on prehistoric Sinagua textiles have been reproduced in rock art of the Wupatki area, considered by Schaafsma to reflect influences from Salado and Hohokam traditions.[5] These patterns, composed of repeated elements without a central focus, are lacking in the Palavayu region (one exception is illustrated in Figure 7.1). A few Palavayu geometric designs resemble blankets, as noted by Christensen, in that they have borders and corner scrolls similar to the "tie-offs" of the warp and weft threads in weavings, but these are not common. Although woven fabrics and baskets have not survived in significant quantity at the open archaeological sites of the Puerco and Little Colorado River valleys, those from other sites of the Plateau Anasazi exhibit many of the same design motifs seen in Palavayu area ceramics and rock art. It is apparent the assemblage of geometric design elements was widespread and freely borrowed among Anasazi groups, and shared by both potter and weaver.

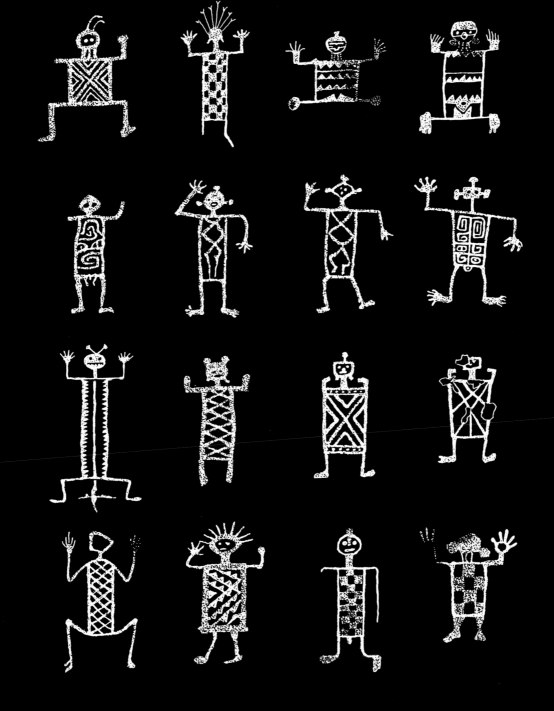

Figure 7.2. Palavayu human figures with decorated bodies (not to scale)

122

The slab paho, a ceremonial object pictured in rock art and described in Chapter Nine, is frequently adorned with patterns seen in ceramic decoration. Preferred design elements are the sawtooth pattern and the rectilinear or curvilinear scroll. Figure 7.11 shows three of the more intricate examples. An interesting variation appears in Figure 7.13, in which an enclosed design of interlocking scrolls is composed around the central shape of a slab paho.

An unusual motif found in rock art of the Petrified Forest area is a geometric shape similar to the Egyptian cartouche. This elongated rectangle encloses various designs and is often finished at one or both ends by an undecorated space within a square or half circle. That it is a material object is suggested by Figure 9.11 where a female figure holds this image aloft. It is the only functional clue noted for this motif, as all other examples are isolated images. Alex Patterson suggests it might represent certain devices worn by participants in Hopi ceremonies, as reported by early ethnographers.[6] They described these shieldlike objects worn on the back as painted animal skins stretched on slender boughs to hold them taut. They are collectively referred to as "moisture" tablets and "sun" tablets. The moisture tablet has been used in the women's *Maraw* ceremony, thus it may be related to the rock art device pictured in the scene showing women apparently engaged in ritual. Painted boards have been found in archaeological sites, and Patterson further surmises that ritualists may have carried them (the placards or banners discussed in Chapter Nine would fit this category), or displayed them at altars. The decorated cartouche image also resembles the slats or sticks which ring the altar set up for the *Maraw* ceremony. Hopi informants told Henry Voth that these sticks represented deceased *Maraw* members,[7] and several rock art cartouche images do bear anthropomorphic features. There is also a resemblance to the *na'tsi*, or board standard, placed on the kiva roof on the fifth day of the Oraibi *Maraw* ceremony described in Fewkes' account.[8] The design presents tantalizing possibilities but cannot be interpreted with any certainty.

Human and animal figures are sometimes attached to or incorporated within geometric designs; an example is seen in Figure 10.2 at the "Royal Flush" site. One petroglyph cartouche at Mountain Lion Mesa in Petrified Forest National Park encloses a lizard. Another curious geometric composition is found at a petroglyph site near the Puerco River. A human head and arms extend from a caterpillar-like sawtooth element with eight legs (Figure 3.12). Fancifully conceived, it suggests a row of concealed men supporting the decorated square above.

A number of human and a few animal images are decorated with interior designs. Although figures with such designs are common in rock art of the Basketmaker Style, they are not characteristic of Pueblo period rock art in the Palavayu region and may represent a concept borrowed from other sources. Human forms with facial features and interior designs are seen in the Quemado area of New Mexico,[9] and may indicate Mogollon origins, with affinities to Jornada and Mimbres art. Although some of the Palavayu petroglyph humans of this type seem to be wearing masks usually diagnostic of the PIV period, others are depicted with simple facial features and suggest an earlier period and style. Some examples of each are seen in Figure 7.2. Decorated sandal and footprints are also occasionally pictured.

A petroglyph design found near the Little Colorado River composed of clustered small squares looks like the floor plan of a many-roomed pueblo (Figure 7.12). Interestingly, a similar design appears on a small Sikyatki Polychrome jar in the Keam's Canyon Collection of Hopi pottery, and was described by Stephen as the ground plan of a "phratry" house (or house built by related clans).[10]

A geometric motif widely depicted in the Southwest and appearing frequently in the rock art of the Palavayu is the outlined or enclosed cross. Parsons states that "the inclosed [sic] cross was a common design on Basketmaker sandals, and on post-Basketmaker (and Hohokam) pottery (Morris [1927], p. 197). It is also an early and widespread petroglyph design."[11] Confirmation of its appearance in "early" rock art came through the discovery of a small rock slab used as a building stone in a Basketmaker III pithouse dwelling at the Twin Butte site in Petrified Forest National Park.[12] Engraved upon the slab is a zigzag line and an enclosed cross. Because part of the zigzag is broken off, the petroglyphs must have been upon the slab before it was used in the structure, thus substantiating its antiquity. Although usually an isolated rock art image, the outlined cross is the focus of the interacting figures found in ritual context in Petrified Forest's "Cave of Life." The petroglyph group in Figure 7.9 featuring a flute player, companion, and a large outlined cross also carries ritual connotations. A handsome variation of the cross design is found at "Slab Crest." The arms of the cross are repeated rather than joined in continuous outline.

Cupules and sharpening grooves are sometimes found in the Palavayu. The grooves may form patterns that seem aesthetic rather than utilitarian, and they are occasionally mistaken for design images. Found throughout the world, cupules are believed to be one of the earliest forms of rock art.[13] In North America, they are particularly common in California where ethnographic research has linked their manufacture with fertility enhancement and weather control.[14] Little is recorded in Pueblo ethnography to account for the cupule's presence in Southwestern rock art except for Matilda Coxe Stevenson's reference to two stone pillar shrines visited by Zuni Indians who wished by certain ritual to aid woman's fertility or to ensure the gender of a future child.[15] The base of one pillar and boulders surrounding it are said to be covered with "female fertility symbols" which include cupules as well as vulva depictions. At one rock art site in the Palavayu region, the cupule may have served another purpose. Several female petroglyph images at "Slab Crest" have hollowed-out depressions close or attached to the figures. Since they are on horizontal surfaces and of ample depth, it seems likely the artisans intended the circular depressions to receive ritualistic offerings. This likelihood is further suggested by the imposing, goddesslike aspect of the images. Small shallow pits also occur there and at other sites, many on vertical faces, ruling out the possibility that they were always used in this manner. Petroglyphs in association with cupules at these infrequent sites present little in the way of additional significance, and the meaning of the cupule in the Palavayu region remains unknown.

The variety of geometric designs in Palavayu rock art and the differing skills and techniques used to produce them indicate this type of artistic expression was important to the prehistoric artisan. Whether the images served some special purpose, communicated a message, or satisfied a creative urge of the maker may never be clear. These designs characterize the distinctive rock art tradition in the Palavayu region, adding a decorative charm as pleasing to the modern eye as it may have been meaningful to the ancient beholder.

Figure 7.3. The equilateral stick cross, more commonly known as "outlined cross," is frequently encountered in Palavayu rock art. Usually enclosed by a single continuous curvilinear or rectilinear outline, multiple-stacked outlines also occur. The quartered emblem, generally believed to represent a star, may also symbolize the four directions, or simply stand for the number four, still treated as a sacred number in modern Pueblo cultures. Height of anthropomorph 43 cm.

▲7.4

▲7.5

◄7.6

◄7.7

◄7.8

Figures 7.4-7.8. Though consistently resisting interpretation, complex geometric designs are among the most aesthetically captivating ingredients of Palavayu "visual rock art feasts." Perhaps part of a sophisticated symbol system, the abstract patterns exemplified here must therefore not be seen as purely decorative, that is, as an end in themselves. Height of Figure 7.4, 52 cm; overall width of geometric squares in Figure 7.5, 110 cm; height of Figure 7.6, 40 cm; overall height of Figure 7.7, 80 cm; and width of Figure 7.8, 60 cm.

Figure 7.9. "The power of two" is conveyed by this scene from a site along Chevelon Creek. Two stars, one in the shape of an outlined cross, hover over two anthropomorphs engaged in playing a single flute. Charming game animals with a magic instrument is a situation in which the flute player is occasionally portrayed. The adjacent deer appears to fit this role. Diameter of cross 13 cm.

Figure 7.10. The geometric images on this panel from "Turtle Back Butte" include an outlined cross and a design reminiscent of a woven blanket, with a textile-like pattern and corner scrolls resembling the tie-offs of warp and weft elements. The tiny human footprint at the lower edge of the design, however, may render this modern, culturally biased interpretation totally meaningless. Width of outlined cross 15 cm.

Figure 7.13. The interlocking rectilinear scrolls of this enclosed geometric surround a slab paho in mazelike fashion. While its striking ornamentation may have been motivated by man's innate desire to realize himself creatively and artistically, its ultimate purpose must elude us. Aesthetic qualities may simply have been thought to render an object more sacred or a site more appealing to the supernaturals. Height of upper geometric 34 cm.

Figure 7.11. Both rock art evidence and Hopi ethnographic information point to a ceremonial usage of the slab paho by members of a religious women's society. Handheld during a ritual performance or possibly placed upright on an altar or at a shrine, the paddlelike board may have embodied a prayer. This slab from the "Lollipop" site is adorned with a total of nine slab pahos. Height of paho on extreme right 30 cm.

Figure 7.12. Two bands of negative zigzags, a stick lizard-man, and a configuration of small clustered squares adorn a cliff wall near Woodruff. The clustered squares look like the architectural blueprint of a Pueblo village with a shrine at the center of the plaza. Height of cluster arrangement 37 cm.

Figure 7.14. Enclosed oblong spaces, filled in with geometric ornaments, are here termed "cartouches." This tablet-shaped example from "Second Flume" along the Little Colorado River is held by a curious figure that, with his horned skull cap, is strongly reminiscent of the Puebloan clown or trickster. Length of cartouche 60 cm.

Figure 7.15. The identity underlying this stylized creature at the "Royal Flush" site is not obvious. Resembling a worm or caterpillar, its ultimate significance eludes the modern observer. Both the conical head, with scroll-like appendages, and the geometrical body lend the creature a dignity that lifts it from the realm of the ordinary. Length 114 cm.

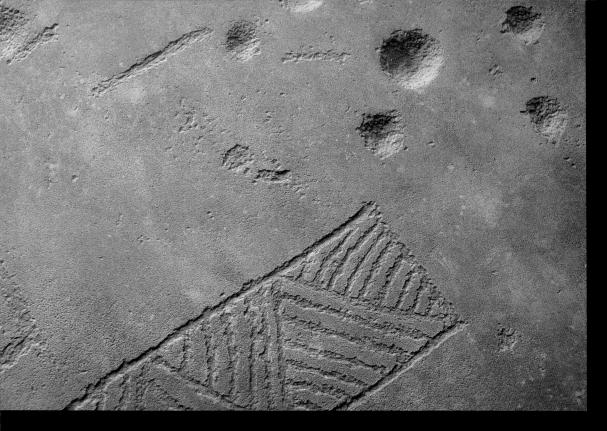

Figure 7.16. Cupule petroglyphs, also known as cupmarks, occur sparsely in Palavayu. Among the hundreds of rock art sites investigated to date, only some two dozen are distinguished by the cuplike depressions. Encountered on a global scale and believed to be part of humankind's most ancient rock art repertoire, most cupules are carved into horizontal rock slabs; however, vertical cliff walls also exhibit the pits. Width of geometric design 13.5 cm.

Figure 7.17. Incised abstract petroglyphs are relatively rare in Palavayu. While solitary grooves generally seem to be the result of tool sharpening, one location south of Holbrook, featuring more than 170 indentations, may reflect a combination of this utilitarian aspect with the creation of petroglyphic imagery. The overall arrangement of the major groove elements suggests a quadruped, perhaps a deer. Many of the indentations are so small and superficial that they appear more decorative than functional. Length of upper grooved edge 50 cm.

Figure 8.1. First appearing to be just a chaotic array of glyphs, the set of concentric circles is actually placed with high calendrical precision. On the day of the summer solstice a shadow line moving from left to right bisects the circles exactly before it merges with the shadow descending from the top of the panel. Diameter of solar marker 22 cm.

"We have increasingly come to realize the richness, complexity, and even accuracy of the understandings of nature developed by 'primitive' peoples. Recent studies of early astronomies have been exceptionally illustrative in this regard."[1] Stephen McCluskey's statement effectively describes the new appreciation for prehistoric man's knowledge of the skies, fostered by an emerging interdisciplinary science called archaeoastronomy. Through ethnographic materials, oral traditions, and iconography, a growing body of evidence shows that the changing positions of sun, moon, planets, and star patterns were well known to ancient sky watchers and used to regulate many areas of their lives. McCluskey's pioneering research with the Hopi calendar and astronomy, and past investigations of ethnologists at Hopi, Zuni, and the Eastern Pueblos over the last 100 years have confirmed the tradition of Pueblo sunwatching in historic times, particularly of the varying sunrise and sunset positions throughout the year.[2] Archaeology and astronomy are now revealing that sunwatching also served as a vitally important mechanism for the Anasazi. As farmers in a marginal agricultural region, survival depended upon a precise knowledge of the relationship between the sun's movement, their local climate, and growth of their crops; thus it became crucial to be able to establish planting dates and time the rituals required to guarantee successful harvests. As with all aspects of Pueblo life the secular intermeshed with the sacred, and the correct timing and procedure of religious ceremony was necessary to keep the people in harmony with their world. No less important is the concern at winter solstice, when the sun stands still, to entreat it by rite and prayer to turn back on the path to summer. Its hesitation might indicate a reluctance to continue the journey, bringing perpetual winter.

In 1977, a rock art site was discovered at Chaco Canyon which displayed precise interaction with the sun at the time of summer solstice by means of a "sun dagger," or narrow shaft of sunlight, as it moved down a shadowed rock face to bisect the center of a large petroglyph spiral.[3] At the times of winter solstice and the equinoxes there were also significant interactions of sunlit shafts with the large spiral and a smaller spiral nearby.[4]

These discoveries prompted a project to determine whether other rock art sites in the Southwest functioned as solar "observatories." Robert Preston and his wife Ann[5] have discovered seventy-six examples of similar solstice events at sixteen petroglyph sites in and adjacent to Petrified Forest National Park, along with twelve sites in other areas of Arizona.[6] Their findings are convincing proof that the Anasazi used certain rock art as calendric markers through the interaction of sunlight and shadow on petroglyph images on the winter and summer solstices. The Prestons determined that certain rock art images, predominantly spirals and circles (including concentric circles), serve to mark solar sites and to interact with sun and shadow. These interactions are remarkably consistent among the various sites. Due to the sun's motion across the sky, a shaft of sunlight or shadow may move across a rock surface to touch the center of a glyph, brush the edge, or trace the outside groove without entering the image. Shadow lines or sunlight dots may suddenly appear or disappear at the center or edges of an image. By examining the play of sunlight and shadow throughout the year on all of the spiral and circular petroglyphs at many of their sites, the Prestons have shown that these types of interactions with the petroglyphs tend to occur much more frequently on the solstices than at other times of the year, conclusively demonstrating that most of the noted solstice interactions are not accidental alignments but are intentional markings of the sun's yearly cycle. Some of the petroglyph markers even display multiple solar interactions on a single solstice, and some mark both solstices. An intriguing question is whether other dates or types of petroglyph images are involved in this phenomenon. The Prestons have noted that in several cases a similar interplay of sunlight and shadow occurs on spiral and circular petroglyphs on the equinox, and that distinctive interactions occur with other petroglyphs (life forms and crosses) on the solstices. One of the Prestons' most impressive discoveries involve a group of petroglyphs in a cavelike rock shelter in the Petrified Forest. Five symbols—three spiral and two circular petroglyphs—display the described solstice sunlight interactions, with both solstices marked by fifteen solar interactions among the five glyphs. In one of the more spectacular events in the cave, forty-five days from winter solstice, a dot of sunlight suddenly appears in one of the spirals and enlarges into a slender sunlit shaft as it moves across the cave, finally disappearing at sunset with its tip at the center of a large outlined cross petroglyph. Simultaneously, the only other pointer on the same rock face disappears with its tip at the end of the tail of a lizard-man figure. In the historical Hopi culture, the important tribal initiation ceremony known as *Wuwtsim* occurs forty-five days before winter solstice, and the time of the ceremony is fixed by solar horizon observations.[7] Symbolizing new beginnings with the "new fire" ritual and initiation of young men into the tribe, the *Wuwtsim* ceremony may have been timed so that a count of days from this date (more easily verified because the sun moves more rapidly along the horizon at this time) may have guided the Hopi sunwatcher in determining winter solstice.[8]

How were these various rock art solar sites actually used? According to Michael Zeilik, if only the solstices or other key dates are definitively marked, then there might not be enough warning to prepare for the accompanying ceremony.[9] "Anticipatory" sunwatching in historical cultures is exemplified by the practice of horizon observation by the Hopi sunwatcher at First Mesa as recorded by Stephen.[10] The official watcher could calculate the progress of the sun's rise or set along the irregular eastern and western skylines in advance of special dates. Perhaps the solar rock art sites used primarily to confirm those dates may mark shrines in which prayer sticks are deposited and offerings made to the sun deity. Of course, the sunlight-petroglyph interactions could also have been used in an anticipatory manner by observing the sunlit images marching across the petroglyphs day by day, slowly approaching ever closer to the ultimate track on the key day.[11]

Light and shadow imaging on rock art elements or on interior walls of prehistoric structures has been documented by archaeoastronomers for other areas of the Southwest, notably in Chaco Canyon and Hovenweep.[12] The method is also known for historic Pueblo structures. Frank Cushing, the ethnographer who lived with the Zuni people from 1879 to 1884, wrote that the Pueblo inhabitants confirmed the announcements of their sunwatching

priest because "many are the houses in Zuni with scores on their walls or ancient plates imbedded therein, while opposite, a convenient window or small port-hole lets in the light of the rising sun, which shines but two mornings in the three hundred and sixty-five on the same place."[13] This venerable custom of sunwatching by Pueblo people has been confirmed by ethnographic data; their forebears' ingenious methods of using sunlight and shadow to mark important dates represents "one of the few empirical avenues to an understanding of the ceremonial life of the prehistoric Indian cultures."[14]

◄8.2

◄8.3

8.4

Figures 8.2-8.4. At the "Cave of Winds" (Figures 8.2 and 8.3), on summer solstice, the tip of a shaft of sunlight breaks off as it crosses the outer edge of the spiral. The point of light then moves across the rock surface until it breaks apart once more before it traverses the "arrowhead" on the extension of the spiral and then disappears. Figure 8.4 represents a winter solstice marker at the "Pinhole Cave" in Petrified Forest. Here a blunt light angle brushes along both the bottom and right pairs of human feet.

Possible archaeoastronomical sites for solstices and equinoxes are easily verified—they can be tested by simple observation on the proper days of the year. Other annually recurring events such as planting dates or dates for ceremonies may also have been tracked by a "sunwatcher." These are more difficult to verify due to the absence of written or oral calendar records from any of the cultures that produced the rock art. Diameter of sunburst in Figures 8.2 and 8.3, 30 cm; width of spiral in Figure 8.4, 7.5 cm

Figure 9.1. The most prominent rock art panel in the Lacey Point area of Petrified Forest pictures an anthropomorphic female flanked by two solidly pecked disks. While the overall context of the associated imagery suggests portrayal of a "Mother of Game" goddess, the function of icons such as the twinned disks, embodying the "power of two," will probably continue to elude us. Height of "game mistress" 53 cm.

Some repeated motifs and scenes in rock art cannot be surely interpreted but they strongly hint at ceremonial events, rites or religious practices, and ritual artifacts. Lines of dancing people, figures with elaborate headdresses, or individuals carrying staffs, rattles, crooks, or other objects are portrayed. Some human images are pictured with "more than human" characteristics: rays or power lines from their heads or hands, birds for heads and feathered wings for arms, bodies of exaggerated size in contrast to smaller surrounding figures. Often associated with these human images are spirals and concentric circles, discs, outlined crosses, and other symbols of equivocal meaning. Flute players are frequently present and sometimes seem to be accompanying or even directing rites. Certain of these scenes and motifs found in Palavayu rock art imagery are discussed in the following pages.

THE MOTHER OF GAME

Despite the knowledge gained from a century of work in the Southwest, archaeologists still know little of the ceremonial customs of Southwestern native people—particularly before the advent of the kachina religion. The most revealing glimpses into the richness of ancient ritual have been through pictorial art: kiva murals, ceramic decoration, and rock art. Because rock art predates decorated pottery and mural paintings, petroglyphs and pictographs have afforded us our only view of early ceremonial life as seen through the eyes of the artist.

Some unrecognizable objects and unusual life forms are repeated in rock art throughout the Palavayu area. These elements, however meaningless they may appear to modern eyes, indicate the artist employed a convention recognizable and significant to his people. Human figures and animals depicted in an uncommon way may represent certain personages or mythic beings, a possibility for one petroglyph image that is repeated at widely separated rock art sites.

The image, a human figure flanked by two solidly pecked disks, is found at two sites within Petrified Forest National Park. Another site is located just outside the park, and others are found at sites along the Little Colorado River. The figure is consistently depicted as female, and in four instances is associated with animals and symbols of the hunt. Her unvarying posture, arms raised and bent at the elbow, legs extended to each side and bent at the knee, gives her a rigidly formal mien; and the disks, though obscure in meaning, may have been meant to signal her identity.

The most informative representation of this female figure is seen on one of the panels within the park (Figure 9.1). Here, she is partly encircled by two animals, two birds, and a flute player. The two animals are in sexually receptive attitudes, with upraised tails. Other elements in the panel include a bow, arrows, and phallic symbols. The content of the panel suggests hunting and animal increase, and these clues point irresistibly toward a deity in the historic Pueblo pantheon known as the "Mother of Game." This deity "owns" the animals, is responsible for their increase, and allows hunters, if they make the proper offerings and follow the prescribed ritual, the right to hunt her children. She is related,

conceptually, to one of the corn mothers of the Keres, the Deer Mother of Taos, and Fire Old Woman of Cochiti. At Zuni, her counterpart is *Chakwena* Woman. But her legend is strongest and her lore most varied at the Hopi mesas. Here, she is known by two names, *Tüküywuuti* and *Tuwapongtumasi,* and although the two are said to be synonymous, they likely are the amalgamation of two "mothers" of different origin. The myths gathered by ethnologists over the years primarily concern *Tüküywuuti,* and from these narratives possible parallels may be discerned in the rock art depictions which may represent this goddess.

Tüküywuuti means "child-sticking-out woman," in reference to a Hopi legend wherein a pregnant woman who died during childbirth was transformed into the deity.[1] This occurred after she was left behind by her people during their migration from the Little Colorado River pueblos to the Hopi mesas. When someone returned to her, they found she had died giving birth to infant game animals. Thereafter, the legend goes, she was a ghostly form wandering the land.

Her role as Mother of Animals is expanded in the various descriptions that Hopi informants gave to early researchers. According to Stephen, she is "mother of the antelope, deer, mountain sheep and both kinds of rabbits;"[2] to Edward Curtis, "a female deity who gave birth to all species of game animals, from rabbits to elk."[3] Hunters make offerings to her for success in the hunt, and prayer sticks are also left at her shrine "that she may increase the supply of game." Her fertility powers also extend to human reproduction; according to Parsons, she "bestows infants," and "sends infants inside women."[4]

Although it seems that *Tüküywuuti,* who bestows infants and permits hunters to kill her children, would be a benevolent and kindly spirit, this is not the case. She is much dreaded and has a ghastly appearance which makes men "freeze in terror." From lore collected by Malotki, it is believed that "if she copulates with a man, he will become a successful hunter who will always get his game."[5] Some modern Hopi believe she is really a beautiful woman who only wears a hideous mask of bones over her face because she doesn't want anyone to see what she really looks like. Her hidden beauty, however, does not seem to outweigh her scary reputation. It is said that after a man has had a frightening encounter with this being and is "petrified with fear," following his recovery he will look for her tracks but will find only the tracks of a jackrabbit.[6] Interestingly, one petroglyph panel along the Little Colorado River shows the female, with disks, commanding the top center of a rock face; at her feet a line of tiny animal tracks stretches across the panel.

Another rock art depiction which seems related to *Tüküywuuti's* legend is located at Crack-in-Rock in Wupatki National Monument. On the cliff face of a mesa a female with disks appears, accompanied by an animal, two birds, and a human figure. Adjacent and at right angles to her, another panel displays four large spirals; on one, human figures seem to follow a path into the center of the spiral. Some Hopi and Zuni regard spirals as migration symbols,[7] and in this instance its association with the female and animals would seem to fit the *Tüküywuuti* myth.

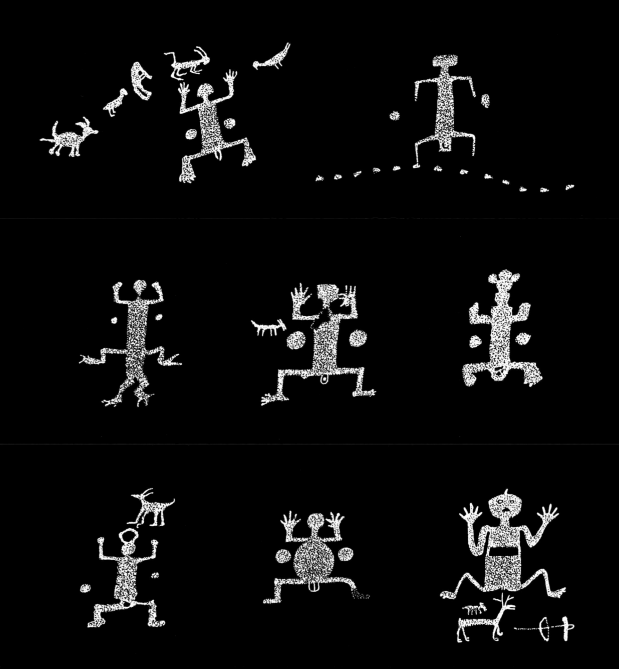

A petroglyph at a Petrified Forest site depicting a woman (flanked by disks) giving birth might refer to the tragic death in childbirth of the woman in the migration legend. Equally possible, it may illustrate her fertility or portray her role as the Mother of Animals (although it is difficult to determine to what she is giving birth). The imagery seems to support either the legend or her persona.

Petroglyphs line a narrow passage through low canyon walls at the base of a rocky escarpment outside the park. Animals and hunting scenes dominate the subject matter of these rock art panels. The funnel of the draw is ideally suited to the "game drive" method of hunting employed in historic as well as prehistoric times. On a boulder against the backdrop of rock art hunters and animals, the female figure with identifying disks is placed.

A final example which may represent this personage is found at a site along the Little Colorado River (Figure 9.9). This petroglyph female lacks the disks and is superimposed on glyphs of another style clearly of a different era. Her staring eyes and bared teeth are similar to features on certain kachina masks, which may imply the figure was made after the kachina tradition was established. The image is in the familiar spread-eagle stance, and a subtle indication of female genitalia verifies her gender. There is an air of the supernatural about her; she is a convincing portrayal of the frightening *Tiikuywuuti*. But other clues also reinforce this possibility. Beneath her a hunter aims his arrow at a deer, and another bowman appears beside her. A flute player salutes her, and a staff bearer can be seen nearby. Some of the glyphs may be contemporary with her; others are obviously older. Close by, on the same cliff face, two small females with disks appear. They are not accompanied by any other glyphs significant to the Mother of Game legend, but their presence shows a familiarity with the disk convention. This may have become an outmoded motif when the later version of the female was made.

The concept of a female spirit who owns the animals is an ancient one, with shamanic roots that may have originated in Siberia in Paleolithic times.[8] Her image and attributes differ from tribe to tribe, wherever she is found. That the evolution of her different aspects has followed many paths is evident at Hopi, where the two deities are said to be one, and whose various names include Mother of Animals, Patroness of the Hunt, Earth Mother, Fertility Goddess, Mother of Kachinas, Wife of *Maasaw* (god of fire and death), and Sister of *Muy'ingwa* (a germination deity).

If it can be concluded that the female pictured in rock art represents this being, an evolution may also be apparent in the way she is portrayed, from the simple enigmatic figure seen at the first site in Petrified Forest to the fearful, nightmarish female at the third site on the Little Colorado River.

THE SLAB PAHO

In 1987, an exciting discovery was made in Petrified Forest National Park. During a survey in a remote area, researchers located a petroglyph panel which seems to show women engaged in a ceremony (Figure 9.11). Such scenes involving women rarely occur in the rock

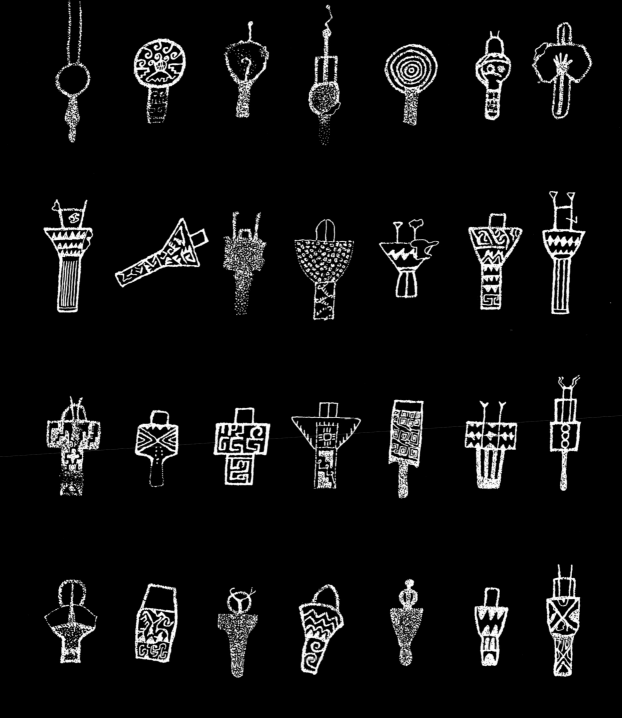

Figure 9.3. Examples of the slab paho in Palavayu rock art (not to scale)

art of this region; indeed, portrayals of females are far less numerous than those of males. But the 1987 discovery is doubly rewarding because an object previously unidentified but often seen in the local rock art is pictured in association with the women, providing a sure context for the element.

This object resembles the dance wands still used in the public ceremonies of a Hopi women's society. Its petroglyphic representation appears with some frequency as an isolated image, formerly regarded as just another of the many geometric rock art designs that abound in the region. Since its probable identification as a dance wand and subsequent investigation into its ethnographic and archaeological history, many more rock art examples have been found in a surprising variety of shapes, decorations, and embellishments. These further variations were identified through a practice of the ancient artist: although the majority of examples are isolated single elements, sometimes one type of "wand" is paired with another of totally different shape and design.

The artifact has also been described as a "slab prayer stick" or "slab paho," due to its function in Hopi culture. Rather than dance wand, paho is a less restrictive designation, as in its different forms it undoubtedly had other ritual uses. Fewkes[9] established the antiquity of the slab paho when he excavated several at Sikyatki, a Hopi pueblo dating from the fifteenth century. The artifact may date even earlier, because many petroglyph representations have been found in association with late Pueblo III (ca. A.D. 1200 to 1300) habitation sites.

The examples in the Petrified Forest panel are held, or displayed, by two women seen in the upper portion of the rock face. Just below them, a third woman holds aloft a cartouchelike design, which is repeated above the group. This element is seen at other sites in the area, but cannot be identified with certainty, although it obviously has significance here. A snake and a large, solidly pecked disk complete the tableau. The formal attitude of the figures in the upper section contrasts with the life and movement of those in the lower half. Here, three women with joined hands are apparently part of a dance group (regrettably, part of the rock surface has spalled away and the scene is incomplete). Parading above and below the dancers are two male staff bearers, one being pushed or pulled by another female.

Although it may be incautious to link prehistoric imagery to historic contexts, there is a striking parallel with the traditions of the women's *Maraw* society at Hopi. The rock art slab pahos, although they have longer handles and simpler abstract designs, are otherwise similar in shape to the *marawvaho*, the wands carried by the *Maraw* women during their public dance performance. Linear extensions on the petroglyph examples resemble the feathers and grasses with which the *marawvahos* are adorned, as seen in the illustrations which accompany articles on the *Maraw* ceremony written by Fewkes[10] and Voth.[11] *Marawvahos* are described by Titiev as being painted "with a great variety of corn, germination, rain, and cloud symbols."[12]

The curious scene of interplay between a staff bearer and the woman who pulls or pushes him is reminiscent of ritualized interaction between *Maraw* women and

Figure 9.4. Varieties of the ceremonial staff in Palavayu rock art (not to scale)

men of the *Wuwtsim* society. According to a myth recorded by Fewkes, both societies claim to have descended from "Taiowa [*Tay'owa*], a sun deity, who met a maid in the underworld and drew her to him by inhalation through a flute. He took her to Tawaki (Sun House), and she bore him many children. To one of his sons he gave the mysteries of the Wuwutcimtu [*Wuwtsimt*], and to one of his daughters those of Mamzrautu [*Mamrawt*]...."[13] They therefore regard each other as brother and sister, and traditionally a number of men, referred to as *marawtaataqt*, or "*Maraw* men," assist at the *Maraw* ceremony. Their relationship is informally dramatized during the rites of both societies, when each side teases and taunts the other with bawdy and sometimes obscene songs, playing tricks and indulging in general horseplay. The petroglyph pair seems to express this sort of playfulness.

A large, solidly pecked disk at the top of the rock could be interpreted as a sun symbol, appropriate to the legend of Taiowa [*Tay'owa*], but a rayed disk is more commonly thought to represent the sun, and is often seen in the local rock art. The solid disk glyph is found in the "Cave of Life" area of Petrified Forest, associated with the ritualistic iconography so abundant at that site. It also may have been used to indicate the subject was of ceremonial import.

Slab paho representations in rock art occur in four basic shapes: the paddle component may be round, square or rectangular, fan shaped, or triangular with tapered base (Figure 9.3). Handles on the first three may be rectangular, or with rounded or pointed ends, much like an old-fashioned hand mirror. Most are surmounted by linear squares, circles, or half-circles, and some have extensions which resemble feathers or grasses. Many are solidly pecked, but an equal number are decorated with geometric designs. It is likely these were flat wooden objects painted and carved with differing designs. Watson Smith describes five objects excavated from an Awat'ovi kiva as "flat paddlelike wooden artifacts...carefully carved and some showed evidences of blue, red, and black paint." He goes on to say that they "resembled certain forms of pahos or prayer sticks used today in some Hopi ceremonies."[14]

The greatest number of petroglyph examples of the slab paho are found near Puerco Ruin within the park, but many are also depicted at rock art sites along the Little Colorado and Puerco rivers. As of this writing, none have been found outside the Palavayu region.

Importance of this ritual artifact and the veneration accorded it is compellingly demonstrated at a rock art site in a remote canyon area. There, a ridge above the valley floor rises to a peak crowned by a massive array of rock slabs. One of these gigantic slabs is covered with petroglyphs, and it projects over all the surrounding glyph-bearing boulders. Uppermost on the same rock face, a single image appears. Isolated at the apex of terrain, ridge, and rock, a magnificent slab paho dominates all.

THE CEREMONIAL STAFF

A petroglyph image abundant in the rock art of Petrified Forest National Park, particularly around Puerco Ruin, is the cross-armed staff, or wand. Often pictured in ritual contexts carried by single or multiple human figures, it also appears as an isolated glyph. This image is found at rock art sites along the Little Colorado River and Silver Creek as well, occasionally featured in elaborate tableaus.

The staff varies in form. The cross bars, occurring up to six in number, may be rectangular, elliptical, or take the form of round discs. As staffs with different shapes of cross bars appear together in the same panel, there may be some significance to each type of staff portrayed.

Staffs are commonly seen as a part of historic Pueblo dance regalia, and have also been found in excavations of prehistoric sites.[15] At least three prehistoric examples of staffs remarkably similar in shape to the elliptical cross-armed variety are known. Among many painted wooden fragments found at Chetro Ketl Ruin in Chaco Canyon is a nearly complete staff and portions of two others. The assemblage of items is believed to be of a ritual nature.[16]

It is impossible to determine the meaning and ceremonial function of the many kinds of staffs pictured in ancient rock art, but a few clues may demonstrate a link between surrounding images and the type of staff depicted.

147

Figure 9.5. A hunting scene possibly depicting a hunt shaman invoking his animal spirit helper

Human figures carrying staffs with cross arms are often seen in conjunction with game animals and sometimes with hunters. Two rock art panels, one near Leroux Wash and one near Silver Creek, show staff bearers presiding over a procession of animals, suggesting the staff might exert control over animals. Near Woodruff, a panel rich in allusion to hunting magic shows a phallic figure pointing a staff at an unidentifiable animal, while in the foreground a hunter pursues a line of deer (Figure 9.5). Although the deer are executed in realistic detail, the creature confronted by the staff bearer is not recognizable, and in contrast to the other animals has a vague, amorphous outline. This panel may picture a hunt-shaman invoking his animal spirit-helper. The same idea may be depicted at other sites by portraying animals transfixed by staffs. On another Leroux Wash panel, a staff bearer levels his staff at a menacing archer (Figure 9.18). This individual is connected by a line to two animals, on one of which the reproductive organs may be defined. It seems likely this scene depicts some esoteric rite concerning hunters and animal procreation. Accompanying this group is a second staff bearer, and the theme of fertility is further emphasized by this subtly delineated figure. Close examination reveals that the figure is female, and a rounded belly suggests she is pregnant. As noted previously, depictions of women engaged in ceremony are most unusual in Palavayu rock art.

The motif of the archer menacing a staff bearer is also seen at a petroglyph site in the park on Mountain Lion Mesa. This scene includes a row of linked human figures, perhaps dancers, and below them parades a variety of animals. The ceremonial setting suggests a drama is being played out, again involving hunters and animals. Similar dramatizations are implied on other rock art panels which depict archers aiming arrows at flute players or at men in ornate headdresses.

The staff with disks, which is as numerous as the cross-armed staff and often pictured at the same petroglyph site, may represent a different sort of device. It could have been ancestral to a type of rattle used in the Flute ceremony at Hopi around the turn of the century, illustrated in Stephen's *Hopi Journal*.[17] Called a "water-rattle," it was composed of gourd disks fastened to a wooden rod; crooked thorns on the back "hook the clouds," which obviously relates to rainmaking ritual.

East of the park is a concentration of petroglyph staffs of a different type. Poles are topped with inverted crescents, some rayed with featherlike projections, some plain. The poles themselves are often ornamented with knobs or small, curving cross bars. First seen as an isolated glyph, investigators did not recognize this image as a staff until the discovery of a rock art site which pictures six human figures carrying these objects. Although the figures seem to be displaying the staffs in a formal stately manner, there is no associated subject matter to imply these figures are participating in any specific kind of ceremony.

In her descriptions of Pueblo ceremonialism, Parsons refers to the staff as a "stick of office" and describes the types which identify the position and authority of chiefs and priests.[18] She also mentions the use of staffs as society standards, placed outside the kiva when a ceremony is in progress. She defines the *mongko*, a narrow rectangular board carried

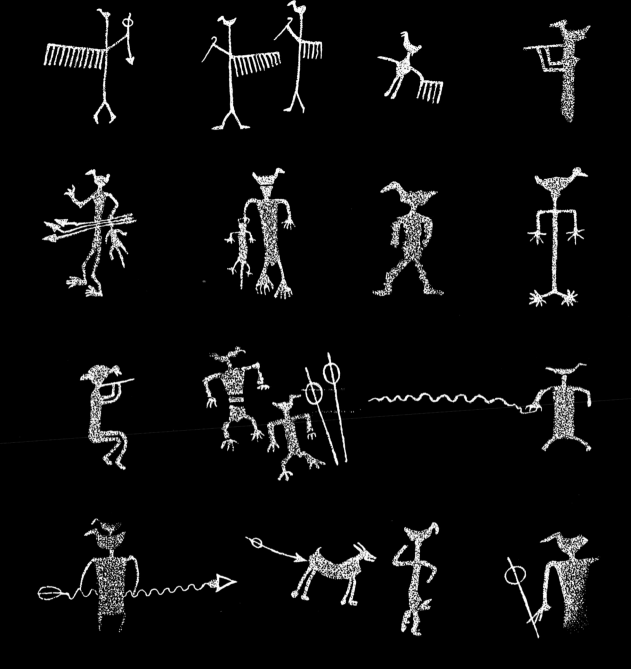

Figure 9.6. Bird-headed figures in Palavayu rock art (not to scale)

by every member of the Agave and Horn society, as a society emblem: an individual sacred possession, which is also a badge of identification. If these historic uses can be related to the prehistoric, it is possible that one of the functions of the cross-armed and crescent-topped staff was to serve as this sort of personal insignia, as panels picturing groups of such staff carriers seem to indicate. Scenes showing the cross-armed staff apparently used as a magical aid in hunting, or in a ritual related to animal increase, suggest that this staff may have been the emblem of a Hunt society. This Society group was important in early Pueblo culture, when the rewards of the hunt played a vital role in supplementing a primarily agricultural economy. The fact that parties of men are shown with particular types of staffs, or that the staffs appear in the rock art of certain areas, may also mean clan or even tribal identification.

Staffs decorated with other forms—pennants, crescents, placards with geometric designs, bird and animal effigies—are also well represented in Palavayu rock art, and some are pictured in Figure 9.4. Bird-topped staffs are depicted at two sites within the park, one near Holbrook, and another near Silver Creek. This type of staff is known archaeologically; Hough describes "ceremonial staffs having birds carved at the upper end," from caves near Blue River, Arizona.[19]

Four staff examples (Figure 9.4) resemble posters or placards decorated with geometric designs, and they are held aloft by human figures. It is not known whether any of these were simulations of an actual staff or whether they were purely decorative petroglyph designs.

One staff, topped by a square on which an animal form is outlined (Figure 9.31), is accompanied by an onlooker brandishing a spear in one hand and apparently giving a "military" salute with the other. This scene, which suggests wholly modern connotations to the present-day viewer, is outdone by an even more puzzling petroglyph. Figure 9.20 shows an individual displaying an animal effigy that resembles nothing so much as a toy on wheels. This image is so evocative of familiar modern-day childhood toys that it is difficult to relate it to an ancient artifact. The wheel, unknown in the pre-Columbian Southwest, seems to be portrayed, and there are no similar objects seen in the rock art of this area to suggest the real meaning of this element. It is unique.

The many types of staffs seen in Palavayu rock art seem to be first represented at petroglyph sites which, on the basis of style and manufacturing technique, are thought to date from the Pueblo III time period (A.D. 1100 to 1300).[20] Their absence in the rock art at Homol'ovi Ruins suggests the cross-armed staff was much less popular during the PIV period. The crescent-topped staff, however, appears in rock art of the eastern Palavayu region in association with masked figures assumed to date from that later time period.

THE BIRD-HEADED MAN

A rock art motif common in Canyon de Chelly, Arizona, and with some distribution through southeastern Utah, has been found in increasing numbers in the Palavayu region. The bird-headed, or bird-topped, man is a mysterious figure whose meaning has prompted much speculation.[21] Campbell Grant recorded scores of bird-head figures during his survey of

Canyon de Chelly rock art and believes the motif originated in that area late in the Basketmaker period.[22] As the majority of the bird elements appeared to be turkeys, Grant concluded that a turkey cult may have developed there, citing examples of other North American people whose economies centered around such animals as the buffalo, salmon, or bighorn sheep. According to Grant, turkeys were domesticated in the Canyon de Chelly area as a food source, which accounts for the seeming preoccupation with this bird in the canyon's rock art. It is portrayed not only as a bird-head component, but is also depicted singly and in large groups or flocks. Other indeterminate types of birds are also pictured on the bird-headed figures.

Bird imagery has a well-known association with shamanism throughout the world. Various peoples believe the shaman is capable of transformation into a bird to make the magical flight to the upper world, where he may retrieve lost souls, commune with supernatural beings, and bring back essential knowledge to his people. The act of transformation is one interpretation for the bird-headed man depicted in rock art, believed to be picturing the moment of metamorphosis of shaman into bird.

A similar, extremely ancient image is the bird on a stick, pole, or staff. A famous cave painting in Lascaux, France, dating from the Upper Paleolithic period pictures a bird-topped pole, a bison, and a falling bird-headed man. The scene was long considered to be anecdotal, the record of a hunting accident in which the hunter was gored by the apparently wounded bison. Reinterpreted from a shamanistic viewpoint, the man is seen to represent a shaman entering the ecstatic trance which releases his spirit for the celestial flight, the bison as a sacrificial animal whose soul he propitiates, and the bird-pole as a shamanic accessory.[23]

Symbolizing shamanic ascent, the bird-pole has been a necessary part of the shaman's paraphernalia through the ages; as Eliade contends, the "'bird perched on a post' is extremely archaic."[24] In the American Southwest, the bird-topped staff is known archaeologically,[25] and it is also pictured in Palavayu rock art. In the "Cave of Life" in Petrified Forest National Park, a petroglyph scene depicts an esoteric rite overseen by an imposing male (Figure 6.4). He holds two staffs, one topped with the image of a bird. Other petroglyph designs apparently representing bird-topped staffs have been found at several rock art sites in the Little Colorado River drainage. On one panel three birds on sticks are pictured, and nearby is a bird-headed man. At a second site, on a panel where bird-headed men are depicted, a short pole with three birds stacked one above another appears in isolation (Figure 9.23).

These petroglyph sites and some with the bird-head motif are found fairly close together in a remote area outside the park. Prominent in the rock art panels are arrows or atlatl-like shafts, some attached to or held by human figures, and one impaling a bird, one an animal, and one a human. Several are pictured as discrete elements. Grant noted the association of the bird-head with the atlatl, a situation which suggests Grant's Late Basketmaker or Early Modified Basketmaker Period (A.D. 400–500) origin for the bird-head motif, although the design apparently persisted into the Great Pueblo Period (A.D. 1100–1300).[26] It is interesting

that the atlatls (and/or arrows) pictured in Palavayu sites are styled like those pictured in the early Basketmaker art of Canyon de Chelly, for much of the Palavayu rock art is almost certainly from late Pueblo times. Other images present in some of the Palavayu panels are typical of the late PIII or PIV periods: females with hair whorls, horned serpents, a humpbacked flute player, a parrot, and a mask. The atlatl image may have become ceremonially associated with the bird-heads in Basketmaker times, enduring as a ritual symbol into the later periods. The connection with hunting weaponry is further carried out at two widely separated petroglyph sites in the Palavayu region. At each site men with birds atop their heads appear to be holding the body or pelt of an animal (Figure 9.6). One of the bird-headed men also carries a bundle of arrows, as if returning from a hunt.

Imagery demonstrating a convincing link with the rock art of Canyon de Chelly has been found at "Dot's Spot," a pictograph site south of Winslow. Pictographs are rare in the Palavayu region, which makes this site even more unusual. Painted in white, black, and shades of pink to dark red, the images include handprints, animal tracks, anthropomorphs, animals, and abstract designs. Especially significant are the portrayals of a bicolored human figure, a bird-headed man (Figure 9.24), and a stick-figure flute player, all motifs common to Canyon de Chelly rock art, and all of the same distinctive style. The bicolored man, whose body is half red and half white (the white much faded but still discernable), has the square-shouldered conformation and stiff bearing of late Basketmaker figures. Grant places these anthropomorphs of the Canyon de Chelly area in his Modified Basketmaker period (A.D. 450–700). This time frame is also likely for the "Dot's Spot" site. The many hand imprints are common in pictograph panels of this period, and the bird-headed man and stick-figure flute player are each strikingly similar in shape to their Canyon de Chelly counterparts, which have been dated in archaeological contexts. The white head and red body of the bird perching on the head of the man are identical to the portrayal of turkeys at Canyon de Chelly sites. Although the reversed legs are not typical, the stick body and curved limbs of the flute player at "Dot's Spot" resemble elements of those figures in Canyon de Chelly. All told, there is compelling evidence that people traveled the 150 miles from Canyon de Chelly to the southern area of the Palavayu. Of additional interest are peck marks which scar almost every pictograph. Just like those marring the petroglyph figures at the "Steps" rock art site, these seem to have been done by later people, perhaps to gain power, perhaps to nullify it.

A panel of rock art near Petrified Forest National Park seems to indicate that the bird-heads may have been members of a society or sect which performed in ceremony. Figure 9.22 shows men carrying crooks and seemingly costumed with one feathered wing. Group participation is suggested by three panels which picture three, four, and as many as seven bird-heads in association. Bird-heads playing flutes have also been found in the Palavayu region (Figure 9.27), further indicating a ceremonial function.

Is it significant that some bird-headed human figures are portrayed with birds resting on their heads, while on others birds actually replace the heads? From a total of forty-four bird-

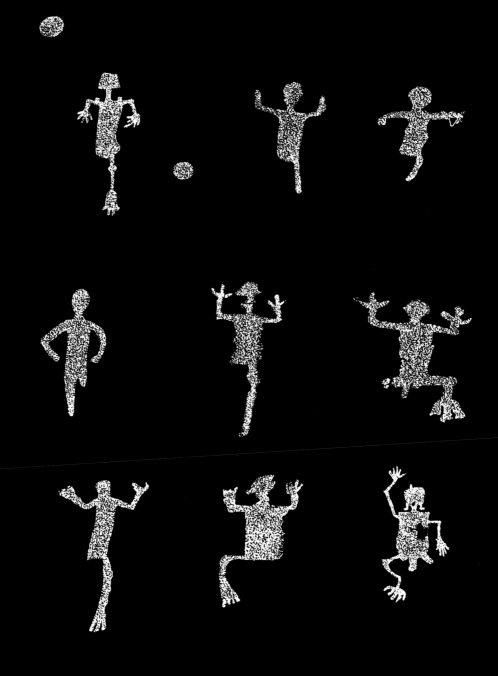

Figure 9.7. The one-legged man in Palavayu rock art (not to scale)

headed figures in Palavayu rock art, there are twenty-three whose heads are replaced by birds and twenty-one pictured with birds placed atop their heads. There seems to be no indication that either type is a dominating figure, differentiated by design, or accompanied by special images. A case could be made for the panel pictured in Figure 9.23, which shows a human with a bird resting on his head and depicted with naturalistic hands and feet, while above him five out of six figures have heads replaced by birds and are lacking hands and feet. This scene suggests the lower human being hasn't yet undergone a shamanic transformation, while those above him have. An examination of bird-heads at other sites, however, reveals that portrayals are mixed and some figures of each type are detailed with realistic hands and feet. The concept of shamanic alteration pictured in rock art should not be ruled out, however; it is an ancient tradition that has been well substantiated. The two methods of depicting bird-headed humans were meaningful to the artists if not clearly understood to us now.

THE ONE-LEGGED MAN

In Petrified Forest National Park, a small rock shelter is situated on the rocky slope of a mesa near Puerco Ruin. Anchor holes for roof beams are visible on one wall of the shelter, and scattered potsherds indicate that this was once a small dwelling occupied in PII–PIII times. On the outer face of a large boulder that forms the south side of the shelter, several petroglyphs stand out in bright contrast to the dark rock surface. A human figure with only one leg is pictured in Figure 9.32. On either side of him is a solidly pecked disk, and a small zigzag design to his left completes the panel. We might assume that the human figure is an unfinished petroglyph—that the artist didn't get around to adding the other leg to the image. But this assumption is contradicted by the careful technique, the lack of scratched guide lines often present in unfinished glyphs, and the precise unbroken line of the torso where the right leg should join.

The "Cave of Life," another rock shelter within the same general area of the park, is noted for its dramatic assemblage of human figures in a ceremonial setting. Two are involved in a phallic rite presided over by a staff-bearing priestly figure. Among the many petroglyphs within the cave, there are two depictions of a one-legged individual. Both are missing their right legs, the same leg missing on the rock art figure at the other rock shelter. Since these petroglyph images were first noted, five more one-legged figures have been located in the Palavayu region; another within the park, one west and one east of the park boundaries, one near the Little Colorado River, and one along a wash which drains into the Little Colorado. Some lack the left leg instead of the right, two are definitely males, and all are depicted in varying styles and techniques. These clues contribute a possible interpretation of this motif: that a one-legged man actually once lived and became a legendary personage—not necessarily seen in the flesh by all who portrayed him in rock art, but renowned nevertheless. It would be an extraordinary event if someone in those times survived such a catastrophic accident as the loss of a leg. It would be an equally singular occurrence if the limb was missing at birth, another possible explanation for this circumstance.

The motif of the one-legged man may have originated in the Petrified Forest area. The majority of the known examples are found there, and the image at the Puerco Mesa site is the most complex, fully realized portrayal. This figure displays realistic details not seen in the others. The bulge above his left leg may represent the different conformation his body would develop as a result of the loss of one leg, and prominent biceps are clearly defined on his arms, suggesting the upper-body strength necessary for those with that handicap. Considering that the two images in the nearby "Cave of Life" are also depicted with the same missing right leg argues for first-hand acquaintance with a fellow man, rather than the portrayal of a mythic figure. A further implication is suggested by the two solidly pecked disks flanking this image. These often accompany figures with supernormal aspects. A shaman, if not acquiring his vocation by inheritance or quest, may be "precipitated" into the shaman role by illness or by an unusual accident in which he is gravely injured.[27] Whether a birth defect or a later accident, such a severe disability would have set this individual apart from other people, one of the first traits which distinguish a shaman candidate. If the one-legged man was believed to possess shamanic powers, it would explain his portrayal with the disks to signify his status, and account for his inclusion in the ceremonial images of the "Cave of Life."

THE FLUTE PLAYERS

No motif in Southwestern rock art arouses as much curiosity and speculation as the humpbacked flute player known popularly, but erroneously, as "Kokopelli." Over a wide area of the Southwest this distinctive figure is portrayed in petroglyphs and pictographs, and sometimes in pottery designs. In addition to his flute and hump deformity, this figure is usually, although not invariably, ithyphallic. In some examples, his legs and feet seem to be deformed. He may be depicted with a feather or projection from the head and occasionally with insect antennae or rabbit ears. Sometimes he appears with animals, especially mountain sheep, and with hunters. Other scenes suggest he is associated with rainmaking, and in some instances the priapic flute player is obviously related to eroticism and human fertility. These unusual traits have given rise to the many labels bestowed upon him— minstrel, hunter, bringer of rain, fertility figure, "Don Juan" —and have generated much lore concerning the origin and meaning of this image.

In Palavayu rock art, the humpbacked flute player is rarely seen. To date, of a total 134 flute player petroglyphs, only thirteen examples have been found which picture the obvious hump considered diagnostic of this icon. Flute players of normal human shape abound, however, in a variety of styles that appear to originate as early as the late Basketmaker period, indicating the "ordinary" image is the older one. Preliminary results of a study of flute players in rock art have yielded significant new information.[28] Drawing upon an inventory of more than 1,000 flute player figures, including those in ceramic design, a pattern of style and distribution has emerged. The study encompasses the geographical extent of images reported by informants and gleaned from published material, and it includes all types of flute players

(those with and without hump, and of differing shapes, attributes, and associations). It has been determined the flute player in all its forms is confined to a limited area of the Southwest. In Utah, the motif is ubiquitous, extending north to Dinosaur National Monument; sparse in Colorado, it appears primarily in the southwestern corner of the state; New Mexico's figures are abundant along the central Rio Grande Valley and the northwest region; Arizona has a high density in the northeast and the Canyon de Chelly area. The image is found as far south as Springerville and the Verde Valley, but is absent below the Mogollon Rim (the flute player appears only on ceramics in the Hohokam area). There are a few in Texas and one has been reported in Oklahoma; it is nonexistent in Nevada and California. Because most "normal" flute players (without hump and nonithyphallic) are concentrated slightly northwest of the Hopi mesas and in the Canyon de Chelly region, this figure may have originated there, spreading outward and acquiring regional traits. The humpbacked phallic depictions, apparently having initially evolved in the Four Corners area, appear to have a geographical focus in the central Rio Grande Valley and northwest quarter of New Mexico. These data, in addition to Pueblo oral literature and ethnographic information, may help identify the source of the "Kokopelli" character.

According to Malotki, the word "Kokopelli" is a corrupted form of the name of the Hopi kachina *Kookopölö*, the masked, humped, and phallic—but fluteless—kachina who appears in various Hopi dances and ceremonies on unspecified occasions. *"Kooko"* is etymologically obscure; *"pölö"* means "ball, hump, lump, or stub."[29] Further complicating the meaning of this word is its Hopi use for the so-called "robber fly" insect noted for its prodigious copulating habits. Kachina, *Kookopölö* insect, and rock art humpbacked flute player are linked in their aspects of sexuality. But there is serious purpose behind the erotic behavior of the kachina and his female companion *Kokopölmana*. They are embodiments of human fecundity, entreated by barren women for offspring in the case of the male kachina, the female representing the desire for human increase.

The kachinas and *Kookopölö* insect are without flutes; the true flute player is the fourth agent involved in this complex intertwining of myth, deities, and traits which seems to have occurred in the Hopi world in the PIV time period. *Maahu*, the cicada or locust, is the musical and curing patron of Hopi Flute societies[30] and the "pet" and clan ancestor of the Spider Clan people on Third Mesa (who also sponsor the Flute Society there). *Maahu* is an ancient deity, as evidenced by his appearance in a Hopi emergence myth.[31] Pictured playing a flute on the altar tiles used in Flute ceremonies, his role is to bring summer warmth to promote crop growth. This connection between locust, his fluting voice, and desirable warmth is recorded in several Hopi tales,[32] the tradition underlaid by the actual phenomenon of the locust's fluting call which heralds the start of warm weather. Also ancient is the Flute Ceremony, possibly predating the kachina religion and certainly the kachina *Kookopölö*. The Hopi never identify the flute player figure as "Kokopelli;" their traditional term for the motif is *Maahu*, or Locust. Malotki believes the locust may have been the prototype for the original rock art flute player.[33] Parsons identifies the humpbacked flute player motif and the kachina as insects, "possibly,

Figure 9.8. Examples of Palavayu flute players (not to scale)

however, not the same insect," going on to differentiate between *Maahu*—Locust—and the *Kookopölö* insect. The humpbacked flute player in rock art, she says, is so obviously an insect [Locust] "once you see it" that no analysis is called for.[34] A number of PII–PIII rock art images of the flute player in the Palavayu and western Anasazi regions exhibit insectile characteristics such as rounded backs and antennae, suggesting that this venerable figure is being represented.

The region encompassing Canyon de Chelly and the area just northwest of the Hopi mesas was likely the cradle of rock art flute players of normal human shape. It is not known for certain, however, where or when the phallic humpbacked flute player originated. The image appears on a pottery sherd from Chaco Canyon excavated from a mound reliably dated to the PI period,[35] and it is definitely present in rock art, ceramic decoration, and kiva murals after A.D. 1000.[36] Spread of this figure may have triggered regional variants and associations such as the rabbit ears, foot and leg distortion, horns, bird heads, and hunting themes. Prevalent in rock art of the central Rio Grande Valley after A.D. 1300, this image with pronounced sexual attributes is thought to have been imported into the Hopi area by the Asa [*Aasa*] Clan, whose original home was near the town of Abiquiu in New Mexico.[37] In the Hopi towns the concept apparently merged with the Locust tradition, becoming the phallic humpbacked kachina deity, losing the flute and gaining an insectile snout. The *Kookopölö* insect with its copulatory habits may have contributed to this image, or may have acquired its name through comparison with the kachina's phallic nature. Florence Hawley points out another possibility for the figure's metamorphosis: the kachina's snout may have derived from the flute, for the snout of a San Juan Pueblo kachina is referred to as a "nose whistle stick," a type of flute which in San Juan ceremony the kachinas "whistle...when they come."[38]

The thirteen examples of the humpback flute player found so far in Palavayu rock art are associated with petroglyphs apparently dating from the PIV period, and this time frame would affirm the likelihood of the figure's arrival and adoption in the Western Pueblo region. It also accounts for the scarcity of the image in an area being slowly abandoned. Characteristics of these humpbacked flute players are not uniformly portrayed, and they differ from the "classic" image seen in the Rio Grande Style of rock art. Of the thirteen, only five are phallic, seven have feathers or projections from the head, five recline while the others stand, and the figure may have an exaggerated hump or a prominently rounded back. One feature is consistent: whether the figure is standing or reclining, the legs are usually bent at the knee.

Other flute players of normal appearance are plentiful in the region, adding weight to the theory that the "hump" was locally a late acquisition. Some seem to be participating in ceremony and many are pictured with accompanying motifs having ceremonial implications. There are two examples of bird-headed flute players (one is seen in Figure 9.27). In one unusual rock art scene a woman playfully hangs on to or carries a flute player (Figure 9.26). But often single or several flute-playing figures appear in isolation and in no special context. As laden with myth and as provocative in concept as the humpbacked image seems to be, the earlier "normal" flute player sometimes appears to be an ordinary human making music for simple enjoyment alone.

158

Figure 9.9. The hunters, animals, and staff bearers on this Little Colorado River rock art panel may indicate that the large female image at the left is a representation of the "Mother of Game." Length of mountain lion at lower right 44 cm.

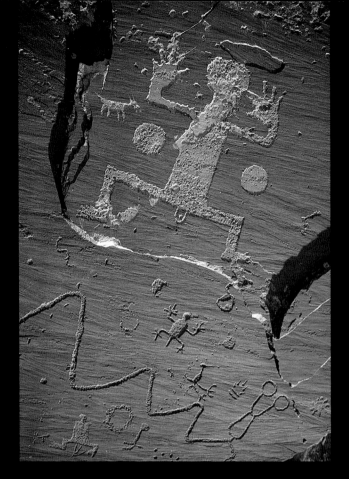

Figure 9.10. Several clues are present in this Petrified Forest rock art panel which might identify the impressive female image as a Game Mother. The mysterious "twinned disk" symbols are present, and at her elbow a small animal is in close attendance. Height 83 cm.

Figure 9.11. This sandstone tableau at "No Name Mesa" in Petrified Forest is adorned with ritual scenes that involve the carrying of staffs and slab pahos or dance wands. Such ceremonial paraphernalia may have been featured in public performances similar to those still staged today at Hopi by the Maraw society. Basically a religious women's organization, its initiated members wave so-called Marawvahos, or "Maraw prayer sticks," up and down in unison during their public dance performance. Note that the figures in both sections of the panel wear side hair bundles which identify them as female. Height of slab paho on right 31 cm.

Figure 9.12. A bright lichen sliver adds a touch of color to a darkly varnished boulder face bearing the design of the slab paho at the "Lone Juniper" site in Petrified Forest. Height 46 cm.

Figure 9.13. A delicately pecked design adorns this slab paho petroglyph at the "Triptych Terrace" site in the Puerco River drainage. Height 31 cm.

Figure 9.14. The esteem accorded the slab paho is well demonstrated by this image's unusually large size and elaborate decoration. The petroglyph dominates a rock art panel at a site alongside the Little Colorado River. Height 78 cm.

Figure 9.15. The slab paho, or dance wand, is one of the diagnostic elements that delimit the geographic perimeter of Palavayu rock art. To date, more than 100 have been found. The portable object was probably used in communal rituals rather than in individual acts of prayer. This example, flanked by an uncoiling serpent, is from a site west of Petrified Forest. Length of wand 84 cm.

9.16

9.17

Figures 9.16 and 9.17. Cross-barred staffs of ceremonial import are
one of the diagnostic hallmarks of Palavayu rock art iconography.
With Figure 9.16 from the "Cooler" site depicting a solitary staff
bearer, Figure 9.17 from "Singing Bat" adds a dramatic element in
that the staff holder is balanced on another figure. Note the
superimposition of the entire scene over the imposing stick figure in
the center whose arced headdress is similar to the head decor of
San Juan Anthropomorphic Style figures (see Figure 2.2b). Height of
staff bearer in Figure 9.16, 40 cm; height of lunate stick figure in
Figure 9.17, 88 cm.

Figure 9.18. A ritual enactment may be depicted in this scene. The staff bearer confronted by an archer is linked to the animal above, while a pregnant woman presides with elevated ceremonial staff. Note the artist's careful attention to detail, such as knee and elbow joints in some of the figures. Width of scene 65 cm.

Figure 9.19. As with many objects pictured in rock art, it is not known whether the spiral carried by the human figure in this panel is a portrayal of an actual staff or if it is a symbolic representation. Height of figure and staff 48 cm.

Figure 9.20. Among the many "standard-bearers" pictured in Palavayu rock art, this one at "Triptych Terrace" stands out. While the true meaning of the figure will never be known, the intriguing configuration may represent the effigy of a divine personage once displayed in a ritual enactment or carried during a ceremonial procession. Note the partial superimposition of the image over a long-tailed quadruped (left disk), and the more deeply revarnished bear and cougar tracks above the body of the pronghorn. Length of effigy 62 cm.

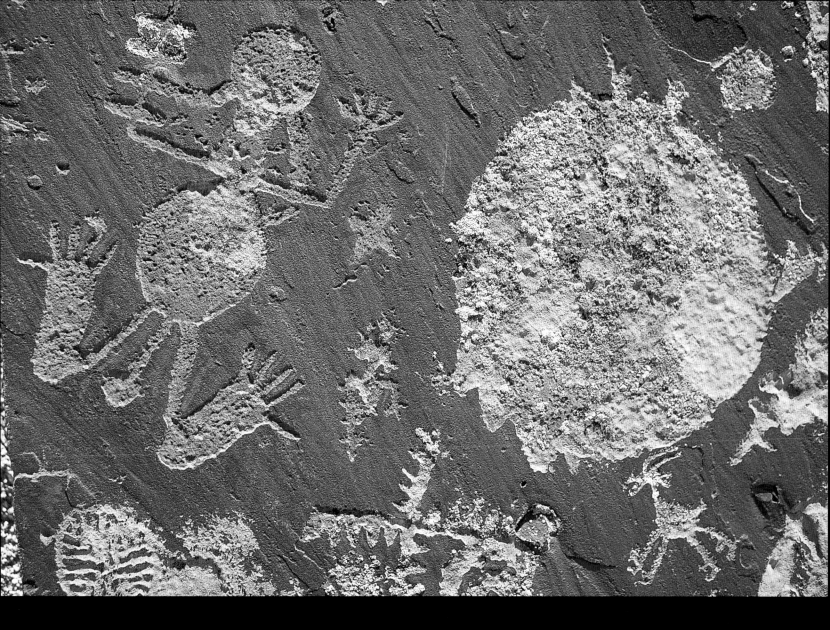

Figure 9.21. The rounded features (head, side hair bobs, torso, tip of phallus) of this cross-barred staff bearer from "Slab Crest" are reinforced by the "lunar" or "solar" disk to his right. While the meaning of the individual symbols is not apparent to us, their interplay nonetheless creates the impression of a sacred spot. Height of staff bearer 46 cm.

Figure 9.22. The shamanic flavor of these bird-headed stick figures at a site along "Daisy Spur" is reinforced by the addition of outstretched wings, typical conveyance symbols of shamanic flight. Furthermore, the figures are endowed with crook staffs or canes which are generally interpreted as symbols of power and authority. Height of birdlike figure on right 29 cm.

Figure 9.23. Bird-headed anthropomorphs are encountered at a number of Palavayu rock art sites. This assembly of bird-topped stick figures in the "Valley of the Flutes" illustrates the attribute of flight, an essential prerequisite for the shaman-artist to contact forces of the supernatural world. The avian imagery in the panel is complemented by two serpents and the solar symbolism of concentric and dot-centered circles. Height of bird-headed figure in lower panel section 70 cm.

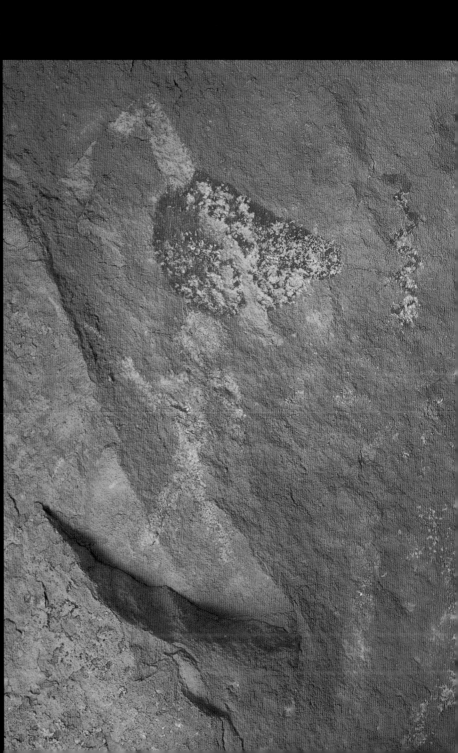

Figure 9.24. While we may never know why the artist produced this turkey-topped anthropomorph, ethnographic analogy strongly suggests that the image of the bird relates to the shaman's practice of magic flight. His soul is believed to change into a bird as it departs from his body. There is a surprising similarity of this motif to bird-headed pictographs of human figures from Canyon de Chelly. Height 56 cm.

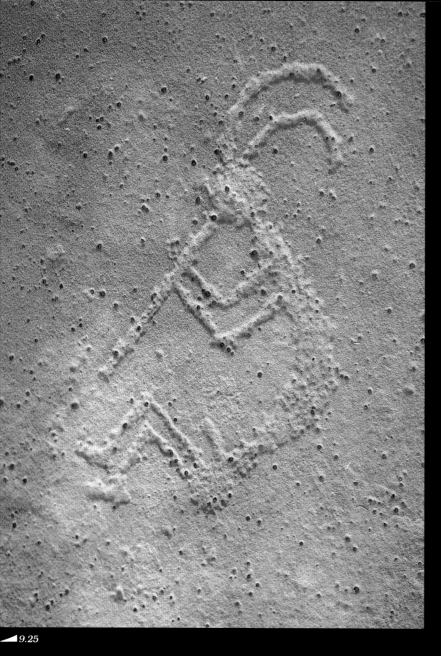

9.25

9.26

9.27

Figures 9.25-9.27. The basic or standard flute player is readily distinguished by the presence of the flute and the absence of phallus and hump. Making up the majority of all Palavayu flute player depictions, the icon occurs in a variety of configurations. Figure 9.25 portrays the ithyphallic flute player (eleven occurrences in Palavayu), Figure 9.26 depicts the motif in conjunction with a female (two occurrences), and Figure 9.27 represents a bird-topped flute player (two occurrences). Height of flute player in Figure 9.25, 32 cm; in Figure 9.26, 15 cm; in Figure 9.27, 25 cm.

Figures 9.28 and 9.29. Among the 130 flute players recorded to date in Palavayu, only 10 percent have a definite hump. Figures 9.28 and 9.29 illustrate both humped and nonhumped variants in a context that shows remarkable similarity in the "rayed recipients" of the flute music. Note, however, that the upright flute player in Figure 9.28 is directing his music toward a phallic "lizard-man," while the reclining flutist in Figure 9.29 is pointing his instrument to an asexual anthropomorph. The radiant aureoles, perhaps indicators of supernatural or extraordinary power, add a ritual dimension to the two scenes. Height of "lizard-man" in Figure 9.28, 27 cm; length of sandal in Figure 9.29, 24 cm.

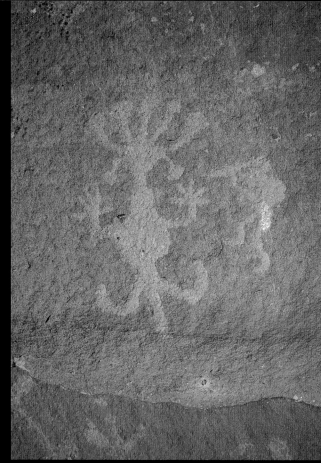

◢ 9.28

◢ 9.29

Figure 9.31. The spear-carrying figure in this panel seems to "guard" the individual holding a banner aloft. Such banners or placards may have functioned as emblems of religious societies in former times and may have been displayed during ritual processions. Height of banner-carrier 41 cm.

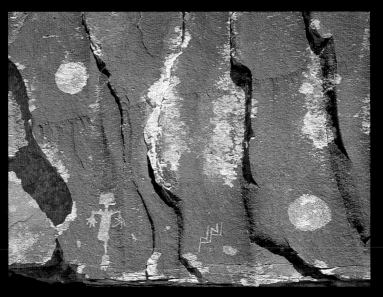

Figure 9.32. The recurrence of a one-legged man motif at Palavayu rock art sites seems to render unlikely the assumption that the artist simply failed to finish the work. This image outside a rock shelter in Petrified Forest may represent a real individual. Height 40 cm.

Figure 9.33. Except for an occasional rattle, the flute is probably the only other musical instrument featured in Palavayu rock art iconography. Like most examples from the Palavayu flute-player complex, these stick-figure portrayals at "Fossil Fold" typically lack the hump. The associated emblems—horned anthropomorph, bird-headed figure with a rake or wing, cougar paw, quadruped, and parrot—lend the entire scene an aura of shamanic potency. Length of supine flute player 27 cm.

Figure 10.1. This arrangement of dots suggestive of a face or mask, together with patches of exfoliated canyon wall and the color of wild roses, combines into an aesthetic whole irresistible to the rock art photographer. Height of dot configuration 22 cm.

One of mankind's earliest and most enduring forms of expression, rock art is a human artistic phenomenon which occurs worldwide. Cave paintings survive from the Upper Paleolithic era in Western Europe, and there are painted and engraved sites in Africa and Australia believed to be between 30 and 40 millennia old.[1] In the New World some petroglyphs and pictographs are thought to date from the Archaic period, and recent research using radiocarbon dating of the rock varnish overlaying petroglyphs may push the age of some rock art back to man's earliest entry into the Americas.[2]

Interest in rock art has exploded throughout the world; the American Southwest, with its superb galleries of rock paintings and petroglyphs, has become one focus of this interest for both professional investigator and layman alike. Because most Southwestern rock art predates written history, the primary questions concern its origin, purpose, and meaning. Who made the art? Are ideas or messages behind the images? Do they represent decipherable codes? What cultural parameters motivated the creators? A multitude of answers have been suggested, ranging from the fantastic or unlikely to the plausible or probable.

In many ways it is easier to define what rock art is *not*. There is no evidence rock art in the Southwest was created by aliens from outer space, members of the lost tribes of Israel, or ancient sailors from Europe. On the other hand it has been amply proven, by research among descendants of the prehistoric people who occupied the region for centuries, that Native Americans are the artisans. The diversity of language, religion, and social order of North American Indian tribes rules out the notion that there is a single universal meaning to the symbols in rock art, and the motives of these differing peoples for producing it must therefore be equally complex. Rock art is not a form of writing, for writing is based upon the spoken language and written symbols must transmit either particular words, syllables, or sounds— none of which underlie rock art symbols in any orderly fashion. It is also a fallacy to think that anyone alien to the social, religious, and linguistic frameworks of a prehistoric culture could decode a system of communication involving images embodying totally unknown ideas and concepts.

How, then, can the function and meaning of Southwestern rock art be interpreted? It is only through comparison with surviving traditions of descendant cultures, long enduring in the case of Pueblo peoples, that the most dependable clues are provided. Practices recorded in early historic times may be presumed to have extended into the past, and archaeological investigation has confirmed this in many instances. Becoming evident in the Pueblo world early in the fourteenth century, the kachina religion has dominated the subject content of regional rock art since that period. Some ancient kachina petroglyph images are similar or even identical to images identifiable in the present-day pantheon of masked deities, and underlying religious principles are reasonably expected to remain relatively unchanged. Myths surrounding gods, heroes, deified creatures, or animals of the natural world represent oral traditions of unknown age; some rock art seems to portray such subjects or illustrate such myths. Certain ceremonial objects and weapons of warfare or the hunt depicted in rock art have also been identified by ethnographic research or—as in the example of the "slab

THE

FUNCTION

AND

AESTHETICS

OF

ROCK

ART

paho"—are even still in use. Historically, rock art was employed at Hopi to mark shrines, record events, illustrate myth, or delineate clan territory; their Pueblo ancestors probably did the same. Analogies between Pueblo societies, both historic and prehistoric, and those of their earlier Anasazi ancestors, however, are more tenuous and difficult to verify.

Of the various purposes and meanings proposed for Southwestern rock art, matters related to religious beliefs are foremost. From the shamanistic images of the Archaic and Basketmaker periods to kachina mask depictions of the late Pueblo period, rock art appears predominantly to represent efforts to communicate with the gods and supernatural forces in order to propitiate, petition, or revere them. The well-being of the individual or the group, success of the hunt, growth of crops and adequate rain to guarantee harvest, fertility of both humans and game animals—all were vital concerns controlled by the deities, requiring the proper rites, prayers, and offerings to insure their benevolence. Rock art itself could become imbued with supernatural power, and repecking or retouching older images, superimposing other images, even defacing or obliterating petroglyphs attest to efforts by later people to take advantage of or negate such power. Springs, caves, rock shelters, and unusual rock formations are often regarded as sacred places or shrines, and rock art identifies them as such or perhaps was a part of ritual or ceremony performed there. Puberty rites and ritual related to fertility and birth may have involved the painting of symbols or carving of certain designs, as recorded in historical times for West Coast Indian tribes.[3] "Sympathetic magic" may have been employed to ensure hoped-for results by depicting successful hunts, human pregnancy, animals with young, and symbols of clouds and rain. Mythical events may have been pictured, and historical events were also probably recorded. Rock art was employed as a calendric device to determine the times of the solstice and the equinox in order to establish planting dates and, most importantly, to time religious ceremonies.

Rock art likely served secular purposes as well. Some marks may have been made as memory aids or tallies. Clan symbols are known historically to represent clan ownership, to denote boundaries, or to signify participation in a pilgrimage or special event. The prevalence of rock art near springs, fords, crossings, and along trails gives credence to the theory that some served as directional or locational markers. However, there is little firm evidence that actual maps are delineated. It has been noted that eagle-capture depictions occur near eagle nesting sites, and animal images and hunting scenes are abundant near game trails, box canyons, or narrow passages where animals could be hunted or ambushed. Such depictions may represent the records of actual kills or captures, visual prayers for success, or mimetic magic to assist either endeavor. Certain images in Palavayu rock art—men brandishing spears, some kachina masks, figures with one upraised hand, depictions of the Hopi god Maasaw[4]—may have conveyed a message of warning to strangers or unwelcome neighbors.

Rock art is often found near habitation sites and areas of human activity, and it has been assumed some petroglyphs were casually created by individuals as a pastime during idle hours. Although crudely executed and apparently meaningless images are found, this category seems to be in the minority. The difficulty of making a petroglyph may have been a deterrent. The

scarcity of unskilled or clumsy drawings possibly associated with children or unpracticed "doodlers" may indicate that rock art sites were off limits to children or ordinary folks; or in other words, the placement, content, and even the act of making rock art had a definite purpose and meaning.

Figure 10.2. Redrawing of bizarre image with anthropomorphic features from Figure 10.6.

One question confronts all rock art researchers, who tend to borrow the art historian's vocabulary for descriptive terms. Often challenged is the implication that rock art has legitimate aesthetic value. Did the making of petroglyphs and pictographs ever become motivated by purely artistic intention? It is generally agreed among researchers that "art for the sake of art" was not the goal of the artisan. However, it is man's nature to perfect his creations, to refine them beyond mere usefulness. Need gives birth to invention: the container, the tool, the weapon, the warm garment. Man's innate desire to "make it better," to improve craftmanship as well as the efficiency of his product, leads further, to please the eye and senses—and art is born. The beginnings of rock art, which may have initially been a means of expressing human and spiritual needs, most certainly moved toward increased technical skill and aesthetic concern. Many rock art panels are outstanding for superior workmanship and a mastery evident in precise execution, graceful design, and stunning imagery. The underlying motives may have had nothing to do with art itself. As with the clay dish which became the beautifully painted bowl, the woven net the intricately worked basket, the skin robe the richly patterned blanket, man transformed function into art.

In this regard, it is fitting to conclude with the example of a rock art site in which a single artisan left striking evidence of creativity and superior talent. In a small box canyon outside Petrified Forest, a remarkable group of petroglyphs appears on a cluster of boulders at the base of a talus slope (Figures 10.4, 10.5, 10.6). Dubbed the "Royal Flush," it is the only site in the small canyon. Although many of the petroglyphs on the twenty-one boulders at the site are obviously of different ages and made by different hands, the work of one artist is clearly apparent in a number of panels. This is seen in the uniformity of style and precision of technique, a deliberate spacing of elements in relation to each other and the boundaries of the rock faces, and a more than usual concern with complex symmetry and balance in the many geometric designs. The boulders themselves provide a special canvas for the art. Light-colored glyphs stand out in dramatic contrast to the dark desert varnish on rock faces. Some larger panels are on smoothly textured surfaces that undulate, adding another dimension to the composition of images. Open exposure to the elements has destroyed a number of petroglyphs and has eroded part of some designs, but enough survives to rank this as one of the most beautiful sites in the region. This site, however, is not accessible to the public, as it is located on private land.

Although personal expression in Western Pueblo rock art is generally limited by a tradition of conventionalized form, the distinctive style of this individual who emerges from the faceless past is compelling proof that not all rock art is subject to this constraint. The beautifully executed images and singular designs suggest the work is not solely functional; there is pride in the mastery of craftsmanship. It is a celebration of artistry and skill beyond the ordinary.

Figure 10.3. Rather than being mere decorations, the antithetical spiral and stacked triangle motifs on this slab at "Lone Juniper" must have been meaningful to their makers. They may have been part of an elaborate prehistoric image system whose complex ideology eludes us. Base of triangle 14 cm.

Figure 10.4. *Although now much eroded away, this entire boulder face was utilized by the artist to compose an assemblage of petroglyphs. A frieze of human figures, underlined by sawtooth bands forming a negative diamond pattern, fills the upper portion, and a large scrolled figure dominates the lower half. Abstract in concept, the figure is vaguely human with its round head and elevated legs ending in five-toed feet. Height of figure 65 cm.*

Figure 10.5. *An intricate trapezoidal design is centered amid a variety of carefully spaced elements which seem to be a display of the artist's geometric creations. Width of trapezoid 26 cm.*

Figure 10.6. This bizarre image, at first sight a complex nonrepresentational form, assumes human characteristics upon close examination. Eyes peer from a head encircled by an elaborate headdress capped with a cloudlike element. Raised arms with five-fingered hands can be seen. Legs terminate in animal figures. The stepped and elongated torso may indicate the figure is female, and the mystical quality of this unusual composition suggests it is the portrait of a deity. Width of figure 93 cm.

PROTECTING
ROCK ART

In these modern times, rock art suffers increasingly from the encroachments of civilization. Petroglyphs and pictographs are drowned beneath the rising waters of reservoirs, destroyed by the bulldozers of housing development or highway construction, and—saddest of all—are deliberately painted over, blasted by gunshot, or defaced by thoughtless individuals. Even well-meaning rock art enthusiasts inflict damage by chalking glyphs or using injurious techniques to make rubbings or impressions of them.

Many archaeological/historical societies and government agencies are responding to growing concern over this problem by increased law enforcement, public education, and work with private and public landowners to protect rock art sites. Two national organizations have been established whose goals are the protection of significant sites. The Archaeological Conservancy acquires rock art and archaeological sites through purchase or donation, for preservation and future study. Ownership of some sites has been transferred to the National Park Service or the U.S. Bureau of Land Management, and some have become state or county parks. The American Rock Art Research Association provides expertise and volunteer assistance to local organizations and government bureaus in recording and documenting rock art, and works to educate the public to the need to respect and preserve this irreplaceable cultural resource.

Rock art is a unique window on the past, our only means of seeing the ancient world through the eyes of the people who inhabited it. Once gone, it is gone forever.

To help minimize impacts to rock art sites, the following etiquette should be observed:

1. Don't touch rock art. Oils from even the cleanest hands can cause deterioration of the carvings or paintings and ruin future dating potential.
2. Don't add graphics to rock art panels by drawing, painting, or scratching on them. Graffiti of this type deface the rock art site.
3. Don't copy petroglyphs by means of charcoal rubbings or latex casts. Residues may adhere to the veneer on the glyphs.
4. Don't build fires in the vicinity of rock art sites. Soot from fires will damage or even destroy the art.

At the "Singing Bat" site near Woodruff, a panel of Archaic engravings is defaced by incised graffiti. Note the anthropomorph beneath the bow of the ship whose hands, in a unique way, are shaped like arrowheads or spear points. Width of ship 50 cm.

At the "Paddle" site southeast of Winslow, the faint shape of an animal figure—visible behind the E in JACEY—is all that is left of the petroglyphs in the entanglement of garish spray paints. Lest other Palavayu sites experience a similar fate, all locational references to them in this book are deliberately vague. Width of animal 27 cm.

FACE OF THE LAND

CHAPTER 1

1. The term Palavayu was suggested by Ekkehart Malotki; it is a Hopi word meaning "red river." An old-time reference to the Little Colorado River, the word was recorded in this sense by Edward Curtis (1922: 185). The Palavayu region includes the lower Puerco River and the central drainage system of the Little Colorado.
2. Excellent descriptions of these geological processes are to be found in the following publications: Ash 1985; Breed and Breed 1972; and Houk 1990.
3. Burton 1990, p. 282.
4. Burton 1990, p. 330.
5. All Hopi words are spelled according to the standardized writing system developed for the Third Mesa dialect in conjunction with the Comprehensive Hopi Dictionary Project jointly compiled by researchers from Northern Arizona University and the University of Arizona.
6. Colton 1939; Reed 1948.
7. Burton 1991.
8. Wells 1989, p. 81.
9. Christensen in Wells 1988, p. 89.
10. Christensen pers. comm.; Pilles 1975; Martynec 1982.
11. Cordell 1984, p. 102.
12. Geib 1990, p. 271.
13. Pilles 1975; Martynec 1982; Turner 1963.

ARCHAIC AND
BASKETMAKER STYLES

CHAPTER 2

1. Huckell 1982.
2. Pilles 1975, p. 5.
3. The reconstruction presented in this chapter is based on present data. Significant changes may result as study continues.
4. Turner 1963.
5. Turner 1971.
6. Schaafsma 1980, p. 72.
7. Schaafsma 1980, pp. 109 - 119.
8. Turner 1963, Figs. 8, 74, 77.
9. Schaafsma 1980.
10. Schaafsma 1980, pp. 109-124.
11. Cole 1990, pp. 111, 113.
12. Jernigan 1978, p. 187, Fig. 91.
13. Cole 1990, pp. 121, 123.
14. Schaafsma 1980, p. 117.
15. Whitley 1994.
16. Burton 1990; Christensen 1991; Ferg 1974; Martynec 1982; Pilles 1975; Schaafsma 1980. John Parsons, of Show Low, Arizona, has also systematically explored the upper part of Silver Creek.
17. Malotki, pers. comm.
18. Hedges 1985, p. 89.
19. Cordell 1984.
20. Turner 1963, p. 7.
21. Burton 1990, p. 263.
22. Schaafsma 1980.
23. Pilles 1975, p. 18.
24. A snake with arms and hands also appears in a Barrier Canyon Style pictograph in east-central Utah, illustrated in Cole 1990, p. 78.
25. Furst 1977, p. 3; Grant 1967, p. 29; Schaafsma 1980, pp. 172-73, 109; Whitley 1994.
26. Hedges 1976, p. 128.
27. Ritter and Ritter 1977, pp. 64-65.
28. Eliade 1964, p. 155; Grant 1978, p. 206; Hedges 1976, p. 128; Schaafsma 1980, p. 71.
29. Bock and Bock 1992; Eliade 1964, pp. 477-82; Grant 1978, pp. 187-89; Hedges 1985, p. 84; Schaafsma 1986, p. 27.
30. Eliade 1964, p. 63.
31. The Barrier Canyon Style also combines "realistic" human figures with abstract "other-worldly" types of anthropomorphs.
32. Turner 1963, pp. 7-8.
33. Pilles 1975, p. 6.
34. Martynec 1982, pp. 38-41.

PUEBLO II—PUEBLO III
STYLES

CHAPTER 3

1. Pilles 1975, p. 7; Turner 1963.
2. Pilles 1975, p. 7.
3. Jones (1987, p. 16) suggests the low population in Petrified Forest National Park between A.D. 750 and 1000 is due to stress from major drought conditions in the 9th century.
4. Schaafsma 1980, p. 71; Wellmann 1976, p. 109; Whitley 1994.
5. Grant 1978, pp. 179-80; Parsons 1939, p. 399.
6. Martynec 1982, p. 43.
7. Parsons 1939, p. 1073, footnote.
8. Pilles 1975, p. 9.
9. Ellis and Hammack 1968, p. 35; Ellis 1975, p. 61; Schaafsma 1987, p. 22.
10. Grant 1978, pp. 209-10.
11. Hunger 1982, p. 4.
12. Christensen 1991b. Most of the material concerning this subject is derived from this study.
13. Heizer and Baumhoff 1962.
14. Heizer and Hester 1978.
15. Ritter and Hatoff 1990.
16. Stoney 1990.
17. Christensen 1991b.
18. Christensen, pers. comm.
19. Burton 1991, p. 17.
20. Wells 1989, p. 75.
21. Stewart 1980, p. 86.
22. Wells 1989, p. 84.
23. Gumerman 1988, p. 3.
24. An exception is the slab paho, which survived into the historic Hopi period. This makes its absence in Winslow area rock art even more surprising, as much of the local population is known to have migrated to the Hopi mesas in the 15th century.
25. Schaafsma 1992, p. 57.
26. Schaafsma 1992, p. 21.
27. Schaafsma 1987, p. 27.
28. Pilles 1975, p. 10.
29. Martynec 1982, p. 60.

PUEBLO IV STYLE

CHAPTER 4

1. Schaafsma 1992.
2. Schaafsma 1992, pp. 76-77 and 1980, p. 237.
3. Hays 1989.
4. Adams 1991.
5. Eggan 1979, pp. 226-30.
6. Malotki 1978, p. 203; and 1991, pp. 50-51.
7. Evidence that the direction of borrowing for "kachina" is clearly from Keres to Hopi is provided by Wick Miller (pers. comm. 1993). According to him, the Keresan term *k'áadzíná* is partially analyzable in Acoma. Constituting a nominal word based on a nonoccurring verb root *-'aadzi* , the *k-* is the third person pronominal prefix which is used in conjunction with the noun-forming suffix *-ná*. The Keres form which begins with a glottalized *k '* is of course rendered as plain *k* in Hopi since Hopi lacks glottalized consonants.
8. Parsons 1933, p. 40.
9. Titiev 1944, p. 109.
10. Fergusson 1931; Luckert 1984; Malotki 1991; White 1932.
11. Malotki 1991, p. 52.
12. Schaafsma 1980; 1992.
13. Pilles 1975.
14. Fewkes 1906, p. 348; Lipe 1970, p. 138; Parsons 1939, pp. 17, 309, 839; Stephen 1936, p. 1077; Turner 1963, p. 32.
15. Cole 1989.

HUNTERS AND ANIMALS

CHAPTER 5

1. Christensen 1988, p. 83; 1989, p. 39.
2. Whitley 1994.
3. Parsons 1939, p. 63.
4. Fewkes 1892, p. 14.
5. Beaglehole 1936.
6. Malotki 1985, p. 4.
7. Beaglehole 1936, p. 7.
8. Parsons 1939, p. 177.
9. Stephen 1936, p. 714.
10. Fewkes 1898, p. 704.
11. Stephen 1936, p. 278.
12. Beaglehole 1936, p. 8.
13. Estimates vary on Navajo entry into the Southwest, but it is generally believed to have occurred early in the 16th century (Cordell 1984, p. 5; Gunnerson 1979.).
14. Kaemlein 1971, pp. 20-52.
15. Beaglehole 1936, p. 4.
16. White 1943, p. 336.
17. Hough 1898.
18. Beaglehole 1936, pp. 4-5.
19. Barnett 1973, p. 97.
20. Grant 1982.
21. Martineau 1973, pp. 48-58.
22. Warner 1982, pp. 125-130.
23. Hedges 1983, p. 55.
24. Whitley 1992.
25. Pilles 1975, p. 16.
26. Beaglehole 1936.
27. Hallowell 1926, p. 149.
28. Hallowell 1926. p. 149.
29. Parsons 1939, p. 170. These paws are actual bear-leg skins, with claws attached, the ritual badge of Keresan curers.
30. Beaglehole 1936, p. 3.
31. Hallowell 1926, p. 77.
32. Parsons 1939, p. 189. Transformation into animals and animals that become humans are common concepts in Pueblo belief.
33. Parsons 1939, p. 188.
34. Stephen 1936, Pl. XLI, pp. 698, 702.
35. Stephen 1936, p. 673.
36. Beaglehole 1936, p. 5.
37. Tyler 1975, p. 14.
38. Burton 1990; Hough 1903; Stewart 1980.
39. Martynec 1982, p. 68.
40. Dutton 1963, p. 105.
41. Tyler 1991. Much of the bird lore in Pueblo belief mentioned here derives from this publication.
42. Fewkes 1900.
43. Tyler 1991, p. 46.
44. Page 1990, pp. 30-35.
45. Judd 1954.
46. Ferg 1974, p. 15.

47. Tyler 1991, p. 22.
48. Fewkes 1900, p. 691.
49. Tyler 1991, p. 71.
50. Tyler 1991, p. 163.
51. Fewkes 1898, p. 677.
52. Parsons 1939, p. 976.
53. Schaafsma 1980, p. 239.
54. Schaafsma 1980, p. 136.
55. Parsons 1938, p. 338.
56. Young 1988.
57. Fewkes 1910, p. 576.

MALE AND FEMALE

CHAPTER 6

1. Turner 1963, p. 29.
2. Kent 1983, p. 115.
3. Hill 1970, pp. 38-39.
4. Pilles 1988, pers. comm.
5. Schaafsma 1980, p. 155.
6. Dorsey 1903, pp. 172-178; Frazer 1922, pp. 139-146.

GEOMETRIC DESIGNS

CHAPTER 7

1. Boas 1955, p. 88.
2. Hedges 1982; Lewis-Williams and Dowson 1988.
3. Kent 1983, p. 201.
4. Christensen, in press.
5. Schaafsma 1987, p. 24.
6. Alex Patterson, pers. comm.
7. Voth 1912, p. 31.
8. Fewkes 1892, p. 235.
9. Schaafsma 1992, p. 21.
10. Wade and McChesney 1980, p. 28.
11. Parsons 1939, p. 1073, note.
12. Wendorf 1953, p. 145.
13. Parkman 1993, p. 3.
14. Hedges 1983; Heizer 1953.
15. Stevenson 1904; p. 294.

ARCHAEOASTRONOMY

CHAPTER 8

1.McCluskey 1987, p. 205.
2. Early documentation includes the research of F. Cushing, J.W. Fewkes, E.C. Parsons, A.M. Stephen, M.C. Stevenson, M. Titiev, and H. Voth. In recent years, Malotki (1983) has added significantly to the record of Hopi sunwatching practices.
3. Sofaer et al. 1979.
4. The site, atop Fajada Butte in Chaco Canyon, has since experienced geological degradation thought to have occurred from the heavy foot traffic of curious visitors. The resulting movement of boulders has destroyed the accuracy of light and shadow patterns which previously marked the astronomical events.
5. Bringing a unique combination of art and science to their research, Robert Preston is an astronomer at the Jet Propulsion Laboratory in Pasadena, California, and his wife Ann is a well-known sculptor on the faculty at the Art Center, Pasadena.
6. Preston and Preston 1993.
7. McCluskey 1977.
8. McCluskey 1982, p. 42.
9. Zeilik 1987, pp. 25-41.
10. Stephen 1936.
11. Preston and Preston 1993.
12. Williamson 1978; 1979; Williamson, Fisher and O'Flynn 1977; Williamson and Young 1979; Williamson, Fisher, Williamson and Cochran, 1975; Sofaer et al. 1979.
13. Cushing 1970, p. 105.
14. Preston and Preston 1985: p. 133.

CEREMONIAL IMAGES

CHAPTER 9

1. Beaglehole 1936, p. 4; Curtis 1907-1930, p. 82; Malotki 1978, p. 208; Mindeleff 1891, p. 32; Voth 1903, pp. 352-53; 1905, p. 141.
2. Stephen 1936, p. 1006.
3. Curtis 1907-1930, p. 103.
4. Parsons 1939, pp. 178, 318.
5. Malotki 1978, p. 208.
6. Malotki pers. comm.
7. Schaafsma 1987, p. 22.
8. Eliade 1964, p. 81.
9. Fewkes 1895, pp. 736-739.
10. Fewkes 1892, pp. 217-245.
11. Voth 1912, pp. 1-88.
12. Titiev 1944, p. 164.
13. Fewkes 1895, p. 447.
14. Smith 1972, p. 31.
15. Ellis and Hammack 1968, pp. 38, 39; Hough 1914, p. 103; Vivian et al. 1978, p. 90.
16. Vivian et al. 1978.
17. Stephen 1936, Figs. 414, 415.
18. Parsons 1939, p. 325.
19. Hough 1914, p. 103, 104, Figs. 211, 212, 213.
20. Pilles 1975.
21. Bock and Bock 1992; Grant 1978; Hedges 1985; Wellmann 1979.
22. Grant 1978, p. 210.
23. Furst 1977, p. 13.
24. Eliade 1964, p. 481.
25. Hough 1914, pp. 103-04, Figs. 211, 212, 213.
26. Grant 1978, p. 210.
27. Eliade 1964, pp. 45, 81.
28. Malotki, Weaver, and Pilles "The Flute Player Project," in progress.
29. Malotki n.d., unpublished manuscript.
30. Parsons 1938, p. 338.
31. Stephen 1929, pp. 5-6.
32. Lomatuway'ma, Lomatuway'ma, and Namingha 1993, p. 323; Voth 1905, p. 217.
33. Malotki 1993, pers. comm.
34. Parsons 1938, p. 337.
35. Hawley 1937, p. 645.
36. Schaafsma 1980, p. 136.
37. Fewkes 1903, p. 86.
38. Hawley 1937, p. 645.

THE FUNCTION AND AESTHETICS OF ROCK ART

CHAPTER 10

1. Bednarik 1993, pp. 5-6; Lewis-Williams 1983, p. 21.
2. Dorn 1992, pp. 10-14.
3. Grant 1967, pp. 29-31.
4. By way of example, Stephen has discussed and illustrated a boundary stone between Second and Third Mesa at Hopi carved with the face of *Maasaw* to keep young people and "Navajos" from removing or destroying it (Stephen 1936, p. 390).

Adams, Charles 1991. *The Origin and Development of the Pueblo Katsina Cult*. Tucson: University of Arizona Press.

Ash, Sidney 1985. *Petrified Forest: The Story Behind the Scenery*, Petrified Forest: Petrified Forest Museum Association.

Barnett, Franklin 1973. *Dictionary of Prehistoric Indian Artifacts of the American Southwest*. Flagstaff: Northland Publishing.

Beaglehole, Ernest 1936. *Hopi Hunting and Hunting Ritual*. New Haven: Yale University Publications in Anthropology 4.

Bednarik, Robert G. 1993. Oldest Dated Rock Art in the World. In *International Newsletter on Rock Art*, No. 4. Jean Clottes (ed.). 5–6.

Boas, Franz 1955. *Primitive Art*. Dover Press, New York.

Bock, Frank and A.J. Bock 1992. The Birdheaded Figure of the Southwest as Psychopomp. In *American Indian Rock Art* 17: 11–28.

Breed, William J. and Carol S. Breed (eds.) 1972. *Investigations in the Triassic Chinle Formation*. Flagstaff: Museum of Northern Arizona Bulletin 47.

Burton, Jeffery F. 1993. Days in the Painted Desert and the Petrified Forest of Northern Arizona. *Western Archeological and Conservation Center Publications in Anthropology* 62. Tucson: National Park Service.

————1991. The Archeology of Sivu'ovi: The Archaic to Basketmaker Transition at Petrified Forest National Park. *Western Archeological and Conservation Center Publications in Anthropology* 55. Tucson: National Park Service.

————1990. Archeological Investigations at Puerco Ruin, Petrified Forest National Park, Arizona. *Western Archeological and Conservation Center Publications in Anthropology* 54. Tucson: National Park Service.

Christensen, Don D. 1991a. Pre-Pueblo Rock Art in the Little Colorado River Drainage. Ms. on file, Western Archeological and Conservation Center. Tucson: National Park Service.

————1991b. Scratched Glyphs in Arizona: A Reevaluation. A paper presented to the San Diego Museum of Man Rock Art '90 Symposium, San Diego, California.

————1989. The Rock Art of Mountain Lion Mesa. In Petrified Forest National Park Boundary Survey, 1988: The Final Season. Susan J. Wells (ed.). *Western Archeological and Conservation Center Publications in Anthropology* 51. Tucson: National Park Service. 37–62.

————1988. Rock Art Sites. In Archeological Survey and Testing at Petrified Forest National Park, 1987. Susan J. Wells (ed.). *Western Archeological and Conservation Center Publications in Anthropology* 48. Tucson: National Park Service. 82-91.

————In Press. Rock Art, Ceramics and Textiles: The Validity of Unifying Art Motifs.

Cole, Sally J. 1990. *Legacy on Stone: Rock Art of the Colorado Plateau and Four Corners Region*. Boulder: Johnson Books.

————1989. *Rock Art Evidence for the Presence and Social Significance of the Katsina Cult at 13th–14th Century Homol'ovi in the Central Little Colorado River Valley, Northeastern Arizona*. MS thesis, Vermont College of Norwich University, Norwich.

Colton, Harold S. 1939. *Prehistoric Culture Units and Their Relationships in Northern Arizona*. Flagstaff: Museum of Northern Arizona Bulletin 17.

Cordell, Linda S. 1984. *Prehistory of the Southwest*. New York: Academic Press.

Curtis, Edward S. 1922. The Hopi. In *The North American Indian; Being a Series of Volumes Picturing and Describing the Indians of the United States, the Dominion of Canada, and Alaska* 12. Frederick W. Hodge (ed.). Norwood, MA.: Plimpton Press.

Cushing, Frank H. 1970. My *Adventures in Zuni [1882]*. Palo Alto: American West Publishing Company.

Dorn, Ronald I. 1992. A Review of Rock Varnish Dating of Rock Engravings. In *International Newsletter on Rock Art* No. 2. Jean Clottes (ed.). 10–14.

Dorsey, George A. 1903. *The Arapaho Sun Dance: The Ceremony of the Offerings–Lodge*. Chicago: Field Columbian Museum Anthropological Series 4.

Dutton, Bertha P. 1963. *Sun Father's Way: The Kiva Murals of Kuaua*. Albuquerque: University of New Mexico Press.

Eggan, Fred 1979. Pueblos: Introduction. In *Handbook of North American Indians: Volume 9, Southwest*. Alfonso Ortiz (ed.). Washington, D.C.: Smithsonian Institution. 224–235.

Eliade, Mircea 1964. *Shamanism: Archaic Techniques of Ecstasy*. Bollingen Series 76. Princeton: Princeton University Press.

Ellis, Florence H. 1975. A Thousand Years of the Pueblo Sun–Moon–Star Calendar. In *Archaeoastronomy in Pre–Columbian America*. A. F. Aveni (ed.). Austin: University of Texas Press. 58–87.

Ellis, Florence H. and Laurens Hammack 1968. The Inner Sanctum of Feather Cave, A Mogollon Sun and Earth Shrine Linking Mexico and the Southwest. *American Antiquity* 33: 25–44.

Ferg, Alan 1974. Petroglyphs of the Silver Creek–Five Mile Draw Confluence, Snowflake, Arizona. Unpublished Ms., Department of Anthropology, University of Arizona, Tucson.

Fergusson, Erna 1931. *Dancing Gods: Indian Ceremonials of New Mexico and Arizona*. Albuquerque: University of New Mexico Press.

Fewkes, Jesse W. 1910. The Butterfly in Hopi Myth and Ritual. *American Anthropologist*, 12 (4): 576–594.

————1906. Hopi Shrines Near the East Mesa, Arizona. *American Anthropologist*, new series 8 (2): 346–375

————1903. Hopi Kachinas Drawn by Native Artists. Washington, D.C.: *21st Annual Report of the Bureau of American Ethnology for the Years 1899–1900*. 13–126.

Fewkes, Jesse W. 1900. Tusayan Migration Traditions. Washington, D.C.: *19th Annual Report of the Bureau of American Ethnology for the Years* 1897–1898, Part II. 573–634.

———1898. Archaeological Expedition to Arizona in 1895. Washington, D.C.: *17th Annual Report of the Bureau of American Ethnology, Part II.* 519–742.

———1896. The Prehistoric Culture of Tusayan. *American Anthropologist*, old series 9 (5): 151–174.

———1895. *The Tusayan New Fire Ceremony.* Boston: Boston Society of Natural History Proceedings 26. 422–458.

———1892. The Mam–zrau–ti: A Tusayan Ceremony. *American Anthropologist*, old series 5 (3): 217–245.

Frazer, Sir James George 1922. *The Golden Bough: A Study in Magic and Religion.* New York: The Macmillan Co.

Furst, Peter T. 1977. The Roots and Continuities of Shamanism. In *Stones, Bones and Skin: Ritual and Shamanic Art.* Anne Trueblood Brodzky, Rose Danesewich, and Nick Johnson (eds.). Toronto: Artscanada. 1–28.

Geib, Phil R. 1990. A Basketmaker II Wooden Tool Cache from Lower Glen Canyon. *Kiva* 55: 265–277.

Grant, Campbell 1982. The Bighorn Sheep—Pre-eminent Motif in the Rock Art of Western North America. In *American Indian Rock Art* 7 and 8: 11–25.

———1978. *Canyon de Chelly.* Tucson: University of Arizona Press.

———1967. *Rock Art of the American Indian.* New York: Thomas Y. Crowell Company.

Gumerman, George J. 1988. The Archaeology of the Hopi Buttes District, Arizona. *Center for Archaeological Investigations Research Paper* 49. Carbondale: Southern Illinois University.

Gunnerson, James H. 1979. Southern Athapascan Archaeology. In *Handbook of North American Indians: Southwest,* 9. Alfonso Ortiz (ed.). Washington, D.C.: Smithsonian Institution. 162–169.

Hallowell, A.I. 1926. Bear Ceremonialism in the Northern Hemisphere. *American Anthropologist* 28: 1–175.

Hawley, Florence 1937. Kokopelli of the Prehistoric Southwestern Pueblo Pantheon. *American Anthropologist* 39: 644–646.

Hays, Kelley Ann 1989. Katsina Depictions on Homol'ovi Ceramics: Toward a Fourteenth Century Pueblo Iconography. *Kiva* 54 (3): 297–311.

Hedges, Ken 1985. Rock Art Portrayals of Shamanic Transformation and Magical Flight. In *Rock Art Papers, San Diego Museum Papers* 18, 2. San Diego: Museum of Man. 83–94.

———1983. The Shamanic Origins of Rock Art. In *Ancient Images on Stone: Rock Art of the Californias.* JoAnne Van Tilburg (ed.). Los Angeles: University of California. 46–51.

———1982. Phosphenes in the Context of Native American Rock Art. In *American Indian Rock Art* 7 and 8: 1–10.

———1976. Southern California Rock Art as Shamanic Art. In *American Indian Rock Art* 2: 126–138.

Heizer, Robert F. 1953. Sacred Rain–Rocks of Northern California. *University of California Archaeological Survey Reports* 22. Berkeley: University of California Press. 33–38.

Heizer, Robert F. and Thomas R. Hester 1978. Two Petroglyph Sites in Lincoln County, Nevada. In *Four Rock Art Studies.* C.William Clewlow, Jr. (ed.). Socorro: Ballena Press. 1–44.

Heizer, Robert F. and Martin A. Baumhoff 1962. *Prehistoric Rock Art of Nevada and Eastern California.* Berkeley: University of California Press.

Hill, James N. 1970. Prehistoric Social Organization in the American Southwest: Theory and Method. In *Reconstructing Prehistoric Pueblo Societies.* William A. Longacre (ed.). Albuquerque: University of New Mexico Press. 11–58.

Hough, Walter 1914. Culture of the Ancient Pueblos of the Upper Gila Region, New Mexico and Arizona. Washington, D.C.: *Smithsonian Institute Bulletin* 87.

———1903. Archaeological Field Work in Northeastern Arizona: the Museum–Gates Expedition of 1901. Washington, D.C.: *Report of the United States National Museum for 1901.* 279–358.

———1898. Environmental Interrelations in Arizona. *American Anthropologist*, old series 11 Volume 11: 135–155.

Houk, Rose 1990. *The Painted Desert: Land of Light and Shadow.* Petrified Forest: Petrified Forest Museum Association.

Huckell, Bruce E. 1982. The Distribution of Fluted Points in Arizona. *Arizona State Museum Archaeological Series* 145. Tucson: University of Arizona Press.

Hunger, Heinz 1982. Ritual Coition as Sacred Marriage in the Rock Art of North America. In *American Indian Rock Art* 9: 1–9.

Jernigan, E. Wesley 1978. *Jewelry of the Prehistoric Southwest.* Albuquerque: University of New Mexico Press, and Santa Fe: School of American Research.

Jones, Anne Trinkle 1987. Contributions to the Archeology of Petrified Forest National Park, 1985–1986. *Western Archeological and Conservation Center Publications in Anthropology* 45. Tucson: National Park Service.

Judd, Neil 1954. The Material Culture of Pueblo Bonito. Washington, D.C.: *Smithsonian Miscellaneous Collections,* 124.

Kaemlein, Wilma 1971. Large Hunting Nets in the Collection of the Arizona State Museum. *Kiva* 36 (3): 20–52.

Kent, Kate Peck 1983. *Prehistoric Textiles of the Southwest.* Santa Fe: School of American Research, and Albuquerque: University of New Mexico Press.

Lewis–Williams, David 1983. *The Rock Art of Southern Africa.* Cambridge: Cambridge University Press.

Lewis–Williams, David and T.A. Dowson 1988. The Signs of All Times. Entoptic Phenomena in Upper Palaeolithic Art. *Current Anthropology* 8 (2): 201–245.

Lipe, William D. 1970. Anasazi Communities in the Red Rock Plateau, Southeastern Utah. In *Reconstructing Prehistoric Pueblo Societies.* William A. Longacre (ed.): Albuquerque: University of New Mexico Press. 84–129.

Lomatuway'ma, Michael, Lorena Lomatuway'ma, and Sidney Namingha, Jr. 1993. *Hopi Ruin Legends. Kiqötutuwutsi.* Ekkehart Malotki (collected, translated and ed.). Lincoln: University of Nebraska Press.

Luckert, Karl W. 1984. Coyote in Navajo and Hopi Tales: An Introductory Essay. *In Navajo Coyote Tales: The Curly Tó Aheedlíinii Version.* American Tribal Religions 8. Lincoln: University of Nebraska Press. 3–19.

McCluskey, Stephen C. 1987. Science, Society, Objectivity, and the Astronomies of the Southwest. In *Astronomy and Ceremony in the Prehistoric Southwest.* John B. Carlson and W. James Judge (eds.). Papers of the Maxwell Museum of Anthropology, No. 2. Albuquerque: University of New Mexico Press. 205–217.

———1982. Historical Archaeoastronomy: the Hopi Example. In *Archaeoastronomy in the New World.* Anthony F. Aveni (ed.). Cambridge: Cambridge University Press. 31–57.

———1977. The Astronomy of the Hopi Indians. *Journal of the History of Astronomy* 8 (2): 175–195.

Malotki, Ekkehart 1991. Language as a Key to Cultural Understanding: New Interpretations of Central Hopi Concepts. *Baessler–Archiv, Neue Folge,* XXXIX: 43–75.

———1985. *Gullible Coyote. Una'ihu: A Bilingual Collection of Hopi Coyote Tales.* Tucson: University of Arizona Press.

———1983. *Hopi Time: A Linguistic Analysis of the Temporal Concepts in the Hopi Language.* In Trends in Linguistics. Studies and Monographs 20. Werner Winter (ed.). Berlin, Amsterdam, New York: Mouton Publishers.

———1978. *Hopitutuwutsi. Hopi Tales. A Bilingual Collection of Hopi Indian Stories.* Flagstaff: Museum of Northern Arizona Press.

Malotki, Ekkehart and Michael Lomatuway'ma 1987. *Maasaw: Profile of a Hopi God.* American Tribal Religions 11. Lincoln and London: University of Nebraska Press.

Malotki, Ekkehart, Donald Weaver, and Peter Pilles n.d. The Flute Player Project. In progress.

Martineau, Lavan 1973. *The Rocks Begin to Speak.* Las Vegas: KC Publications.

Martynec, Richard J. 1982. The Archeology of Petrified Forest National Park: A Rock Art Perspective. Ms. on file, Western Archeological and Conservation Center, National Park Service, Tucson.

Mindeleff, Victor 1891. A Study of Pueblo Architecture in Tusayan and Cibola. Washington, D.C.: *8th Annual Report of the Bureau of Ethnology for the Years 1886–1887.* Smithsonian Institution Press. 3–228.

Page, Jake 1990. Hyeouma. *Native Peoples* 3 (4): 30–35.

Parkman, E. Breck 1993. Lungumari Puntilla: A Cupule Petroglyph Occurrence on the South Coast of Peru. Paper Read at the Annual Meeting of the American Rock Art Research Association, June 5–7, Reno, Nevada.

Parsons, Elsie Clews 1939. *Pueblo Indian Religion.* Chicago: University of Chicago Press.

———1938. The Humpbacked Flute Player of the Southwest. *American Anthropologist* 40: 337–338.

———1933. Hopi and Zuni Ceremonialism. Menasha, WI: *Memoirs of the American Anthropological Association* 39.

Pilles, Peter J. Jr. 1975. Petroglyphs of the Little Colorado River Valley, Arizona. *In American Indian Rock Art* 1: 1–26.

Preston, Robert A. and Ann L. Preston 1993. Consistent Forms of Solstice Interaction between Sunlight and Petroglyphs Throughout the Prehistoric American Southwest. Unpublished Ms.

———1985. The Discovery of 19 Prehistoric Calendric Petroglyph Sites in Arizona. In *Earth and Sky.* A. Benson and T. Hoskinson (eds.). Thousand Oaks, CA: Slo'w Press. 123–133.

Reed, Erik K. 1948. The Western Pueblo Archaeological Complex. *El Palacio* 55 (1): 9–15.

Ritter, Dale W. and Eric W. Ritter 1977. The Influence of the Religious Formulator in Rock Art of North America. In *American Indian Rock Art* 3: 63–79.

Ritter, Eric W. and Brian W. Hatoff 1990. Symbols for Explanation: Scratched Petroglyphs at the Pistone Site in Western Nevada. Paper presented at the 22nd Great Basin Anthropological Conference and Nevada Archaeological Association Meeting, Reno, Nevada, October 1990.

Roberts, F.H.H., Jr. 1932. The Village of the Great Kivas on the Zuni Reservation, New Mexico. Washington, D.C.: *Bureau of American Ethnology Bulletin* 111. Smithsonian Institution Press.

Schaafsma, Polly 1992. *Rock Art in New Mexico.* Santa Fe: Museum of New Mexico Press.

———1987. Rock Art at Wupatki: Pots, Textiles, Glyphs. In *Exploration, Annual Bulletin of the School of American Research.* David Grant Noble (ed.). Santa Fe: School of American Research. 20–27.

———1986. Anasazi Rock Art in Tsegi Canyon and Canyon de Chelly: A View Behind the Image. In *Exploration, Annual Bulletin of the School of American Research.* David Grant Noble (ed.). Santa Fe. School of American Research.

———1980. *Indian Rock Art of the Southwest.* Santa Fe: School of American Research, and Albuquerque: University of New Mexico Press.

Smith, Watson 1972. Prehistoric Kivas of Antelope Mesa, Northeastern Arizona. Cambridge: *Papers of the Peabody Museum of American Archaeology and Ethnology, Harvard University* 39 (1).

Sofaer, Anna, Volker Zinser, and Rolf Sinclair 1979. A Unique Solar Marking Construct. *Science* 206: 283–291.

Stephen, Alexander M. 1936. *Hopi Journal* 1 and 2. Elsie Clews Parsons (ed.). New York: Columbia University Press.

———1929. Hopi Tales. *Journal of American Folk–Lore* 42: 5–6.

Stevenson, Matilda Coxe 1904. The Zuni Indians: Their Mythology, Esoteric Fraternities, and Ceremonies. Washington, D.C.: *23rd Annual Report of the Bureau of American Ethnology for the Years 1901–1902.* 3–634.

Stewart, Yvonne G. ed. 1980. An Archeological Overview of Petrified Forest National Park. *Western Archeological and Conservation Center Publications in Anthropology*, No. 10. Tucson: National Park Service.

Stoney, Stephen A. 1990. The Scratched Style Mystery Re–examined: Is It Illusion or Reality? Paper presented at the 22nd Great Basin Anthropological Conference and Nevada Archeological Association Meeting, October 1990.

Titiev, Mischa 1944. Old Oraibi: A Study of the Hopi Indians of the Third Mesa. Cambridge, MA: *Papers of the Peabody Museum of American Archaeology and Ethnology, Harvard University* 11 (1).

Turner, Christy G., II 1971. Revised Dating for Early Rock Art of the Glen Canyon Region. *American Antiquity* 36: 469–471.

———1963. Petrographs of the Glen Canyon Region. Flagstaff: *Museum of Northern Arizona Bulletin* 38. 469–471.

Tyler, Hamilton A. 1991. *Pueblo Birds and Myth*. Flagstaff: Northland Press.

———1975. *Pueblo Animals and Myths*. Norman: University of Oklahoma Press.

Vivian, R. Gwinn, Dulce N. Dodgen, and Gayle H. Hartmann 1978. *Wooden Ritual Artifacts from Chaco Canyon, New Mexico: The Chetro Ketl Collection*. Anthropological Papers of the University of Arizona 32. Tucson: University of Arizona Press.

Voth, Henry R. 1912. The Oraibi Marau Ceremony. Chicago: *Field Museum of Natural History Publication* 156, *Anthropological Series*, 11 (1): 1–88.

———1905. Traditions of the Hopi. Chicago: *Field Columbian Museum Publication 96, Anthropological Series*, 8.

———1903. The Oraibi Summer Snake Ceremony. Chicago: *Field Museum of Natural History Publication* 83, *Anthropological Series*, 3 (2): 262–358.

Wade, Edwin L. and Lea S. McChesney 1980. *America's Great Lost Expedition: The Thomas Keam Collection of Hopi Pottery from the Second Hemenway Expedition, 1890–1894*. Phoenix: The Heard Museum.

Warner, Jesse E. 1982. Concepts and Significance of Two and One Horned Sheep. In *American Indian Rock Art* 7 and 8: 112–131.

Wellmann, Klaus F. 1979. *A Survey of North American Indian Rock Art*. Graz, Austria: Akademische Druck– und Verlagsanstalt.

———1976. Some Observations on the Bird Motif in North American Indian Rock Art. In *American Indian Rock Art* 2: 97–108.

Wells, Susan J. 1989. Petrified Forest National Park Boundary Survey, 1988: The Final Season. *Western Archeological and Conservation Center Publications in Anthropology* 51. Tucson: National Park Service.

———1988. Archeological Survey and Testing at Petrified Forest National Park, 1987. *Western Archeological and Conservation Center Publications in Anthropology* 48. Tucson: National Park Service.

Wendorf, Fred 1953. Archaeological Studies in the Petrified Forest National Monument. *Museum of Northern Arizona Bulletin* 27. Flagstaff.

White, Leslie A. 1943. New Material from Acoma. Bureau of American Ethnology Bulletin No. 136. Washington D.C.: Smithsonian Institution Press.

———1932. The Acoma Indians. *47th Annual Report of the Bureau of American Ethnology for the Years 1929–1930*. Washington D.C.: Smithsonian Institution Press. 17–192.

Whitley, David S. 1994. Ethnography and Rock Art in the Far West: Some Archaeological Implications. In *New Light on Old Art: Recent Advances in Hunter–Gatherer Rock Art Research*. David S. Whitley and L. Loendorf (eds.).Monograph 36. Institute of Archaeology, University of California: Los Angeles. 85–98.

———1994. By the Hunter, for the Gatherer: Art, Social Relations and Subsistence Change in the Prehistoric Great Basin. *World Archaeology* 25 (3): 356–373.

Williamson, Ray A. 1979. Hovenweep National Monument—Field Report. In *Archaeoastronomy, the Bulletin of the Center for Archaeoastronomy* 2 (2): 11–12.

———1978. Pueblo Bonito and the Sun. *Archaeoastronomy, the Bulletin of the Center for Archaeoastronomy* 2. 5–6.

Williamson, Ray A. and Mary Jane Young, 1979. An Equinox Sun Petroglyph Panel at Hovenweep National Monument. In *American Indian Rock Art* 5: 70–80.

Williamson, Ray A. and H. J. Fisher and D. O'Flynn 1977. Anasazi Solar Laboratories. In *Native American Astronomy*. Anthony F. Aveni (ed.). Austin and London: University of Texas Press. 203–217.

Williamson, Ray A. and H. J. Fisher, A. F. Williamson and C. Cochran 1975. The Astronomical Record in Chaco Canyon, New Mexico. In *Archaeoastronomy in Pre–Columbian America*. Anthony F. Aveni (ed.). Austin: University of Texas Press. 33–43.

Young, M. Jane 1988. *Signs From the Ancestors. Zuni Cultural Symbolism and Perceptions of Rock Art*. Albuquerque: University of New Mexico Press.

Zeilik, Michael 1987. Anticipation in Ceremony: The Readiness is All. In *Astronomy and Ceremony in the Prehistoric Southwest*. John B. Carlson and W. James Judge (eds.). Papers of the Maxwell Museum of Anthropology, No. 2. University of New Mexico Press. 25–41.

Italic numbers indicate pages with plates

A

abraded technique, 6
abstract elements, 13–14, 16, 35, *126–27, 131, 180*
aesthetics, *43–44, 174,* 175–81, *180*
American Rock Art Research Association, 77, 182
Anasazi
  migrant populations of, 51
  Plateau, 40, 51
  sunwatching by, 133
  Western, 4
  Winslow Branch, 39
animal images, 8, 13, 19, 40, 54, 67, *73,* 89, *90. See
  also* zoomorphs
  badgers, 67, 76
  bats, 35, 77, *79,* 96
  bear, 67, 74–75, *92*
  bison, *25*
  composite, *44, 62*
  deer, 19, *72,* 74
  dogs, 34, 76–77, *95*
  elk, 19, *29,* 67, *72*
  in geometric designs, 122
  mountain lions, 34, 36, 67, *68,* 75–76, *86, 88,
    93–94, 98, 112, 159*
  mountain sheep, 13, 14, 19, 34, 71–72, *91*
  in Palavayu Linear Basketmaker Style, 19
  pregnant, *91*
  pronghorn, *24, 30,* 34, *72,* 74, 88
  rabbits, 76
  in relation to human figures, 22, 67, 89
  as spirit helpers, *20, 46*
  supernatural, 68
animals
  as clan symbols, 67–68
  as guardian spirits, 67, 76, *91*
  hunting of, 68–71
  in Pueblo culture, 67–68
animal track images, 8, 13, 34, 40, 68, 88
anthropomorphic images, *10,* 22, *25, 30, 44, 117,
  180. See also* female images; male images
  androgynous, *115*
  Barrier Canyon (Utah) Style, 18
  Basketmaker Style, 18, 22
  bird-headed, 36, *149,* 150–52, 154, *168–69*
  body art of, *45*
  couples, *107, 108, 113, 116*
  decorated bodies, *121*
  enclosed in geometric designs, 122
  facial features of, 36
  family grouping, *107–8*
  Glen Canyon Linear Petroglyph Style, 13, 18
  groups of, *48*
  headdresses on, *23*
  heads of, 14, 18
  horned, 18–19, *27, 46*
  hunters, 66, 67
  intercourse between, *110*
  kachina image, *61*
  lizard men, 36, *42,* 82, *129, 171*
  movement depicted, 34
  one-legged man, *153,* 154–55, *173*
  outlined, 36
  oversized, 106
  Palavayu Linear Basketmaker Style, 18, 22
  partial, 35
  pattern-bodied, *30,* 45
  phallic, 18, 22, 49, *115*
  in pictographs, *11*
  rake-bodied, 16
  in relation to animal figures, 67, 89
  San Juan Anthropomorphic Style, 14
  sexual intercourse depiction, *110*
  shield figures, 60
  skeletalized, *28*
  snakes, 19, *25,* 184
  with staffs, 147–48, *165–67*
  stick figures, 34
  supplicant, *28, 63*
  turkey-topped, *169*
arachnids, 83
archaeoastronomy, 132–37
Archaeological Conservancy, 182
archaeological sites of Palavayu region, 2, 4, 6
Archaic period, 5, 13
  Palavayu rock art in, 16
  peoples of, 18
  rock art style, 5, 8, *12, 24*
archers, 66, 87–88, 97, 99, 148, 165
astronomy, primitive. *See* archaeoastronomy
atlatls, 6, 8, 18, 35, 151–52
Avanyu (Horned Serpent), 82

B

badger images, 67, 76
banner images, 35, 36, *173*
Barrier Canyon (Utah) Style, 18, 184 n2:31
Basketmaker habitation sites, 23
Basketmaker II-III period, 5, 13
Basketmaker II period, 4
Basketmaker Linear Style, *22, 28*
Basketmaker Style rock art, *12,* 13–14, 16, 33
  Palavayu Majestic Style, *17, 23, 29, 30*
  Palavayu motifs, *32*
  transition to Pueblo II styles, *32,* 34
basket weaving designs, 120
bat images, 35, 77, *79,* 96
Baumhoff, Martin, 38
Beaglehole, Ernest, 68, 70
bears
  as guardian spirits, 67, 68
  images of, 74–75, *92*
  in medicine societies, 75
  paws, *10, 99*
  tracks, 34, 36, 40, 68, 74–75
  veneration of in Hopi culture, 74, *92*
beetle images, 83
bighorn sheep. *See* mountain sheep images
bird-headed men, 36, *149,* 150–52, 154, *168–69*
bird images, 19, 22, 34, 54, 64, 77–81, *79*
  capture of, 97
cranes, 80
ducks, 80
eagles, 34, 40, 65, 78, 97
  macaws, 78–80
  owls, 19, 34–35, 81, 98
  parrots, 34, 78–80
  quail, 34, 81, *103*
  shamanism and, 151, 154, *168–69*
  symbolic functions of, 77, 151
  tracks of, 34
  turkeys, 34, 80, 151
  wading, 80
birthing scenes, 34, *107, 111–12,* 142
bison images, 25
Blue Mesa, *2,* 75
Boas, Franz, 119
bouquets, *26*
bows and arrows, 6, 35, 66
burial traditions, 106
butterfly images, *43,* 84, *103*

C

calendars, seasonal, 133, 176
Canyon Butte Ruins, 40, 56, 57
Canyon de Chelly, 14, 80, 150–51, *152,* 158, *196*
Canyon Diablo, 1
Carr Lake Draw, *62,* 82
cartouche designs, *91, 122, 130*
caterpillars, 83
Cedar Mesa, 14
centipede images, 19, 35, 83, 99, *102*
ceramic designs, influence on rock art images, 5, 35,
  40, 57–58, *59,* 119, 120
ceremonial object images, 14, 36, 138–73, *160*
  banners, 36, *173*
  staffs, 36, *45,* 147–48, 150, *164–66*
ceremonies
  bird-headed men and, 152
  dates of seasonal, 133–34
  depiction of, 36, *166*
  flute, 156
  in life of Palavayu region, 139
  male responsibility for, 106
  rainmaking, 52
  women's *Maraw* (Hopi), 122, 144, 146, *160*
  women's *Owaqöl* (Hopi), 84
Chacoan people, 4, 39
Chaco Canyon, 133, 134, 147, 186
Chavez Pass, 51
Chetro Ketl Ruin, 147
Chevelon Creek sites, 5, 22, 74, *128*
Chevelon Ruins, 51
Chinle Formation, *2,* 9
Christensen, Don, 38, 120
chronology of cultural stages, 5
chute and pound hunting method, 70
Cibola people, 4, 39
cicadas. *See* locusts and flute player images
circles
  concentric, 13, 14, 35, 45, 132, *169*
  dot-centered, *7, 169*
  as solar site markers, 133

clan insignia, 35
Clear Creek, 57
cloud imagery, 35, 47, 51, 56, 62
coils, 45
Cole, Sally, 14
Colorado Plateau, 1, 13, 40
copulation, symbolic, 34, 36, 108, 115
corn. See maize
Cottonwood Creek, 5
cougars. See mountain lion images
Crack-in-Rock site (Wupatki National
    Monument), 140
craftsmanship, decline of, 5, 33, 41, 58
crane images, 80
creatures
    geometric, 130
    hybrid, 44, 62
crosses, outlined, 33, 40, 123, 125, 128
cupule images, 123, 131
Curtis, Edward, 140, 184 n1:1
Cushing, Frank, 134–35
D
dancers, 46–47, 95, 108, 144
dance wands. See slab pahos
dating methods, 5, 6, 13, 175
Dead Wash, 41
deer
    hunting of, 69, 71
    images of, 19, 72, 74
deity images, 14, 22, 28, 45, 108, 138, 139–41,
    176, 181
desert varnish. See rock varnish
destruction of images, 48, 182, 183
dinosaur fossils, 2
disks, twinned, 138, 139, 160
dog images, 76–77, 95
dragonfly images, 19, 84, 103
duck images, 80
Dutton, Bertha, 77
E
eagles, 34, 40, 65, 97
    capture of, 36, 78
    Hopi rituals and, 36, 78
elk images, 19, 29, 67, 72
engraved technique, 6, 9, 118
entoptic images, 20, 25, 119
equinoxes, tracking of, 133–34, 137
erosion effects on rock art, 7
F
Fajada Butte, 186
feathers
    eagle, 78
    quail, 81
    turkey, 80
female images, 44, 57, 59, 62, 101, 112–13, 138, 159,
    165. See also anthropomorphic images;
    women
    in ceremonial scenes, 142, 144, 148, 160
    as goddesses, 63, 104
    identifying markers, 34

Mother of Game, 139–42, 159–60
    pregnant, 108, 114, 140, 148, 165
    Pueblo II-III Style, 34
    Pueblo IV Style, 57, 59
    San Juan Anthropomorphic Style, 14
fending sticks, 6, 18, 28
fertility shrines, 111
fertility symbols, 109, 113, 123, 140, 156
Fewkes, Jesse Walter, 70, 84, 144
flowers, 26
flute player images, 40, 54, 128, 155–58, 170–73
    humpbacked, 34, 155, 158, 171
    locusts and, 156, 158, 172
    origin of, 156, 158
    phallic, 34
    in Pueblo II-III period, 34
Flute Societies (Hopi), 156
footprints, human, 13, 35, 40, 128
fossils, 2
frogs, 82–83, 103
function of images, 4, 176
G
game
    animals, 88, 91
    corrals, 85–86
    deities, 90, 94, 112
    drives, 85, 142
gender based activities, 105–6
geometric creatures, 130
geometric designs, 7, 13, 33, 40, 41, 46, 119–31
    animals within, 122
    cartouche-shaped, 122
    ceramic art and, 35
    derivation of, 119
    elements of, 119
    entoptic forms, 20, 25, 119
    function of, 124, 126–27
    human figures in, 11
    limitless, 120
    in Pueblo II-III Style, 38
    squares, 118
Glen Canyon area, 13, 105
Glen Canyon Linear Petroglyph Style, 13–14, 15, 18,
    19
goddess images, 63–64, 111, 116, 138, 139–40, 141,
    142
    Old Spider Woman, 104
    tutelary game images, 112
gouged technique, 6, 10
Grant, Campbell, 150–51
Great Basin Scratched Style, 38
grinding technique, 41
grooves, sharpening, 123, 131
guardian spirits, 67
H
hallucinogens, effect on rock artist, 28, 119
handprints, 14, 152
Hatoff, Brian, 38
Hawley, Francis, 158
headdresses, 14, 23, 32
heads, 14, 30

heart line motif, 65
Hedges, Ken, 16
Heizer, Robert, 38
heron images, 80, 97
Hisatsinom, 4
Hohokam influence on Palavayu rock art, 40
Holbrook (Ariz.) area, 1, 82
Homol'ovi area, 40
Homol'ovi Ruins, 5, 51, 57
Hopi Buttes district, 39
Hopi culture, 4
    eagles and rituals in, 36, 78
    hunting practices in, 68–69, 71, 72
    kachinas and, 47, 52, 54, 60
    language of, 184 n1:5, 184 n4:7
    legend about Mother of Game, 140, 141
    Maasaw (deity), 56, 81, 186
    masks in belief structure, 60
    Ogre kachina, 56, 57, 65
    origin myths of, 52
    Owaqöl women's ceremony, 84
    Snake Dance, 16, 24, 81, 99
    uses of rock art, 176
    veneration of bear, 74, 92
    Wuwtsim ceremony, 134
Hopi Journal (Stephen), 69, 148
horned images
    snakes, 51, 54, 62, 82, 101
    as symbol of shamanic powers, 19, 22, 46, 67
Horned Water Serpent (deity), 81–82
Hough, Walter, 57
Hovenweep, 134
human figures. See anthropomorphic images; female
    images; male images
humor in rock art, 49
hunter figures, 66, 67
hunting practices
    bird-headed men and, 152
    chute and pound method, 70
    communal game drives, 70–71, 85
    depictions of, 36, 67–71, 85–86, 95, 99, 147, 159,
        176
    in Hopi culture, 68–69, 71, 72
    nets, 70–71
    Pueblo cultures, 70–71
    for rabbits, 71, 88
    use of animal disguises, 71
    in Zuni culture, 71
I
iconographic elements in rock art, 7, 20
incised technique, 6, 41, 118
insect images, 7, 19, 35, 79, 83–84
interpretation, difficulties of, 179
Interstate 40, Northern Arizona portion, 1–2
J
Jack's Canyon, 57, 60
jewelrymaking, 106
Jornada Style, 51, 54, 82
Joseph City (Ariz.), 62

INDEX

K

kachina religion
 Pueblo culture and, 39–40, 51–52
 rituals of, 52
 rock art and, 50, 51, 175
kachinas, 64
 definition of, 52, 54, 185 n4:7
 as Hopi clan ancestors, 54
 images of, *42*, 51–52, 57, *60–61*, 175
 Kokopölmana, 156
 Kookopölö, 156, 158
 Longhair, 47
 Manangya (Collared Lizard), *42*
 masks of, 52
 Owl, 81
 Putskoomoktaqa, 102
 Toho (Mountain Lion), 94
Kayenta people, 4, 39
Keresan culture, 52
kiva murals, influence of rock art images, 5, 57, 59
Kokopelli. *See* flute player images
Kwaatoko (mythical eagle), 68

L

Lacey Point site, *138*
ladder images, 13
Leroux Wash, 148
lichen growth
 as dating agent, 33
 effect on petroglyphs, *43*, *48*, *98*, *104*, *161*
lines
 sawtooth, *32*
 ticked, 13, *32*
 zigzag, 13, *27*, *32*, *129*
Little Colorado River, 1, 5, 39, *163*
Little Colorado River drainage area
 petroglyphs in, 13
 rock art sites in, 14
 Western Anasazi in, 4
Little Colorado River Style, 39
Little Colorado River Valley, 13, 51, 56
lizard images, 34, 36, 82–83
lizard men, 36, *42*, 82, *129*, *171*
location of images. *See* placement of images
locusts and flute player images, 156, 158, *172*

M

Maahu (Hopi deity), 156
Maasaw (Hopi deity), 81, 186
macaw images, 78–80
magic, sympathetic, 85–88
maize, 13, 18
making of images, 5, 176–77
male images, 105–16, *113*, *115*. *See also*
 anthropomorphic images
Malotki, Ekkehart, 14, 16, 52, 54, 140, 156, 184 n1:1
man, one-legged, *153*, 154–55, *173*
Manangya (Hopi kachina), *42*
manufacturing techniques, 6, *10*
 abraded, 6
 engraved, 6, 9, *118*
 gouged, 6, *10*

grinding, 41
 negativism, 38, *100*
 pecked, 6, 19
 percussion, indirect, 33, 36, 38, 41
 scratched, 38
Maraw ceremony (Hopi), 144, 146, *160*
marawvahos, 144
Marsh Pass, 14
Martynec, Richard, 23, 41, 77
mask images, 30, *50*, 51, 54, 55, 56, 57, 60, 64
material culture images, 4, 6, 35
mazes, squiggle, 13, *28*
McCluskey, Stephen, 133
meander images, *27*, *43*
meaning of images, 175, 176, *179*
Mesoamerican art, 51
Mexican religious influence on Pueblo culture, 51
migration imagery, 35
Mimbres
 ceramic art, 51
 rock art, 40
Mogollon culture, 40
moisture tablets, 122
mongko, 148, 150
Mother of Game, 76, *138*, 139–42, 159–60
moth images, 83, 84
mountain lion images, 34, 36, 67, 68, 75–76, 86,
  88, 93–94, 98, *112*, *159*
Mountain Lion Mesa, 56, 57, 77, 122, 148
mountain sheep images, 13, 14, 19, 34, 71–72, *91*
Mt. Trumbull, 38
mythology, rock art depictions of, 175

N

narrative scene depictions, 36
natural elements, 13–14, 35
Navajo Indians, 4, 185 n5:13
negativism technique, 22, 38, *100*
nets used in hunting, 70–71
Newspaper Rock, 2, 77, 82
nodule clubs, 66, 69
number symbols, *125*
Nuvakwewtaqa, 51

O

one-legged man, *153*, 154–55, *173*
orientation of sites. *See* placement of images
owl images, 19, 34–35, 81, 98

P

Paalölöqangw (Hopi Water Serpent), *62*, 82
Painted Desert (Ariz.), 2
painted rock art. *See* pictographs
Palavayu Linear Basketmaker Style, *17*, *18*, *20*, *25*,
  50
 animal images in, 19
 functions of, 23
 manufacturing techniques of, 23
 pecked images, 19, 22
 snake images, 19
Palavayu Majestic Basketmaker Style, *17*, *20*, 23,
  29–30
Palavayu Pueblo IV Style, *53*, *55*, 58
 anthropomorphic images, 56

masked images in, *55*
 subject inventory of, 54, 56
Palavayu region
 archaeological sites of, 2, 4
 boundaries of, 1, 39, 184
 cultural chronology within, 5
 map of, xi, 3
 name of, 184 n1:1
 Pueblo population within, 4–5, 33
 terrain of, 1–2, 39
Paleo-Indian period, 5, 13
parrot images, 34, 78–80
Parsons, Elsie Clews, 83, 123, 148, 156, 185 n5:32
patina. *See* rock varnish
Patterson, Alex, 122
percussion, indirect (technique), 33, 36, 38, 41
Petrified Forest National Park (Ariz.), 1–2
 archaeological excavations in, 4, 39
 Cibolan ceramics in, 39
 dinosaur fossils in, 2
 rock art surveys in, 67
Petrified Forest region
 depopulation of, 39, 40, 58, 184 n3:3
 settlements within, 40
petroglyphs, 4, 6
 dating of, 33
pictographs, 4, 6, *11*, 14, 152
Pilles, Peter, 13, 23, 33, 35, 39, 41, 56, 58
Pilot Rock, 1
placement of images, xii, 6, 8, 176–77
plantlike images, 13, 19, *26*, 105
pottery. *See* ceramic designs
Pottery Mound kiva murals, 57, 59, 64
prayer sticks. *See* slab pahos
pregnant
 animal images, *91*
 human figures, 108, *114*, 140, *165*
Preston, Ann, 133, 134, 186 n8:5
Preston, Robert, 133, 134, 186 n8:5
pronghorn images, *24*, 30, 34, 72, 74, 88
protection of rock art sites, 182
Pueblo I rock art, 33
Pueblo II period, 5, 33
Pueblo II-III styles, 5, 33–34, 38–39, 41, 56
Pueblo IV period, 5
Pueblo IV style, *10*, 50–65
 archaeological sites of, 56–57
 kachina religion and, 51
 Palavayu style, 53
 Western Pueblo area, 51
Pueblo people
 animals in cultural context, 67–68, 69
 hunting season of, 71
 kachina religion and, 51
 Mexican cultural impact on, 51
 prehistoric subgroups, 4
 social organization of, 106
Puerco River, 1, 4, 39, 122, *162*
Puerco Ruin, 4, 40, 51, 57, 82, 84, 105, 146, 154
 location of, 2, *3*
 Pueblo IV style at, 5, 54, 56, 58

193

Q

quail images, 34, 81, *103*
Quemado district (New Mex.), 40, 122
Quetzalcoatl (Mexican deity), 51, 81–82

R

rabbits, 76
  hunting of, 71, 88
rabbit sticks, 71, *102*
rainfall, importance of, 18, 52
rainmaking ceremonies, *46*, 52, 148
rain symbols, 16, 18, *24*, *27*, 96
rake images, 13, 14, 16, 18
religion and rock art, 8, 41, 176 *See also* kachina
  religion; shamanism
reptile images, 81–83. *See also* snake images
Reserve Petroglyph Style, 40
retouching of images, 22, *31*
revarnishing, effects of, 6, 8, *12*, *24*, *27*, *31*, 117,
  166
Rio Grande Style, 51, *53*, *54*, 60
Rio Grande Valley, 51
Ritter, Eric, 38
rock art designs
  ceramic arts and, 57–58, *59*
  kiva murals and, 57, *59*
rock varnish, *xi (inset)*, 6, 10, 175

S

sacred places, 8, 20, *42*, *58*, 167
safe treatment of images, 182
Salado influence on Palavayu rock art, 40
salamander images, 82–83
Salmon Ruins (New Mex.), 82
San Juan Anthropomorphic Style, 13, 14, *15*, *164*
San Juan River area, 14
Schaafsma, Polly, 13–14, 40, 51, 54, 82, 108
scorpion images, 83, *102*
scratched technique, 6, 38–39
scroll images, 122, *192*
serpents. *See* snake images
sexual intercourse images, 34, 36, 108, *110*
sexual symbolism, 108, *113*
shamanic images, *20*, *28–29*
shamanic vision quests and rock art, *44*
shamanism
  in Basketmaker culture, 19
  bird imagery and, 151, 154, *168–69*
  one-legged man motif, 155
  rock art and, vi, 8
shamans
  hunt, 86, 89, *147*, 148
  rock art and, 8, 14, 19, 20, 22, 25–26, 28, 34, 46, 86
  as rock artists, ii
sheep. *See* mountain sheep images
shield figures, 54, 56, 60
Sikyatki (Hopi pueblo)
  pottery of, 84, 123
  slab pahos at, 144
Silver Creek, 14, 19, 81, 148

Sinagua culture
  rock art compared to Palavayu, 40
  weaving tradition of, 40
sipapu, 35
slab pahos, *42*, *58*, 98, 122, *129*, 142–44, *160–63*,
  184 n3:24
  shapes of, 146
Smith, Watson, 146
Snake Dance (Hopi), 16, *25*, 81, 99
Snake Gulch, 38
snake images, *7*, *11*, *28*, *44–45*, 79, 81–82, *99–101*
  anthropomorphized, 19, *25*, 184 n2:24
  anthropomorphs pictured with, 19, *24*
  horned, 51, 54, 62, 82, *101*
  knob-headed, *12*, 16
  Palavayu Linear Basketmaker style, 19
  shamanistic spirit helpers, *12*, *24*
  water symbolism of, 16, 18, *24*, *27*
solar markers, *132*, 133–34
solstices, tracking of, 133–34, *136–37*
spear throwers, 8
spider images, 83
Spider Woman, 83, *104*
spirals, 14, *25*, 35, *41*, *45*, 95, *112*, *137*
  migration symbols, 140
  as solar site markers, 133, *137*
  triangles and, *179*
spirit helpers, *24*, *46*, 67
spirits, supernatural, 22, 28
squares, 35, 123, *126*, *129*
staff bearers, 95, *115*, *145*, 148, *164*, 166
staffs, 35, *145*, *164–65*, 167
  bird-topped, 150, 151
  ceremonial, 36, 45, 147–48, 150, *164–66*
  crescent-topped, 150
  forms of, 147, 148, 150, *166*
  uses of, 148, 150
star images, 54, *125*
Stephen, Alexander, 69, 140, 148
Stevenson, Matilda Coxe, 123
stick figures, 34, 60, 152, *164*
Stone Ax Ruin, 40, 56
Stoney, Stephen, 38, 70, 148
sunburst images, 14, 120, *136*
sun symbolism, 35, *45*, 146
sun tablets, 122
sunwatching, 133, 134–35
superimposition of images, ii, 14, *29*, 38, *164*, 166
supernatural power images, 19
surveys, rock art
  in Little Colorado River area, 58
  in Petrified Forest National Park, 67
symbolism in images, 35

T

Taawa (Hopi deity), *xii*
tablets
  moisture, 122
  sun, 122
techniques. *See* manufacturing techniques
textile patterns and rock art, 40, 119–20, *128*

theocodont fossils, 2
throwing sticks, 18, 69
Tiikuywuuti (Hopi goddess), 140, 142
Titiev, Mischa, 52, 144
Tlaloc (Mexican deity), 51
toad images, *25*, *46*, 82–83, *103*
trapezoidal designs, *180*
turkeys, 34, 80, 151
Turner, Christy, 13, 14, 18, 23, 58, 105
turtle images, 19
Twin Buttes, 1

U

uses of rock art, 175–76

V

vandalism of rock art, 8, *183*
violent images, 87
Virgin people, 4

W

Wallace Tank, 56, 57
wands. *See* slab pahos, staffs
water imagery, 35
weapons, 66, 69–71
  atlatls, 6, 8, 18, 35, 151–52
  bows and arrows, 6, 35, 66
  hunting, 69
  nodule clubs, 66
  rabbit sticks, 71
weaving patterns and rock art designs, 40, 106, 120
Wells, Susan, 39
Willow Springs, Ariz., 68, 83, 84
wind symbolism, 35
Winslow (Ariz.) area, 1
  population growth of, 39–40
  rock art style of, 39–40, 41
Winslow Branch Anasazi, 39
women. *See also* female images; goddess images
  pregnant, 108, *114*
  under-representation in rock art, 105–6
  status of in Pueblo culture, 106
Woodruff, Ariz., 57, *129*, 148
Wupatki National Monument, 140
Wuwtsim society, Hopi men's, 134, 146

X

x-ray skeletal effect, 22, 57

Y

Young, Jane M., 83
yucca plant images, 105

Z

Zeilik, Michael, 134
zoomorphs, *25*, *31*, *33*, *43*. *See also* animal images
Zuni people
  hunting practices of, 71
  insect symbolism of, 83
  sunwatching by, 134–35
  traditions of, *7*